Christ, Capital & Liberty

A Polemic

Anthony Flood

Christ, Capital and Liberty: A Polemic

Copyright © 2019 by Anthony Flood

For permission requests, please contact:
Anthony Flood
Box 7156, F. D. R. Station
New York, NY 10150

Printed in the United States of America

ISBN 9781077874817

Also by Anthony Flood

Herbert Aptheker: Studies in Willful Blindness (2019)

Contents

Part One
Setting the Table

Part Two
Main Course

Part Three
Dessert and Leftovers

Appendices

Foreword

A nthony Flood's *Christ, Capital and Liberty: A Polemic* is a spirited and detailed defence of the fundamental compatibility of Catholicism and Austro-Libertarianism. Its point of departure and its intellectual sparring partner throughout is Christopher A. Ferrara's *The Church and the Libertarian*, the central theme of which is a supposed fundamental incompatibility between Austro-Libertarianism and Catholicism. "[T]he principal features of the Austro-libertarian system, reflecting 'classical liberalism' in general," writes Ferrara, "have been explicitly condemned as errors in a long series of papal pronouncements summed up by Pope Pius XI under the description 'moral, legal, and social modernism.'" It follows that Christian orthodoxy is incompatible with the "grave moral, philosophical and even theological errors" of Austro-Libertarianism.

In respect of this thesis, Flood begs to differ.

Flood is critical not only of Ferrara's conclusion, but also of the argumentative methods that Ferrara employs. "Several thorough readings," writes Flood, "have convinced me that it is such a bad book, morally as well as stylistically, that it arguably ought to be ignored rather than critically reviewed. Its tone is continuously inflammatory, its arrangement of material lopsided... and his use of sources tendentious. The last-mentioned trait includes either unawareness or evasion of evidence relevant to his topic but inconvenient to his purpose." Flood is especially critical of Ferrara's epistemically uncharitable failure to employ responsible internal criticism of his opponents' positions and also of his inadequate grasp of various historical controversies.

Flood, then, rejects Ferrara's contention that Catholic orthodoxy and Austro-Libertarianism libertarianism are incompatible. To the contrary, his ringing conclusion is that "Catholics are within their rights to be Austro-libertarians in their political and economic thinking. There is no necessary cognitive dissonance between the Gospel and the libertarian prohibition against the initiation of force." He continues:

> I would go further, however, by suggesting to my fellow Austro-libertarians—Catholic or not, Christian or not, theist or not—that the Catholic worldview is a congenial philosophical home for libertarianism. Catholicism should move out of the shadows of libertarian discourse and onto center stage. Catholics can make a difference to the libertarian movement by stressing their distinctive worldview.

Tony's book will be of interest to many people, but perhaps especially (but not only) to those who are Catholic and who are also attracted to the intellectual coherence of Austro-Libertarianism, but are concerned that the two systems of thought may be irreconcilable. Polemical writing is not everybody's favourite form of reading, but the multiple, mostly short, chapters of *Christ, Capital and Liberty* provide so many insights, engage the perspectives of so many thinkers and attack the central topic of the compatibility of Catholicism and Austro-Libertarianism from so many angles that no reader can fail to achieve a greater insight into the matter after reading it than he had before he began.

Gerard N. Casey MA, LLM, PhD, DLitt.
Professor Emeritus, University College Dublin
Associated Scholar, The Mises Institute, Auburn, Alabama
Fellow, Mises UK

Preface:

The Origins of a Polemic

S ocialism is back in the news. Americans born after the collapse of the Soviet Union have not learned the hard lessons of interference in markets. And they never will, if the new breed of so-called democratic socialists get their way. The masses will be fed slogans and dreams; those who dissent will be smeared, shamed, subjected to lectures on "social justice." The gullible and willfully blind will drink it in; opportunists will benefit in the short run; we'll all pay the price.

The intellectual case for socialism was refuted long before its latent horrors were made patent. An armory of refutation is available on mises.org, the site of the Ludwig von Mises Institute. Almost a century ago Mises wrote the book against it: *Socialism: An Economic and Sociological Analysis.*[1] Mises led the Austrian School of Economics (ASE) for half a century until his death in 1973. Its lessons, especially developed by Mises' student, the brilliant and prolific polymath Murray N. Rothbard, has informed my political and economic thinking from the time I met him in 1983, shortly after reading his *Man, Economy and State.*

---

[1] The original title of this 1922 study was *Die Gemeinwirtschaft: Untersuchungen über den Sozialismus.*

From March 8, 2011 to September 10, 2012, nineteen months in all, I blogged my criticism of *The Church and the Libertarian*,[2] Christopher A. Ferrara's slanderous and ignorant attack on the ASE. He argued that no faithful Catholic could be a sincere libertarian of the ASE persuasion. One day I had promised Mr. Ferrara that if he published a book to that effect, I'd answer it. Across almost ninety posts I fulfilled that promise, and this book reincarnates them.

After a year and a half, however, I decided that life was too short to sacrifice other projects on the altar of this polemic.[3] The issues were (and are) important, and I found researching and writing about them congenial, but I could no longer sustain the effort. Dr. Thomas E. Woods, Ludwig von Mises Institute Senior Fellow and former co-author of Mr. Ferrera's, encouraged my efforts, and for that I thank him.[4] The appreciation of faithful readers was also gratifying.

This book is the record of an effort in pro-market apologetics (in the classic sense of "defense against intellectual attack"). All interference in market exchange, *not* only outright state control of the "means of production," but also violent robbery, involves

---

[2] The blog was "anarcho-catholic: fisking Christopher A. Ferrara's *The Church and the Libertarian*, while delimiting, defining, and defending an Austro-libertarian option for Catholics." The full citation of targeted book is *The Church and the Libertarian: A Defense of the Catholic Church's Teaching on Man, Economy, and State*. Forest Lake, MN: The Remnant Press, 2010. iii + 383 pp. Foreword by John C. Médaille.) Hereafter, to as TCATL. In the book you're reading, numbers in parentheses refer to pages of TCATL.

[3] "[H]owever forcefully its arguments are presented in places, [TCATL] is also meant as a fraternal appeal to Catholic proponents of the errors at issue, that they might abandon all error and return to the path the Church has marked out for them and for every soul that seeks true happiness in this world and the next." (5) An early salvo in this polemic is Ferrara's "Fury in the Cult of Rothbard," *RemnantNewspaper.com*, June 24, 2011. For a Catholic critique of Médaille's *Toward a Truly Free Market: A Distributist Perspective on the Role of Government, Taxes, Health Care, Deficits, and More*, which predates Ferrara's book, see Kishore Jayabalan, "Distributism is not Free-Market," *Acton Institute PowerBlog*, September 1, 2010.

[4] See the following on TomWoods.com: "Lawyer's Anti-Market Case Dismantled," April 29, 2011; "How Not to Write a Book," June 14, 2011; "The Skewering Continues," July 1, 2011; "Propaganda, Meet Modern Research," July 18, 2011; "It's OK to Like the Industrial Revolution," July 26, 2011; "Keep Digging that Hole," July 27, 2011.

a degree of "socialization" of the costs of acquiring a good or service. To impose costs on individuals who have not chosen to bear them, be they contemporaries or later generations, is to "socialize" those costs. Calculating these (usually hidden) costs falls to the economist. "Socialism" and "communism" are but frank labels for the systematic, territory-wide state interference with the market exchanges of individuals. That is, it differs in degree, not of kind, from the predations of garden-variety gangsters.

Conservatives who object to socialized medicine seem never to have a problem with socialized defense, police or courts. Or socialized (i.e., "central") banking. In these instances, nominally "anti-socialist" conservatives somehow forget that prices go up and quality down whenever government gets involved in the provision of *any* product or service. And, as in the case of military mis-adventures, people can get killed, by the tens of thousands if not by the millions.

Among such conservatives may be found traditional Roman Catholics who further identify themselves as "Distributists." They advocate "Catholic Social Teaching" (CST), that is, warmed-over social democracy arrayed in Catholic terminology. For them as for all other socialists, voluntary exchange is insufficient to ensure the morally mandatory "just price" (exchange rate) of at least some justly acquired goods or services. Christopher Ferrara promotes what amounts to *de facto* social democracy combined with the intense moralistic shaming and ridicule we've come to expect of the radical Left in the Age of Trump. Indeed, his book models, if not presages, the kind of "fake news" that is the stock and trade of Trump's enemies: throw it against the wall, see if it sticks; if it doesn't, proceed to the next smear.

Markets are networks whose nodes are persons and ties are exchanges or trades of title to scarce resources. These networks arise out of trade, not from historically transitory social conventions. Trade is what people spontaneously engage in, everywhere and always, under conditions of scarcity (that is, between Eden and the Kingdom of God) as they form families and create wealth to provide for them. The label "capitalism," a staple of anti-free market propaganda since the days of *Das Kapital,* reinforces the idea that history consists of a series of stages of which "capitalism" is but one, scheduled for displacement by another. It's a misnomer but, as Hayek suggested, it's one we're probably stuck with. (See Chapter 20.)

Capital is what wealth becomes when traders do not consume the yield of their labor or trade, but invest it in an enterprise so as to earn interest or (as it was once called) "usury."[5] Capital is a factor of production, alongside the two original factors, land and labor. "Capitalism" should clang in our ears as would "landism" or "laborism." There is no justification for referring to any stretch of human history as "capitalism," as though once upon a time people did not exchange property titles and will one day "return" to a marketless, and propertyless social order, all the wiser for having passed through the hell of "class society."

Markets flourished and property rights were protected more in some places and times than in others. The *libido dominandi,* the lust for power over others, however, will find more and more avenues of expression as the present dispensation draws to a close, until God shoots at evildoers as with an arrow (Psalm 64:7-8), halting their progress (2 Timothy 3:9). *We* cannot halt it, whether or not we take up the sword against them, but God can and will. Or so I hold in opposition to my optimistic Rothbardian friends.

Protests to the contrary notwithstanding, CST's "principle of subsidiarity"—a larger and more complex organization should do nothing that a smaller and simpler organization can do well— is a fond wish that offers little resistance to the "socialism" they

---

[5] As Jesus taught in His parable of the talents, earning interest [Greek, *toko*] is sometimes morally imperative. Matthew 25:27. Mosaic law, however, prohibited an Israelite from charging interest *to fellow Israelites*. Deuteronomy 23:20. In effect, the Israelite lender was obliged to make a gift to his brother of the foregone use of the loaned money.

claim to abhor. It was of little value to the Catholic Church during its centuries-long acquiescence in chattel slavery, condoning it long after those whom its leaders formally branded "heretics" abolished that "peculiar institution" in their countries. (It didn't govern Pius XI's regard for Mussolini as a "man sent by Providence" a few decades after *Rerum Novarum*. Or did it?) The protests of Distributists against "socialism" ring hollow. Taken in by Dickensian fractured fairy tales, they've missed the profoundly pro-life story of the Industrial Revolution.

But is hope in defeating socialism reasonable? I no longer think so, and I realize such thoughts can be bad for business in certain political circles. I pray for the divine assumption of sovereignty, prophesied from one end of the Bible to the other. That is, I pray for God to put His judgments, His government, *in the earth* (Isaiah 26:9, 42:4). This He has not yet done. For man (which I stipulate is shorthand for "humankind") has demonstrated that he has no judgment. Every victory is but a holding operation, a finger in a dyke. Man has failed, and from his failure and propensity to repeat and recapitulate failure he must be liberated and saved. Man needs to be set free (Luke 4:18).

We may be unable to resist the urge to theorize about political economy, but we cannot systematically implement our best theories. We stumble from crisis to crisis. Socialism and other forms of collectivism and state-ownership are based on errors, but what they promise remains seductive. Yet we— myself included, here and now— battle on quixotically. States may be overthrown, but only by other states. We acquiesce in statism even as we fight it (if we do). The State, as confessional or secular as you please, we shall have with us always—or at least until Kingdom come. Only then will we have government done right (Psalm 67:4).

I believe we're living in the last days of the dispensation of grace (Ephesians 3:2), the last one before the Kingdom. It began at the time marked by Acts 28:28, when the salvation-bringing

message of God was freely authorized to the nations (whereas
before it had been restricted, with rare exceptions, to the Jews).
The 21 symptoms of the present syndrome of wickedness that
the Apostle Paul foresaw (2 Timothy 3) are on full display and
intensifying in their malignancy. Politics will not reverse it any
more than politics can accelerate or delay God's assumption of
sovereignty. The latter will not be an anarcho-capitalist political
economy. But until then, God's policy is strictly *laissez faire*: if
He doesn't act in grace, He doesn't act at all. No one could stand
if He should mark iniquities (Psalm 130:3); He'll mark them,
however, when He governs those who'll be privileged to live in
the Kingdom.

Analyzing Ferrara's diatribe led me into historical matters
whose potential interest to others transcends our spat and, in
my opinion, justifies reincarnating blog posts as chapters of a
book. Informing my side of the dispute was a concern over how
Christians should disagree with each other. He should have
honored the principle, not of subsidiarity, but of charity in all
things, including debate. The latter, and not any desire to kick
a hornet's nest, comprise this book's *raison d'être*.[6] If I have failed
to honor the principle of charity, I expect to be held to account.

When working out my Rothbardianism as well as my
salvation in fear and trembling, I found broad compatibility—
"commonality" is Thomas Woods's word for it—between Catholicism and libertarianism. But although I found it intellectually
attractive and psychologically satisfying, the likeness never
seemed to amount to more than a happy coincidence. Suppressing
that impression, I forged ahead. I learned much along the way, and
this collection of posts salvages the fruits of my education.

"Catholic Social Teaching" builds on solid rock only when
it builds on the Scriptures. This, however, it hasn't always done;
in fact, it has diluted the Living Water of Christ's Word with

---

[6] For my rejection of Rothbard's defense of abortion, see Appendix A, "Murray Rothbard:
on my late friend's lamentable error," first published on *anthonygflood.com*, January 7, 2019.

the bathtub gin of alien philosophy, betraying the good intentions of CST's advocates. (Aristotle's rationale for slavery comes to mind; defenses of it can be found in Catholic moral manuals as late as 1958, almost 70 years after *Rerum Novarum*, CST's marching orders. See Chapter 28 below.)

An understanding of free trade and an affirmation of its goodness are ever in conflict with the *libido dominandi*, to which some people succumb more easily than others. On the so-called "left" and "right," we find those whose sensibilities are offended by lectures about markets. My fear, now my reluctant conclusion, is that this desire to intervene in markets with violence or the threat thereof, the insane hostility to the obstacles that free markets pose to political fantasy, is central to the fallen human condition. It is an expression of the sin of the world, to take away which the Lamb of Christ was crucified.

Of course, saying this won't make politics go away. It will remain our misfortune until the Kingdom comes; when it does, it will be within us, that is, God will govern us *internally* (Isaiah 30:21) and every transgression will receive its just recompense of reward (Hebrews 2:2)—which is obviously *not* happening now! He will legislate *and* judge *and* execute His judgments. Enjoying an abundance of all goods—God will open His hand and satisfy the desire of every living thing (Psalm 145:16)— we'll have no need for buying and selling and therefore no need for money. When, during the last days of the centuries' long Kingdom, the Holy Spirit lifts the King's internal restraints for seven years to test His subjects, buying and selling, i.e., markets, will return (Revelation 13:17), as will wars and rumors thereof (Matthew 24:6). There will be a defection from, a revolt (*apostasia*, 2 Thessalonians 2:3) against the Kingdom. These things will be signs that the Day of the Lord and of His *Parousia* approaches. (Having been continuous for all of recorded history, they cannot be "signs" now.) Until then, we can only opine about how to respond to the foreign and domestic barbarians at our gates.

xviii | Christ, Capital &Liberty

The inclination to wield political power is as inevitable as the effort to resist it is ephemeral and bootless. My political mentors wed an eschatological agnosticism to a this-worldly optimism; my eschatological optimism is independent of my political temperament, which happens to be pessimistic. As Rothbard once told me, "You know, we're Manichaeans, not Augustinians." That is, he didn't believe in a God who will one day stanch the flow of evil. The victory of good over evil, the end of iniquity, is was not inevitable, not divinely guaranteed. So, it's up to us. My journey from Herbert Aptheker[7] to Murray Rothbard and beyond has convinced me, almost against my will, of the futility of politics.

That futility is one great, if negative, mark of the present dispensation. The latter's end will also conclude the Day of Man (*anthropines hemeras*, 1 Corinthians 4:3), the age that stretches from the debarkment of Noah and his family to the moment God assumes sovereignty and inaugurates the Day of Christ (*hemeras Christou Iesou*, Philippians 1:6, 10; 2:16). God will once again inject Himself into the flow of history, this time pouring out His Spirit upon all flesh (Joel 2:28; Acts 2:17) to govern all the nations upon the earth (Psalm 67:4). There will be no anarcho-*anything* after God blazes forth (*epiphaneia*, 2 Timothy 4:1, 8). (My interpretation of Scripture, whose assertion here many will find tendentious, will be the focus of my next book.)

I expressed my grasp of Austrian economics and Christian ethics in a polemic that, in my biased opinion, has contemporary relevance. Regardless of the gloomier view I now have of its practical import, I cannot bring myself to consign these chapters to the flames. Perhaps others, if they find anything in them worth developing, will develop it or consign the whole thing to the flames themselves.

---

[7] See my *Herbert Aptheker: Studies in Willful Blindness.* Independently published, 2019. Available on Amazon.

A polemic is a living thing: to have uprooted these essays from their soil, disguised their origins, and displayed them in the journalistic equivalent of tubes on an assay tray would have almost certainly evacuated them of any force they may have.

There are four appendices: (A) a critique of Murray Rothbard's defense of the alleged "right" of a woman to procure an abortion; it originally appeared on anthonygflood.com; (B) a review of Thomas E. Woods's ground-breaking *The Church and the Market*, which first appeared on LewRockwell.com, as did (C), my appreciation of Lord Acton.

Finally, written during my anarcho-catholic years, but not overtly Christian, is (D) my defense of a free market order against philosopher David Ray Griffin's charge that it is a "cause" of war; the Libertarian Alliance (UK) published it as an issue of *Philosophical Notes* (No. 81), in 2009.

I'm honored and gratified that the Foreword that graces the reader's entrance to this volume was provided by Dr. Gerard N. Casey. He exemplifies integral anarcho-Catholicism at its most rigorous, as his many publications demonstrate.[8]

Who was the first anarcho-Catholic (at least of the Austro-liberatarian persuasion)? Probably James A. Sadowsky, S.J. (1923-2012). I first phoned him in his Fordham University room in 1983. (Later that year I'd meet Murray Rothbard, whom *he* had looked up in the early 1960s after reading *America's Great Depression*.) As I wrote elsewhere, "I never feel I have reached a defensible position until I have found words that swat the Sadowskyan mite who squirts in my mind's ear devastating

---

[8] Including *Born Alive: The Legal Status of the Unborn Child In England and the U.S.A.* (Barry Rose Law Publishers Ltd, 2005); *Libertarian Anarchy: Against the State* (Continuum, 2012); *Murray Rothbard* (Bloomsbury Academic, 2013); *Freedom's Progress?: A History of Political Thought* (Imprint Academic, 2017); and the forthcoming *Zap! Free Speech and Tolerance in the Light of the Zero Aggression Principle* (Societas, scheduled for publication October 1, 2019). See Marcus Grodi's Catholicism-themed interview of Casey on EWTN's The Journey Home, August 19, 2013. https://www.youtube.com/watch?v=O1QjUjcFTeI See also the Wikipedia entry for Casey: https://en.wikipedia.org/wiki/Gerard_Casey_(philosopher)

refutations of my cherished positions."[9] But even these words dilute the affection that the memory of our many conversations evoke. He died shortly before the blog behind this book did. To the memory of our friendship of almost thirty years I dedicate this volume. I miss you, Jim.

I didn't answer every point Mr. Ferrara made; I'll let others speculate about whether I couldn't. This book isn't the "fisking" I wanted the blog to be. He is free to drive that point home in any review he may write. I wish him well, for I am sure Jesus Christ is His Lord and Savior as He is mine.

Perhaps He is yours as well, dear reader. If He isn't, or you don't even think you need one, you have no ground for your understanding of either capital or liberty: along with you, it's floating in a void. (An argument for another book.)

I once believed we could immobilize fools, but no longer. Again, only God can and will do that (Psalm 64:7-8; 2 Timothy 3:9). With our well-doing, however, we can put their ignorance to silence (1 Peter 2:15). May this book serve that end.

Anthony Flood
July 15, 2019

---

[9] http://www.anthonyflood.com/sadowsky.htm

Part One

Setting the Table

Chapter 1

A Question of Tone

Amusician may have mastered the melodic, harmonic, and rhythmic elements of a composition, but if he cannot produce tones of the appropriate timbre and texture, he will undermine rather than promote his purpose. By contrast, the most banal of tunes in the hands of a great instrumentalist or vocalist might mesmerize millions. In an important sense, then, we perceive a performance's texture "before" (esthetically, if not temporally) we hear the notes, so much so that if we don't like the former, we are biased against the latter. We may consequently misjudge the musical content in which we might have delighted were another to deliver it to our senses.

Sometimes, however, cacophony simply signals the activity of a tone-deaf composer. No one who has read more than a few pages of Christopher A. Ferrara's *The Church and the Libertarian* can take it seriously as a "fraternal appeal" to Austro-libertarian Catholics.[10] Several thorough readings have convinced me that it is such a bad book, morally as well as stylistically, that it arguably ought to be ignored rather than critically reviewed. Its

---

[10] *The Church and the Libertarian: A Defense of the Catholic Church's Teaching on Man, Economy, and State.* Forest Lake, MN: The Remnant Press, 2010.

tone is continuously inflammatory, its arrangement of material lopsided (the second section being longer than the first and third combined), and his use of sources tendentious. The last-mentioned trait includes either unawareness or evasion of evidence relevant to his topic but inconvenient to his purpose.

Even while rummaging through memories of my Marxist days (1969-1975), I cannot recall ever having encountered between two covers such a barrage of uncharitable construction, sarcasm, gratuitous assertion, name-calling, motive-questioning, playing to the gallery, assumption of facts not in evidence, digressive appeal to unqualified expert opinion, citing overvalued credentials, stereotyping, redefining key terms, abuse of scare-quotes, innuendo, misleading references, and theatrical laughter. I could support this impression with any three consecutive pages of the reader's choosing. Passages from the writings of Herbert Aptheker in his worst mood rival it, but even that historian-cum-propagandist never sustained his invective for hundreds of pages.[11]

In other words, reading it will likely be a chore for any one not predisposed to the author's point of view. The only thing that is clear after more than three hundred pages is that Mr. Ferrara is angry that any Catholic, and especially his erstwhile collaborator Thomas E. Woods, would enter into the thought of Murray Rothbard and allow it to interact with his faith.[12]

* * *

[11] See my "Herbert Aptheker: Apothecary for a Red Teenager," *AnthonyGFlood.com*, October 25, 2018. Republished in Flood, *Herbert Aptheker: Studies in Willful Blindness,* Amazon, 2019.

[12] In a video interview Mr. Ferrara said that both "love for what the Church teaches" and "deep, serious and . . . righteous anger . . . about a certain kind of sophistry that has taken hold of the Church today, the sophistry of the so-called modern libertarian movement and its advocacy of radical *laissez faire* as the basis for social order" motivated him to write the book under review." A Lake Garda Interview with Chris Ferrara, July 20, 2010. http://www.youtube.com/watch?v=ymtCyf8XvLQ

By "propaganda" I mean a communication of information, ideas, and opinions that the communicator wishes its recipient to accept uncritically. His intention is to persuade and dissuade, not by surveying the evidence, weighing alternative hypotheses potentially explanatory of it, and submitting to his readers merely fallible judgments. It is, rather, to filter that evidence and then emotionally charge selected portions of it in a way that convinces his audience to submit themselves willingly to *his* judgment.

The challenge facing a reviewer of a work of propaganda is to reveal it to be such without engaging in it himself. While he must note the intellectual issues that the propagandist raises and critically evaluate the latter's handling of them, he must not (a) appear to grant the propagandist's conceit that his is a work of intellectual merit, (b) give the propagandist a victory by appearing to evade the alleged force of his "devastating" arguments, or (c) get into the gutter with him.

The propagandist who has chosen the book as his medium has his reviewer at a disadvantage. In order to marshal evidence for identifying the book's genre as propaganda, he must risk appearing as uncharitable toward its author as he can easily show the author to have been. The responsible reviewer must weigh that risk against that of granting the propagandist's conceit that he is a fellow seeker of truth. Unfortunately, he must risk trying his readers' patience (again advantaging the propagandist) by begging them to accept, at least provisionally, his conceit that it *is* propaganda and should be reviewed as such.

While steeling myself to write this essay, I was struck by the similarity, at least on one point, of my situation with that of 20th-century Catholic convert, Bishop Basil Christopher Butler, when he took on a Protestant critic of the Church:

> . . . a complete and exhaustive answer to [George Salmon's *Infallibility*] would need to be a much longer treatise than this. It is easy to pack into half a dozen pages enough clever charges against the Catholic

Church to require a thousand pages in reply. In this kind of warfare the aggressor always has an enormous advantage.[13]

Or as one contemporary theologian more succinctly put it: "It's almost always tedious to refute tendentious reporting."[14] But sometimes it's necessary.

---

[13] Basil Christopher Butler, *The Church and Infallibility: A Reply to the Abridged "Salmon,"* New York: Sheed and Ward, 1954, vi. http://www.philvaz.com/apologetics/num11.htm It was a reply to Anglican divine George Salmon's *The Infallibility of the Church: A Course of Lectures Delivered in the Divinity School of the University of London*, a book first published in 1888, one which some Reformed apologist still claim has "never been answered." I am moved to ensure that *that* will never be said of TCATL.

[14] R. A. Reno, "How Do You Spell Tendentious," *First Things,* July 2, 2010.

Chapter 2

In Few Things, Charity?

There is a substantial academic literature on the imperative to construe charitably another's position. In philosophy and rhetoric, the principle of charity requires interpreting a speaker's statements to be rational and, in the case of any argument, considering its best, strongest possible interpretation. In a narrower sense, the goal is to avoid attributing irrationality, logical fallacies, or falsehoods to the others' statements when a coherent, rational interpretation of the statements is available.

According to philosopher Simon Blackburn, this principle "constrains the interpreter to maximize the truth or rationality in the subject's sayings."[15] Philosopher Nigel Warburton defined the principle as follows:

> Interpreting arguments or positions adopted by others in the best possible light. Rather than setting an opponent's pronouncements up as an easy target, those who adopt the principle of charity look for the best case that this person could consistently be making rather than the worst. Adopting the principle of charity

---

[15] Simon Blackburn, *The Oxford Dictionary of Philosophy*, Oxford University Press, 2008, 59.

is the opposite of setting up a straw man. Rather than caricaturing an opponent's position, charitable thinkers give everything about it the benefit of the doubt. The appropriateness of this depends entirely on the context.... There is no obligation to adopt a principle of charity, and in many cases it would be entirely inappropriate, labour-intensive, and unrewarding. But it can provide an occasional antidote to knocking down straw men, and the kind of relentless negativity that clear thinkers are sometimes accused of.[16]

Almost every page of TCATL provides evidence of Mr. Ferrara's sin against this principle. Because he is a Catholic, this exercise in mockery is a disgrace: not only is grace absent from its pages, but so is charity, even according to the standards of secular discourse. By the standards one has the right to expect of a Catholic, for whom charity ought to be the chief virtue, it is scandalous. Because that tone infects his case against Austro-Libertarianism, however, it is hard to tweeze out the content from the form in which he encases it. That tone poisons the atmosphere within which an exchange of ideas might take place, one that has the potential of benefiting both Austro-libertarians and their critics.

The common meaning of "in all things, charity" is apparently so alien to him that referring to his adversaries as "charlatans" (301) who promote a "form of lunacy" (251) is his idea of "a fraternal appeal."(5) Mr. Ferrara is of the opinion that "spokesmen of the Austro-Libertarian movement . . . have much that is good and true to say concerning the benefits of free enterprise and private property." (309) The preceding 308 pages do not convey that impression. Fourteen pages later in the same chapter, however, he writes: "Catholics ought to have nothing to do with the Austro-Libertarian movement." (323)

---

[16] Nigel Warburton, *Thinking from A to Z*, Third Edition, Routledge, 2007, 34.

One would think Catholics ought at least to have "something to do with" the "good and true things" that Austro-Libertarians say by acknowledging that their spokesmen say them and finding out why they say them. After all, the Austro-libertarian movement is an educational movement and not, say, a paramilitary one. That is, the only way one could have anything to "do" with it is to consider its ideas. Therefore, he who deems some of them "good and true" cannot avoid having something to do with that movement. This self-imposed dilemma is not a deceptive appearance created by juxtaposing out-of-context quotations.

I shall argue that Catholics are within their rights to be Austro-libertarians in their political and economic thinking. There is no necessary cognitive dissonance between the Gospel and the libertarian prohibition against the initiation of force. I would go further, however, by suggesting to my fellow Austro-libertarians—Catholic or not, Christian or not, theist or not—that the Catholic worldview is a congenial philosophical home for libertarianism. Catholicism should move out of the shadows of libertarian discourse and onto center stage. Catholics can make a difference to the libertarian movement by stressing their distinctive worldview.

An integration of Austro-Libertarianism with Catholicism should replace the current gentlemen's agreement of settlement whereby one politely notes either (a) the Catholicism of several leading Austro-libertarians as a mere biographical detail or (b) Murray Rothbard's positive assessment of the role of the Roman Catholic Church in the history of Western liberty. In short, Austro-Libertarian Catholics should clarify that, for them, "Catholic" is the substantive and "Austro-libertarian" the adjective and, when appropriate, make their case for the greater intelligibility of the Catholic worldview as libertarianism's wider context of meaning compared to any rival worldview.

Of course, non-Catholic Austro-Libertarians, after considering the case for Catholicism as that nurturing home for their economic and politics, may lack the grace necessary for conversion (as a Catholic might interpret the situation) and yet be enriched by the encounter. Even if they take a pass on Catholicism, their Austro-Libertarianism still needs a framework, and they should not want for Catholic associates ready to challenge them to justify their choice of any other.

I forget exactly how Christopher Ferrara learned of my views, but do remember his approaching me during the intermission of a talk we had attended and his subsequent e-mails in which he tried to draw me into an argument over the just wage. After a few attempts on my part to make sense of his complaint, I begged off with the promise to review any book that might result from his series of articles for *The Remnant* newspaper. Our encounter occurred shortly before the appearance of my review of Thomas Woods's *The Church and the Market*, near the end of which I wrote:

> My repeated references in this review to "seven consecutive popes" reflect a recent conversation with a Catholic critic of Austrianism [i.e., Christopher Ferrara]. He used that phrase several times as if to underscore its centrality to his case against Catholic free-market defenders like Woods. As I mentioned [earlier in the review], we are not going to find popes handicapping sporting events. And when it comes to faith and morals, it would not take seven but only one pope speaking *ex cathedra* to bind a Catholic's conscience. If it does not pertain to those matters, if it is instead about, say, music, architecture, or economics, then not even the considered opinions of 265 consecutive popes, in themselves, would suffice to bind it. Especially ironic about this critic's line of argument was its sharp contrast with his powerful defense, delivered in a lecture just before he and I chatted, of Archbishop Marcel Lefebvre's 1988

consecration of bishops without the Pope's explicit permission (and arguably against his wishes). According to this critic, therefore, a faithful Catholic may withstand Paul VI to his face on *Novus Ordo Missae*, but not on the living wage, or John Paul II on episcopal consecration, but not on "consumerism.[17]

Since he initiated email correspondence with me, and since I subsequently (but long before he completed TCATL) praised both Woods and Lord Acton on LewRockwell.com, I wonder why Mr. Ferrara declined to treat me as one of the usual suspects.[18] Since Mr. Ferrara managed to write a book on the Catholic reception of Austro-Libertarianism without evaluating the writings of James A. Sadowsky, S.J., however, it is a small matter for him to have overlooked me. More on Father Sadowsky presently.

---

[17] Anthony Flood, "A Profound Philosophical Commonality," *LewRockwell.com*, April 23, 2005. www.lewrockwell.com/orig6/flood1.html Reprinted as Appendix B.

[18] See also Anthony Flood, "Lord Acton: Libertarian Hero," *LewRockwell.com*, April 4, 2006. www.lewrockwell.com/2006/04/anthony-flood/lord-acton-libertarian-hero/ Reprinted as Appendix C.

Chapter 3

A Question of Competency

E ven if one pushes past the unrelieved sneer that colors Mr. Ferrara's brief, one may raise questions about the evidence he adduces and his use of it. His every venture into a field in which he is not expert is a contrived garden path to a foregone conclusion.

An early-warning sign of trouble is the number of disparate areas of study that its author, not a specialist in any of them, presumes to treat. Land enclosure in 18th-century England; the loss of Church lands in Europe; the Greek ingredient of the medieval Greco-Christian synthesis; consequentialist ethics; praxeology as a method of the social sciences; the moral status of lending money at interest ("usury"); the financial crisis of 2008; distributism—these are but a few of the topics I can call to mind without consulting his book afresh. His opinions are delivered with an arrogance that might be tolerable if displayed by a polymath, but insufferable when exhibited by a dilettante.

Not surprisingly, given our author's profession, his book is redolent of a prosecuting attorney's brief. That is, it assumes the form of reasoning while denying the power thereof, which requires one to be on the lookout for possible flaws, not only in another's hypothesis, but also in one's own. For attorneys at trial are not engaged in mutually enriching dialog. Whether prosecuting or defending, they are under no obligation to disclose to their curial adversaries a weakness in their case. In fact, they may be under obligation *not* to. To dispose his opponents' case in the most favorable light, then, to raise questions for their consideration, and to be genuinely open to their responses is not a concern of Ferrara's, if this book is any evidence.

Because TCATL never engages the body of thought with which I am conversant as an advocate, I must comment as much on its rhetorical performance, even theater, as on the content of his few arguments, which only betray his ignorance. What the book does parade before the reader is one external criticism after another, each resting on the author's superficial grasp of (a) the historical controversies to which those criticisms refer and (b) the literature that evaluates those controversies.[19] Of course, had Mr. Ferrara tried to evaluate that literature, he would have had either to confine his scope restrict himself to a narrower scope of topics or write many volumes the size of TCATL. To achieve judiciousness in all of them in a mere 326 pages, however, the caliber of one's mind would need to rival that of Jacques Barzun. Alas, Christopher Ferrara is no Jacques Barzun.

And neither is the reviewer. Apart from four years of graduate school in philosophy, this cradle Catholic, who intellectually converted to Austro-Libertarianism in 1983 and enjoyed the friendship and guidance of Murray Rothbard (1926-1995) for the last dozen years of his life, claims no expertise in any of the fields

---

[19] A criticism may be "internal" or "external." An internal criticism takes the writer's case on its own terms and tries to ascertain whether, on those terms, it stands or falls. An external criticism presupposes something to be the case dogmatically—much as a court of law might "take judicial notice" of the fact that the sun rises in the east and sets in the west without demanding justification for it—and then notes whether or not the text under review contradicts the presupposition. If it can be shown that it does, then it has *ipso facto* been refuted. While both kinds of criticism can be effective, the efficacy of external criticism varies inversely with the controvertible character of what the critic presupposes. Internal criticism relies on no controvertible propositions other than those supplied by the writer.

for which our author presumed to play tour guide. As we shall see, however, expertise is not required in order to discern that Mr. Ferrara does not have any. We merely aim to examine the disservice he did his readers by way of inexcusable omissions and distortions. That is, our case is primarily moral: the author is not to be trusted on his chosen topic. Unfortunately, showing it will cost me many more sentences than the one of dismissal TCATL deserves solely on its content.

Finally, this review-essay is intended to be a resource for Catholics in Mr. Ferrara's camp or orbit who, although inclined to agree with his *prima facie* case against Austro-Libertarianism, are curious about what might be said in reply. To that end, readers will be referred to the literature, much of which was arguably Mr. Ferrara's responsibility to bring to their attention and from which they may infer fuller answers to his charges.

Chapter 4

Sound Bites, Panic Buttons, Scare Quotes

M r. Ferrara's "Author's Introduction" begins with a true enough reminder that "[w]e live in an age of demagogues and sound bites," as opposed to the "reasoned polemics that once characterized public discourse" on important matters." (1)

Perhaps he is tacitly promising his readers that the book they are about to enjoy is a specimen of reasoned polemic. As his rhetorical style puts one in mind of the sound bites that characterize electoral campaign ads, his complaint is a case of the pot calling the kettle black. For in that opening paragraph he announces, with no hint of irony, that he will occasionally interrupt his discourse to post sound bite-sized "panic buttons" to which Austro-libertarian advocates allegedly resort when confronted with inconvenient facts and arguments. Here are the eleven "buttons":

- "Industry is evil, evil, evil! (21)
- "So, corporations are evil, evil, evil. What about all the good they have done?" (26)
- "So, you want to soak the corporations!" (29)

- "Socialism!" (137)
- "Minimum wage laws! Mandatory health insurance! Crushing burdens on business!" (172)
- "Socialism! Government-imposed caps on executive pay! Envy of the rich! Class warfare!" (197)
- "OSHA! OSHA! OSHA! Government bullying of small businesses and a further expansion of the 'nanny state'!" (200)
- "AFL-CIO! TEAMSTERS! UNION THUGS!" (206)
- "You're making excuses for the Fed" (221)
- "Government regulation of business! Burdensome requirements! More bureaucracy!" (281)
- "The abolition or breakup of big business!" (284)

It is hard to interpret these imputations of panic as anything other than rhetorical sound effects intended to enhance the perceived impact of Ferrara's attempts at argument. The sputterings he puts into the mouth of his adversaries add nothing to those attempts, but instead detract from their presentation. By his resort to these theatrical cues he shows contempt for the reader's intelligence, for although he "identifies" the buttons, he does not source them, that is, he does not name the "opponents of the arguments to be presented here" who might "activate" those buttons. (1)

That is, before he has presented one word of his opponents (or before he has even told the reader who they are), he characterizes them as purveyors of "bugaboos" that serve only as "distractions from real issues." (2) For all Mr. Ferrara has shown to the contrary, none of the Austro-libertarians he names, none of the anarcho-Catholics who have provoked him to write TCATL, have ever pushed those buttons in an actual exchange of views. Yet somehow they are supposed to "prepare the reader" for such an exchange.

We also get a first look at his mixed message to libertarian readers. He wants to explore "common ground" with libertarians in an effort to dismantle "the modern state" (but not the state as such), which "was built on the ruins of former Christendom *by the very principles doctrinaire libertarians defend* as essential to what they think is Liberty." ([2] Emphasis in the original.)

Ah, Christendom. The man who insists that his argument is not with libertarianism as such, but only with the "Austro" brand—and any suggestion to the contrary is but a "diversionary tactic"—puts no distance between himself and that phase of Christianity's history during which so many un-Christ-like things transpired in His name. Mr. Ferrara will not entertain the possibility that the ruins of Christendom were forecast in the venal stupidities and crimes of so many doctrinaire Catholics of Christendom who defended them as essential to Christianity.

Mr. Ferrara excoriates, for example, the revolutionary expropriation of ecclesiastical property in France, but not the absolutist state of Louis XIV who reserved to Catholics the privilege of owning human beings in France's colonies, provided the slaves were baptized and their families not broken up. His Royal Highness was only acquiescing in contemporary Catholic Social Teaching which, thank God, contrary to Mr. Ferrara, *can* change. Continuing in the introduction, we find one of the first of countless instances of mocking scare quotes redundantly combined with "so-called":

> This book originated in a series of articles for the Catholic bi-weekly *The Remnant* examining the opposition between Catholic teaching and the so-called "Austro-libertarian movement," a combination of radical libertarianism with the so-called "Austrian School" of economics . . . . (3)

Does his criticism have a real object? For if he accepts the label by which it is commonly referred to, there is no need for punctuation that only renders his reference uncertain. The tic-like use of scare quotes renders many of his statements ambiguous. To a critic of any of those uses, Mr. Ferrara can always retort:

"I wasn't referring to x! I was referring to 'x'!" Or: *"I didn't say S's assertion was heretical! I said it was 'heretical'!"*

And so when we read that "this book is not an attempt to 'excommunicate' anyone from the Catholic Church" (2) we face a problem of interpretation, for no one seriously believes that Mr. Ferrara has the power either to excommunicate or even to set in motion a series of events that would result in excommunication.

My surmise? His use of "excommunicate," like "heresy," contributes to an atmosphere of suspicion without his appearing to arrogate any authority to himself (which conceit would cost him credibility). But then what we have here is nothing more than polemical theater. Despite the accusatory tone that permeates his book, Mr. Ferrara denies that he wrote it "to make accusations against the persons who have uttered them." (3) Either he does not know what an accusation is, or some other defect accounts for his use of that word.

*   *   *

In *The Aims of Education,* Alfred North Whitehead argued that "Style is the ultimate morality of mind," and in *On Writers and Writing,* Walter Raleigh held that to "write perfect prose is neither more nor less difficult than to lead a perfect life." Mr. Ferrara is certainly not the only writer who relies heavily on the italic font, the typographical equivalent of table-banging, to enhance the performance of his prose. He is, however, the only one I know who italicizes the words of others without bringing that alteration to the reader's attention *at the time.* He could have defended this departure from good practice in his "Author's Introduction" to TCATL, or in one of its footnotes—that is, *notes at the foot of the page*—where it would be hard to miss. He chose instead merely to stipulate, in the fourth note to Chapter 1, on page 327: "Emphasis added, here and throughout the book unless otherwise indicated."

I suppose Mr. Ferrara believes it was reasonable of him to expect his readers to find and retain this stipulation early in their reading. I do not believe it was, but I may be wrong. After all, my late discovery of it (well into my second reading) may not be typical. Until I saw that note, however, my impression was that those many emphases *were* in the original—i.e., *not added*—unless Mr. Ferrara indicated otherwise. Consequently, in those cases where I knew that was *not* the case—the cited books were on my shelf—Mr. Ferrara appeared to me to be guilty of multiple counts of misquotation. I now see he was merely guilty of the lesser offense of amplifying the perceived "volume" of his evidence while obscuring the agency of the amplification. Apparently, Mr. Ferrara could not trust readers to "get" the meaning of his quotations without help, and yet also realized that to din "emphasis added" in their ears as many times as necessary would risk highlighting only his low opinion of his readers rather than his point.

Chapter 5

An Inconvenient Jesuit

M r. Ferrara dedicated TCATL "to all the great Jesuits at Fordham [University] in the Seventies," where he matriculated, specifically Francis Canavan, S.J. (1917-2009). Another great Jesuit of that time and place was James A. Sadowsky, S.J., S.T.L. (1923-2012), to whose memory this book is dedicated, a professor of philosophy, who began teaching there in 1960.

A convert to Roman Catholicism from Anglicanism (1939) and a priest of the Society of Jesus (1957), Father Sadowsky apparently did not have the opportunity to mold our author's young mind. A friend of Murray Rothbard's since the early '60s, Sadowsky frequently celebrated Mass in the Tridentine Rite at St. Ann's Shrine in New York during the decade before that church's 2005 tragic demise.

Although many of Sadowsky's writings are germane to Mr. Ferrara's topic, either his research didn't lead him to them, or it didn't serve his propagandistic purpose to bring them to his readers' attention. This is so even though Tom Woods cited those writings several times, and even though Rothbard endorsed Sadowsky's definition of rights.[20] My review of Woods's *The Church and the Market* praises its use of Sadowsky, a review that (a) Mr. Ferrara almost certainly knows and (b) provides links to the text of many of Sadowsky's papers. The failure to confront this Catholic moral philosopher's Austro-Libertarianism is inexplicable except in terms not favorable to Mr. Ferrara's reputation as a researcher. Take, for example, this passage from a 2004 lecture of Woods's:

> When dealing with wage rates, a moral question that is hardly ever asked, but should be by those who advocate "living wage" legislation is why the obligation of charity should fall entirely upon the shoulders of the employer. Fr. James Sadowsky explains that the very fact that an employee has accepted employment is an indication that he expects to be made better off than he would have been had he attempted to go into business for himself. Thus in the case of a worker in dire need, while "certainly from a Christian point of view we ought to help him meet his needs," the question that *ought* to arise is this: "Why, however, should it be precisely he *employer* on whom this obligation falls, if in fact the employer is not worsening but bettering the condition of his employee?"[21]

Except for the word "moral," this passage reappears in Woods's 2005 *The Church and the Market*, page 73.[22] But this is how Mr. Ferrara presents it in TCATL:

---

[20] Sadowsky's formulation appears in his 1966 article, "Private Property and Collective Ownership," which Rothbard cites in his *The Ethics of Liberty* (1982), which Mr. Ferrara certainly knows.

[21] Thomas E. Woods, Jr., "Morality and Economic Law: Toward a Reconciliation," Lou Church Memorial Lecture, Austrian Scholars Conference, Auburn, Alabama, delivered March 20, 2004. www.lewrockwell.com/woods/woods25.html

[22] Thomas E. Woods, Jr., *The Church and the Market*, 2006, 73.

When dealing with wage rates, a *moral* question that is hardly ever asked, but should be by those who advocate "living wage" legislation is why the obligation of *charity* should fall entirely upon the shoulders of the employer. . . . [I]n the case of a worker in dire need, while "certainly from a Christian point of view we ought to help him meet his needs," the question that *ought* to arise is this: "Why, however, should it be precisely he *employer* on whom this obligation falls, if in fact the employer is not worsening but bettering the condition of his employee?" (193)

Mr. Ferrara preserves the internal quotation marks indicating Sadowsky's words, but replaces with an ellipsis the sentence that (a) attributes them to Sadowsky and (b) implicitly invites the reader to compare and contrast the costs and benefits of being an employee and going into business for oneself. (Mr. Ferrara added the italics in the first sentence without remark; the other two italicizations are Woods's.)

Woods quoted from Sadowsky's "Capitalism, Ethics, and Classical Catholic Social Doctrine,"[23] cited in his book's third chapter, note 85. Since Mr. Ferrara paid special attention to that chapter, he must have noticed Sadowsky's name in its first paragraph and the citation of this article in the first and last reference notes as well as in the 85th (not to mention elsewhere, and in the bibliography).

Had he done due diligence, Mr. Ferrara would not have referred to Woods's source as "a Jesuit economist." (Does Sadowsky's question strike you as one an economist would ask?) Had he performed an internet search for "James Sadowsky," he would have discovered that he could access the text of every Sadowsky article mentioned by Woods. When we turn to the

---

[23] James A. Sadowsky, "Capitalism, Ethics, and Classical Catholic Social Doctrine," *This World*, Fall 1983, 115-125. www.anthonyflood.com/sadowskycatholicsocialdoctrine.htm

just wage, we will ask Sadowsky's question again and evaluate Mr. Ferrara's answer.

I would remind readers who think I pay too much attention to the "little things" of Mr. Ferrara's attack on Austro-Libertarianism that the way one manages little things can be an excellent predictor of how one manages big things. (Matthew 25:14-28) They may think me fussy. But perhaps they misunderstand the point of this enterprise.

Mr. Ferrara's noisy, everything-but-the-kitchen-sink style of "argument" *is* his substance. The few matters that require thought and research could be listed on an index card. His objections were answered long ago in print, in some cases before Mr. Ferrara was born. He did not look for those answers or, if he did, he kept his research to himself.

I care very much about the ideas he distorted and the people he held up for ridicule, especially since he did so in the name of Christ and His Gospel. It is therefore my purpose to subject Mr. Ferrara's every polemical twitch to common standards of truthful communication. Once we document Mr. Ferrara's departure from those norms, the errors and sloppy scholarship with which it is rife will be seen as symptomatic of ethical lapse. The complaints he brings to the bar of reason are but so many tithes of mint and anise and cummin. Justice in one's communication pertains to the weightier matters of the law.

That's a rather Big Thing. This he ought to have done, without leaving the other undone. (Matthew 23:23)

Chapter 6

An Overview of an Overview

In his "Author's Introduction," Mr. Ferrara lists five concerns of his to clarify what his book is *not* about. It is not about the propriety of Christians' voting for libertarian candidates, nor even about libertarianism "in the broad and benign sense of a call for limited governments consistent with the Catholic teaching on man, economy and state to be defended here." (1) Perhaps any other sense might not be so benign. In fact, his proviso rules out most libertarian philosophies, for what Mr. Ferrara means by "the Catholic teaching on man, economy and state" is "libertarian" in the weakest possible sense, that is, non-totalitarian.

Mr. Ferrara proposes a narrow definition of "socialism" such that his book is "not a defense of any form thereof," even though he supports policies that would hamper markets no less than any socialist program, and for much the same reason socialists offer for their schemes: justice allegedly requires it.

Again, early in the book, before one has read one word of his opponents or even knows who they are, Mr. Ferrara has characterized them as purveyors of "bugaboos" that serve only as "distractions from real issues." (2)

John C. Cort was a Catholic gentleman who sincerely, eloquently, and prolifically argued that the social teaching of the encyclicals and non-Marxist democratic socialism converged on the same goal. Having read his *Christian Socialism*, I'm persuaded of that fit. When reading Ferrara, I get the impression that the only reason why a Catholic mustn't be a socialist is because a pope said so. Catholics who reason that way tend not to perceive the democratic socialism implicit in what some popes *actually wrote* and, ironically, in what writers like Ferrara actually believe (i.e., Distributism).

Mr. Ferrara rests his alleged opposition to socialism on what he views as a God-given right to property as the basis of a "rightly ordered liberty." ([2]; or "real liberty" or "true liberty" as he will later refer to it). He also sends mixed messages to libertarian readers. He wants to explore "common ground" with them in an effort to dismantle "the modern state" (not the state as such), which "was built on the ruins of former Christendom *by the very principles doctrinaire libertarians defend* as essential to what they think is Liberty." ([2]; emphasis in the original). Mr. Ferrara's appeal is presumably to non-doctrinaire libertarians whose libertarianism us compatible with Catholicism as he understands it. It also provides a glimpse of his causal hypothesis about the origins of the modern state.

Mr. Ferrara will explain the 2007-2009 economic "meltdown," presupposing his confusion regarding free markets and capitalism introduced in Chapter 1, a confusion that, by then, we will have exposed.

To anyone in the economics profession, "Austrian economics" is a perfectly intelligible label for a respectable body of thought, even to its opponents, such as Paul Krugman, a Nobelist in that field. Friederich Hayek's sharing of the 1974 Nobel Prize in economics removed any justification for casting doubt on the legitimacy of the Austrian School. The Wikipedia entry for it describes the latter as "heterodox," or "non-mainstream," that is, not owing its distinctive ideas to the "orthodox" synthesis of neo-classical microeconomics and Keynesian macroeconomics. Another heterodox school is the Marxian, around few would think it necessary to put scare quotes. The origin of the appellation is of interest to our story. Too bad Mr. Ferrara declined to tell it.

Mr. Ferrara is concerned that some Catholic Austro-libertarians portray their school "as compatible with orthodox Roman Catholicism," whereas, he claims,

> the principal features of the Austro-libertarian system, reflecting "classical liberalism" in general, have been explicitly condemned as errors in a long series of papal pronouncements summed up by Pope Pius XI under the description "moral, legal, and social modernism." (3)

The mute premise of Mr. Ferrara's syllogism is that orthodox Roman Catholicism includes these papal condemnations so that what is inconsistent with the latter is also inconsistent with the former. We will contest Mr. Ferrara's facile theological equation.

The "Author's Introduction" concludes with two sections entitled "The Negative Case" and "The Positive Case." The gist of the former is that "no orthodox Christian can abide" the "grave moral, philosophical and even theological errors" of Austro-Libertarianism "if he would be faithful to Christ and the Gospel." (3)

Observe the broadening scope of Mr. Ferrara's defense: no longer merely Roman Catholicism as articulated in a century's worth of papal pronouncements, it is (small "o") orthodox Christianity itself, even the very meaning of the message of the Gospel and of Christ. We will contest that claim.

Mr. Ferrara refers to "the triumvirate that rule the world today," i.e., "Big Government, Big Business, and Big Finance" (4), but it is important to his case against Austro-libertarians that they be seen as obscuring that alliance, rather than being, as is the case, among the first to have highlighted it, indeed among the thought leaders who first drew out its implications for scholarship. Mr. Ferrara's unfortunate subscription to Kevin Carson's epithet "vulgar libertarian" and the underlying notion is foreshadowed. (4)

As for the "positive case," TCATL has the "far more important positive aim" of defending "the Catholic vision" of social order "presented in the papal encyclicals." (4) Implicitly, at least, Mr. Ferrara offers an interpretation both of those encyclicals and of their importance. As we shall see, however, he does not anchor his claims about their meaning and importance in anything more reassuring than his own grasp of history and theology, but does not admit that limitation.

Mr. Ferrara claims that "real freedom means only that freedom made possible by the truth of the Gospel and that the only really free society is one built on the law of the Gospel." (4–5) We note only his referring to what is to be defined in his definition, but also those qualifiers ("real freedom," "really free") by which he conflates political libertarianism with libertarianism in both the metaphysical sense ("free will") and spiritual (cf. Romans 7). That "real freedom" is to freedom as military music is to music is something we hope to make clear.

The Catholic understanding of fallen humanity's need for grace and the latter's variable active presence in all of us, regardless of our degree of depravity or sanctity, must inform what Catholics say about political liberty, but it hardly justifies the illiberal political regime of which Mr. Ferrara seems to approve. His claim that

> Christian civilization, which stood for 1,600 years
> and can exist again if only we seek to restore it,
> already contains every morally legitimate element of
> the libertarian position . . . . (5)

raises several questions. Exactly which 1,600 years does he mean?

That there is a libertarian core to the Gospel, and that this has implications for ordering our use of interpersonal violence, I have no doubt. What is in doubt is the libertarianism (except in the most attenuated sense) of anyone who seeks to restore what Mr. Ferrara means by "Christian civilization."

Christendom, I shall argue, was a "mixed bag" at best, its own worst enemy at worst, and not something that anyone who names the name of Christ would want to restore without the most stringent of qualifications, of which Mr. Ferrara offers not one.

Mr. Ferrara made it clear what he means by "the law of the Gospel." (4) It is not the compelling quality of Christ's personality and divinity as it given us in the Gospels unmediated by the teaching authority of the Catholic Church. No, that *magisterium* is, according to Mr. Ferrara, the cognitive mediator between Christ and man. As he quotes Pope Pius XI:

> Because the Church is by divine institution the sole depository and interpreter of the ideals and teaching of Christ, she alone possesses in any complete and true sense the power effectively to combat that materialistic philosophy which has already done and, still threatens, such tremendous harm to the home and to the state. . . . [T]he Church is able to set *both public and private life* on the road to righteousness by demanding that everything and all men become obedient to God "Who beholdeth the heart" to His commands, to His laws, to his sanctions.[24]

This passage sounds the theme of Mr. Ferrara's book. What he calls for is hardly libertarianism minus "liberal errors." But misstatement is nothing compared to his claim that TCATL,

---

[24] In this quotation from Pius XI's *Ubi arcano dei* (1922), Mr. Ferrara italicizes what he wishes His Holiness had emphasized (but did not) without referring to that alteration. That is, Mr. Ferrara will not alert his reader to to this unexpected departure from honest practice in the introduction. As we noted earlier that announcement does not occur, assuming one is sharp-eyed enough to catch it, until the fourth note of the first chapter on page 327 and its force is assumed for next 300+ pages.

however forcefully its arguments are presented in places, is also meant as a fraternal appeal to Catholic proponents of the errors at issue, that they might abandon all error and return to the path the Church has marked out for them and for every soul that seeks true happiness in this world and the next. (5)

Again, as a Catholic proponent of what he deems error, not the faintest tincture of fraternity emanates from this self-appointed hammer of heretics. The author of a truly fraternal appeal would normally ask, in all humility, that those whom he criticizes show him, if they can, where he might have gotten something wrong and join him in a common search for truth, especially if they are fellow Catholics. But, then, one does not search for something one thinks one already securely has, does one?

* * *

Like Roman Gaul *circa* 58 B.C., TCATL is divided into three parts, but its total area is hardly as well-distributed as was that provincial territory. The only thing "Roman" about its organization are its numerals. The book's contents are allocated over 22 chapters as follows:

Section I: Encountering the Austro-Libertarian Movement, 35 pages, two chapters

Section II: Austro-Libertarianism contra Ecclesiam, 214 pages, 15 chapters

Section III: A Catholic Response, 69 pages, five chapters

In other words, the middle section bulges with more than twice as many chapters and pages as the other two combined.

Section I effectively consists of only one chapter, namely, the second, "The Illusory Free Market," to which we will, of course, pay special attention. I say this because one-and-half pages out of the first chapter's five, ostensibly dedicated to "meeting" Mr. Ferrara's flesh-and-blood targets, do not in the least serve that purpose. Instead they articulate two "caveats" about what TCATL does *not* concern, material that for some reason he left out of the "Author's Introduction" where it clearly belongs. Of course, that would have left three-and-a-half pages (out of 326) to summarize a century of the scholarly thought one is going to spend the rest of the book critiquing. (No, those three-and-a-half pages are not a judicious précis.)

Section II is a grab bag of topics, ranging from the sublime ("Man and God: Opposing Views") to the ridiculous ("A Defense of Scrooge"), all in some way purporting to show how Austro-libertarian Catholics fail Mr. Ferrara's test of Catholicity (or, as he sometimes adds, even human decency). With a little effort, however, he might have broken it into two sections, one more philosophically oriented, the other more "applied philosophy." The latter would have served nicely as a transition to Section III, Mr. Ferrara's brief for Distributism. The placement of a repetitive "summary" chapter ("The Market Can Do No Wrong"), fourth from that section's end, signals organizational trouble. It is a distracting waste of space that could have been conserved to beef up the skimpy first chapter. What we have instead is an aggregate of topics.

Section III is modestly subtitled "A Catholic Response" (as opposed to "*The* Catholic Response"), although arguably the whole book is one Catholic gentleman's "response" to the phenomenon of Austro-libertarian Catholics. "A Catholic *Alternative*" would have been more accurate. Where it is not stumping for Distributism, this section repeats many charges made earlier. When we get to those repetitions, we will simply refer back to posts that addressed them sufficiently the first time.

Finally, it is worth noting that in his "Acknowledgements," Mr. Ferrara didn't discharge the customary authorial duty of taking full responsibility, and absolving others, for "any remaining errors." I have always enjoyed seeing how many different ways authors can creatively reword that boilerplate. Mr. Ferrara may have deprived me of that sample of his literary powers, but his silence reveals much more: he will not acknowledge even the possibility of his own error. But what propagandist ever had?

No, for remaining errors I won't be blaming Professors Médaille, McCall, or McArthur. Not even Mr. Obriski, his "eagle-eyed" proofreader.

Chapter 7

Demonize and Delete the Austrians

M r. Ferrara's first chapter, "Meet the Austrians," reveals
almost nothing about history the Austrian School of
Economics (ASE), but a great deal about how Mr.
Ferrara wants his readers to perceive its key figures.

Ostensibly about "meeting the Austrians," it manages to
ignore the role in American intellectual life of *The Quarterly
Journal of Austrian Economics* (founded as *The Review of Austrian
Economics* in 1987) and *Libertarian Papers* (founded as *The
Journal of Libertarian Studies* in 1977). Hundreds of scholars have
written for just these three peer-review publications, to name no
others. You would never know that from reading TCATL.

In Mr. Ferrara's opinion, the ASE is not a respectable body
of heterodox (non-mainstream) economic thought with which
one may reasonably disagree, but an academic put-on. His
opening salvo:

> Within due moral limits, private property and the
> market economy are indubitably essential components
> of a rightly ordered liberty that the Catholic Church

can and does approve. The easiest way to lose the argument in favor of property and market, however is to take extreme positions in defense of them— positions contrary to the social teaching of the Church, common sense and even basic human decency.[25] (8)

Let's ignore the emotionally charged terms "extreme" and "human decency" (redolent of political campaign attack ads). Mr. Ferrara sounds as though he is giving lawyerly advice to Austro-libertarian Catholics on the topic of how to not to lose arguments, even though the motivation for writing TCATL was that they are winning too darn many of them and persuading too many educated Catholics with them!

As we shall see, donning easily punctured pretensions to authority and expertise is one of Mr. Ferrara's preferred methods of losing arguments. His truncation of the history of the Church's social teaching, including its not altogether reassuring relationship to human decency, will prove to be another.

Mr. Ferrara introduces, in one sentence, the names of Carl Menger, Eugen von Böhm-Bawerk, and Ludwig von Mises, economists whose writings mark the history of the ASE from the last third of the nineteenth century to the second half of the twentieth. He accurately enough identifies them as representatives "of the 'fin-de-siècle Viennese modernism' of the last years of the Hapsburg Empire" (8), although he does not clarify the meaning of "modernism" in this context.

But then, "modernism" is not his word. In sourcing this brief description, he does not cite any of the histories of the ASE

---

[25] I grant that one may make converts with bad arguments (at least in the short run, until the fallacies are exposed: the blurbs on the back of TCATL attest to that). That admission, however, does not address Mr. Ferrara's claim. It suggests that an "extreme position," *just because* it is extreme, undermines any argument that may be advanced in its favor. One would think that embattled Catholic traditionalists, having been on the receiving end of sound-bite epithets like "extreme," would have resisted the temptation to hurl one at fellow Catholics. Like "beautiful," "extreme" is in the eye of the beholder. (*"I'm principled; you're stubborn; he's pig-headed."*) It serves only to stir up emotions that block thought and raise a cloud of suspicion over any reasoning about the position itself.

that the Mises Institute has made freely available online.[26] He does not even cite Wikipedia's article. To draw upon such sources would have honored the principle of charitable construction (as well as exposing his impressionable readers to them). It would not have prevented him from also citing surveys favorable to Mr. Ferrara's point of view.

No, his source is "Carl Menger and Viennese Modernism," a "Study Project" of the European Forum of Hebrew University.[27] (327, Chapter 1, note 1) It is an undated abstract. There is no evidence that it has ever been published or, for that matter, even finished. The researcher, a young scholar of Hebrew University's Center for Austrian Studies, is Sharon Gordon. Then a doctoral candidate in history at that institution, Ms. Gordon, as she is still identified in her online university profile, does not list this research in her profile's short publications list. The study's abstract refers to it in the future tense: "This research will explore how Carl Menger (1840-1921) related to fin-*de-siécle* Viennese modernism."

There's no evidence that Mr. Ferrara read further. No citation at all, however, supports his assertion of a broad thesis morally implicating thought leaders of the ASE in the downfall of Christian civilization.

Mr. Ferrara chose to convey his view of the import of *laissez faire* at the expense of defining it. It is, in the first place, opposition to a government's use of its monopoly of the means of coercion to regulate economic exchange, to determine whether

---

[26] To name just three such works: Ludwig von Mises, "The Historical Setting of the Austrian School of Economics," Auburn, AL: Ludwig von Mises Institute, 1984 [1969]; David Gordon, "The Philosophical Origins of Austrian Economics," Auburn, AL: Ludwig von Mises Institute, 1996; and Hans-Hermann Hoppe, "Economic Science and the Austrian Method," Auburn, AL: Ludwig von Mises Institute, 1995. All freely available on mises.org.

[27] Sharon Gordon, "Carl Menger and Viennese Modernism," a "Study Project" of the European Forum of Hebrew University. The link to this abstract that I provided in the original post no longer works. A search of the title will yield its citation as a "working paper" in two books.

something may be produced or not, at what rate, and sold for what price. That is, he allowed a particular connotation—"the primary dogma of economic liberalism that emerged as part of the Enlightenment's overall attack on the Christocentric social order of Catholic Europe" (7)—to crowd out its denotation in his exposition.

The words "emerging as part of" an "overall attack" on "Christocentric social order" can excite the Christian reader's glands, but his or her exigent mind may wonder what role Carl Menger and the ASE played in those events or their aftermath. He or she may also wonder, as do we, about the viability of an allegedly Christocentric social order that was so easily undone and ask about any role that agents of that order unintentionally played in the unraveling.

In vain does one search in TCATL for a causal story that shows how one may impute to opponents of interventionism even partial culpability for the demise of a putatively healthy social order. (I find such a possibility improbable.) Identifying Anne Robert Jacques Turgot (but only by his last name) as a leader of the Physiocrats (undefined), who in turn "helped" (somehow) the Encyclopaedists (also unidentified) "pave the way" to the French Revolution is a flabbily expressed opinion, not a carefully framed hypothesis.

Mr. Ferrara translates *"Laissez faire, laissez passer!"* as "Let do [or "let be"] and let pass!," but doesn't tell us what he thinks of the forced cartelization and privileges (and suboptimal consequences for the consumer) that mercantilism represented and against which *"Laissez faire!"* was a protest. If his counterrevolutionary proposal is not something like, "Restrain and obstruct!," he should have made that clear.

In his essay on Turgot, which I recommend as an antidote to Mr. Ferrara's gossip, Murray Rothbard showed how Turgot anticipated many insights of the ASE.[28] (But Mr. Ferrara both claims that his book "is not concerned with 'economics' as an academic discipline" [11], and yet he will make exceptions, unavoidable in a book critical of the ASE.) Mr. Ferrara takes a swipe at "the fallen bourgeois minister Turgot," without telling his reader what it means for something to be a fallen bourgeois minister.

Unlike Mr. Ferrara's book, Ms. Gordon's abstract at least *mentions* Menger's tutelage of Rudolph, Crown Prince of Austria. "So what?," you may ask. Well, His Imperial and Royal Highness, Carl Menger, and Eugen von Böhm-Bawerk were Catholics, and the environment of their marginal revolution in economics was the Catholic Austro-Hungarian Empire; that of the anti-liberal, Junker-supported German Historical School (GHS), Protestant. (Again, Ms. Gordon mentions the GHS, Mr. Ferrara does not.)

In other words, Mr. Ferrara missed an opportunity to link his own, early 21st century concerns to their close parallel in late 19th, inevitably referred to in the literature by the misleading tag *Die Methodenstreit.* Rather than a "debate" over "method," however, it was a bitter polemic over the very nature of economics. Is economics a value-free (except for the value of truth, of course[29]) science, or a political instrument of extra-scientific interests (framed, of course, in the language of ethical concern)?

Ironically, Mr. Ferrara and his modern Catholic Social Teaching camp have championed the Protestant rather than the Catholic side of this divide. We will return to this theme. For now,

---

[28] Murray N. Rothbard, "Brief, Lucid, Brilliant," mises.org/about/3244, excerpted from Rothbard, *An Austrian Perspective on the History of Economic Thought, Vol. I: Economic Thought before Adam Smith,* 385-403. Freely available on mises.org.

[29] Frank van Dun, a Belgian professor of the philosophy of law in the ASE tradition and a member of the Academic Advisory Board of Antwerp-based Rothbard Institute, argues that no science can be absolutely value-free because every scientific pursuit presupposes the value of truth. See Frank van Dun, "Economics and the Limits of Value-Free Science," *Reason Papers,* No. 11 (Spring 1986) 17-32.

http://users.ugent.be/~frvandun/Texts/Articles/LimitsValuefreeScience.pdf

let a passage from an unedited transcript of a lecture of Murray Rothbard provide us with a marker for such future reference:

> It's no accident that the ... epistemological value and value climate in Austria is completely different than it was in Germany and Britain . . . Austria was Catholic and always had been Catholic, whereas northern Germany was Protestant. . . . Menger and Böhm-Bawerk were . . . steeped in natural law and natural rights and Aristotelian epistemology in general. Northern Germany and England and Britain were influenced by Calvinism and Protestant Evangelicalism, which tossed out the so-called scholastic method. . . . . So we have the Austrians steeped in a very different tradition, religious and philosophical tradition than either the Germans or the British.[30]

Rothbard then praises Barry Smith's work on this philosophical division. Smith noted:

> Austrian philosophy is marked ... by the absence of entrenched Kantian and Hegelian elements, philosophical education in the Habsburg lands having been dominated instead by textbooks whose content was drawn from Catholic school-philosophy and from the Leibnizian-Wolffian *Popularphilosophie* that had been current also in Germany until the time of Kant. It is against this background that both the Brentanian movement and the Austrian school of economics grew up and became established.[31]

---

[30] Rothbard, "Menger and Böhm-Bawerk." Fourth in a series of six lectures on the History of Economic Thought. Transcribed and donated by Thomas Topp.
https://mises-media.s3.amazonaws.com/Menger%20and%20Bohm-Bawerk%20Murray%20N%20Rothbard_2.pdf

[31] Barry Smith, "Carl Menger: On Austrian Philosophy and Austrian Economics," *Austrian Philosophy: The Legacy of Franz Brentano,* Open Court Publishing Company, 1995, 300.
http://ontology.buffalo.edu/smith/book/austrian_philosophy/CH10.pdf

In the same lecture, Rothbard highlighted the importance of this background:

> . . . Menger . . . was reacting against the historical school, which was dominant in German-speaking countries, headed by Gustav Schmoller, who believed there were no economic laws, partly because he was interested in building up the state power in Prussia and the rest of Germany. *It was inconvenient to have any economic laws out there which might contradict or confound government degrees and actions.* As a matter of fact, the famous phrase of Schmoller, which Mises liked to mention from time to time, is that the function of the University of Berlin—which, of course, was the creation of the Prussian state—the function of the professor of the University of Berlin is the intellectual bodyguard of the House of Hohenzollern. That was the dynastic Prussian monarchy. When Menger's *Principles of Economics* was published, it was greeted with hatred—bitter derision and hatred—by the Schmollerites of Vienna, that organized a contrary campaign against it. Then Menger got [caught?] up in the mythological conflict, explaining why there is such a thing as economic law. [My emphasis.—A.F.]

Mr. Ferrara's attack on the ASE only mirrors the "bitter derision and hatred" of his ideological forebears in the GHS. He fails to mention that the ASE got its name when Menger's German sparring partner, Gustav Schmoller, head of the German Historical School (GHS), contemptuously bestowed that label on them in the 1870s.

Menger picked a fight with Schmoller and his GHS over its approach to social science, and the resultant squabble was misnamed *Die Methodenstreit* (or "debate over method"). The propositions commonly referred to as modern Catholic Social

Teaching (CST), which Mr. Ferrara takes as oracular, presuppose the philosophical approach to economics of Heinrich Pesch, S.J., his GHS teachers, and his students.

It is ironic that what has come to be called modern Catholic Social Teaching has been largely influenced, not by the Catholics in that skirmish, but rather by the Protestant Schmollerites and their students, including Richard T. Ely.[32] By contrast, the ASE's cultural seedbed was the neo-scholastic Catholic intellectual atmosphere of Vienna.

Although Heinrich Pesch, S.J. had enough solid Catholic training not to be taken in by Schmollerism, he nevertheless effectively took the latter's side in the "debate" with Austrians over the nature of economics. When we arrive at the relevant section of TCATL, we will comment further on Father Pesch's attempted marriage of Christian ethics to methodological collectivism and document his influence on the writing of Pius XI's *Quadragesimo Anno*.

The convergence of nominally anti-socialist CST and nominally anti-Communist democratic socialism in their economic presuppositions was complete by about 1950. (Once again, I recommend John C. Cort's *Christian Socialism*.) Having ignored this convergence and its roots, Mr. Ferrara cannot shed light on such things as, say, *Freedom and Economic Justice for All*, the democratic socialist document issued by the United States Conference of Catholic Bishops in 1986 and reaffirmed by that body a decade later.

---

[32] Ely, the godfather of American Progressive and Institutionalist social thought, wrote the introduction for *A Living Wage* by John A. Ryan, S.J.—"The Right Reverend New Dealer," as Father Charles E. Coughlin affectionately dubbed him—one of Mr. Ferrara's favorite authors in this field. See Gary North, "Millennialism and the Progressive Movement," *Journal of Libertarian Studies*, 12:1 (Spring 1996): 121–142. https://mises-media.s3.amazonaws.com/12_1_6_0.pdf

Chapter 8

Value-Laden and Value-Free

In the chapter in which he is supposed to be introducing Austrians, Mr. Ferrara prefers to begin mounting a positive case (supposedly reserved for the book's third part). This has forced us to foreshadow our response. And so as we turn the first page of that chapter, we find him asserting that the Catholic Church has always insisted that

> the marketplace, no less than any other field of human action, is entirely subject to the requirements of the moral law, including the dictates of natural justice in both the distribution of goods (distributive justice) and transactions between individuals (commutative justice).[33] (8)

Mr. Ferrara does not specify the sense in which a "field of human action" can be "subject to the requirements of the moral

---

33 We ought to be able to deduce from this categorical assertion that the Church subjected the market for human chattel slaves to those requirements. Unfortunately, she viewed that market as part of the "natural order" in the Aristotelian sense and subjected the "Peculiar Institution" to those requirements only on the edges, as it were, until the second half of the nineteenth century, that is, well after Congregationalists, Baptists and others (whom successive Supreme Pontiffs deemed heretics) had helmed an effective abolitionist movement.

law." The "field" that is the marketplace is ontologically nothing over and above the "transactions between individuals" who alone are subject to the moral law.

The market is a complex process consisting exhaustively of innumerable free offers and free responses thereto, opportunities for profit and discoveries or thereof or their oversight.[34] Those offers and responses are in the hands of the individuals who offer and respond responding. He who would take them out of their hands bears the burden of argument.

(The contrary assumption—no one may act unless another gives him permission—would lead us quickly to extinction, for permission-giving is itself an action.)

Individuals may arrogate to themselves the prerogative of making decisions for others (and give themselves fancy titles). After individual transactions are concluded, however, nothing remains to be "distributed." All the actions that carry out individual (decentralized) decisions allocate the total product without remainder.

Mr. Ferrara tries to make out a charge against the Austrian School (or at least create an impression that a charge is lurking):

> For Austrians, as we shall see, within the market "framework" freedom of action is the ultimate moral criterion and only outright violence, theft or fraud should be prohibited, even if "personal morality" might call for a higher standard of behavior outside the "framework." (8. Commas added to improve clarity. A.F.)

Mr. Ferrara does not source this scare quote-laden generalization. (The market is not really a framework? There's

---

[34] Here I borrow the language of Israel Kirzner, who also happens to be a strict-observance Orthodox Jew, and another authoritative Austrian economist to whom Mr. Ferrara never introduces us.

really no such thing as personal morality? He sneers, but he does not explain.)

Now, the "prohibition" of certain behavior usually refers to *governmental* prohibition, and I have little doubt that *that* is what he means. Since such prohibition is not cost-free, however, Austrians *as economists* will demand that those attendant costs be counted (Luke 14:18). As *libertarian* political thinkers, Austrians have a moral objection to authorizing an intrinsically force-initiating institution to prohibit certain immoral behavior (whether or not that behavior involves the initiation of force); or to force individuals to incur costs they do not wish to incur. Austro-libertarians do not acquiesce in the view that the government is exempt from the presumption against initiating force. Rather, we hold that the burden of proof is on those who would grant that exemption. We also happen to think that bar for overturning it is high, in fact, impossibly so.

If Austrian-libertarians happen to be Catholic Christians, the content of their moral objection is the liberating message of the Gospel. They are therefore especially averse to sanctioning patterns of interpersonal interaction that violate the dignity of persons, all created in the image of God, to do evil that good may come (Romans 3:5-8). They argue that the State is such a pattern, no matter how many holy people have been associated with it, and no matter how fine their raiments, glorious their music, their art, and their dwellings.

Vague reference to an "emerging attitude" now follows:

Theirs is the attitude which first emerged as an explicit ethic in late 16th century Protestant England: "trade is one thing and religion is another . . . . business affairs should be left to be settled by businessmen, unhampered by the intrusions of an antiquated morality or by misconceived arguments of public policy." (8)

No scare-quotes this time, but rather real quotation marks. In the main text Mr. Ferrara does not reveal the identity of the authority he's citing. An Austrian? A 16th century English Protestant?

No, he's citing (approvingly) the characterization of an attitude provided by economic historian and social reformer R. H. Tawney (1880-1962), the most influential Christian socialist of his time. How fitting, and how exemplary of Mr. Ferrara's use of sources.

We wish to stress that Mr. Ferrara is no socialist. He's very sensitive to that smear. He just likes quoting socialists and left libertarians and Protestants who have no authority, but who occasionally say things he agrees with.

The claim about economics around which its practitioners may honestly disagree is over its definition. The Austrians proffer a formal object free of the admixture of ethical or other value judgments: it is the science of human action, with specific reference to the allocation of scarce resources to achieve imagined ends.

Now, instead of weighing the pros and cons of this criterion of demarcation, Mr. Ferrara wastes his and his reader's time by noting that a certain Austrian economist has also made a value judgment. He obscures the fact that the allegedly offending Austrian economist was not making ethical evaluations as part of an *economic* analysis, as he or she understands the latter.

The *value-freedom* of economic analysis is not in conflict with the *value-laden* reason why that discipline exists. On the contrary, it is just because we want to promote certain values that we must prescind from them if we would understand causal relationships. But both interests, cognitive and ethical, motivate the same person.

Chapter 9

Adventures in Meta-Ethics

To continue with Mr. Ferrara's mood-setting (long on assertion, short on documentation and argument):

The Austrian defense of the "laws" of economics, however, consistently judges moral abuses in the market according to the supposed greater good that accrues or greater evil that is avoided if these "laws" are allowed to operate unhindered—a morally invalid consequentialist and utilitarian ethic the Church condemns. (See Chapter 8) (8)

What are we to read into the scare quotes this time? That economic laws are figments of the imagination? Or that they are real, but Austrian economists have not correctly identified them?

Since he announces a few pages later that he has no intention of dealing with the "technical matters" of economics—except for the "seemingly technical matter" of Austrian utility theory! (11)—we'll never know. A convenient inconsistency, as I see it, which we will examine in due course.

In the sentence under scrutiny, the meaning of its subject, "the Austrian defense," is ambiguous. The predicate is "judges." Now, who or what judges? Why, the "Austrian defense." Which one? No answer is possible, because "defenses" don't judge: people judge when they defend, and Austrians do not form a philosophical monolith.

I have never met, read, or heard of an Austro-libertarian who, in "defending" (expounding?) the laws of economics and *having ascertained that a particular market transaction constituted a moral abuse, judged its occurrence as morally acceptable* because it transpired "in accordance with" the unhindered operation of those laws—excuse me, "laws."[35]

What I have found is that Austro-libertarian Catholics find the recommended market-hampering or market-hindering to be an intrinsic evil that we cannot countenance "that good may come" or another evil averted (Romans 3:8). Mr. Ferrara never cites the allegedly offending Austrians. He cites Austrians right and left, to be sure, but *not* as having done what he slanderously insinuates.

To the sentence we are parsing Mr. Ferrara appended an opinion that implies that the Church takes a position on the terms set by his confusion. Since that appendix has so far receded from our view, I will reproduce it here:

> . . . a morally invalid consequentialist and utilitarian
> ethic the Church condemns. (8)

Mr. Ferrara will later elaborate upon what he means by this, but for some reason in a skimpy (i.e., five-page) chapter professedly dedicated to "meeting the Austrians," he felt the need to throw in the proverbial kitchen sink, i.e., meta-ethics. Our response in this already overlong post can only glimpse the longer examination we will undertake at the appropriate time.

To express the matter with almost intolerable compact-ness: the consequentialist-deontological dialectic—the false alterna-

---

[35] Mr. Ferrara may seek wiggle room in the fact that he did not use the words "morally acceptable," but I submit that that is the clear meaning of "judges moral abuses in the market according to the supposed greater good . . ." I leave it to the reader to decide if Mr. Ferrara would be successful in that effort.

tive alleged between looking *only*, or *never*, to consequences— is a modern dilemma. Since Mr. Ferrara knows that the Church predates modernity by a few centuries, he should never create the impression that She simply condemns one side of a modernist spat, because that impression might suggest that She supports the other.

That is, if one asserts without qualification that the Church "condemns" utilitarianism or consequentialism, one invites the inference that She favors some form of deontological metaethics, because that is the option to which utilitarianism is dialectically tied.

No one seriously argues, however, that a Catholic must be Kantian if he or she is not a Benthamite. Good consequences are generally the fruit of acting upon good principles, and the attractiveness of good consequences is germane to the thinking by which we arrive at good principles (Matthew 7:16-24). But we'll have to leave the matter there for now.

* * *

Mr. Ferrara continues:

> At any rate, the "laws" of economics are not moral laws, violation of which would have moral consequences for the "violator." (8)

Watch those darn scare quotes! Strictly speaking, Mr. Ferrara didn't deny that the laws of economics are moral laws. Rather, he denied that the "laws" of economics are moral laws! Worse, will not address his ambiguity of reference to law. Does he mean law as universal principle? Or law as legislation expressing the will of the legislator?

Our "inconvenient Jesuit," James A. Sadowsky, answered Mr. Ferrara's ideological forebears this way:

> One detects at times a certain impatience with economics. Talk is heard about "so called laws of economics." I read recently of a clergyman's saying that we

ought not to treat the laws of economics as if they
were the laws of God. But the laws of economics are
the laws of God. They are in the same way that the
laws of physics are the laws of God. They are laws,
however—not legislation. They are the laws of God
because He it is that decrees the existence of the
entities whose nature it is to obey those laws: had He
wanted other laws He would have had to create other
things. He can create beings that observe other laws,
but He cannot legislate alternative laws for the same
kind of being. This shows how nonsensical it is to ask
why God did not make the laws of nature different
from what they are. To ask for a different set of laws
is to ask for a different universe![36]

While it is logically possible to violate legislation, it is
impossible to violate a universal principle. A person obeys or
disobeys legislation, insofar as it issues from a person, but not a
principle: to the latter people can only wisely adjust their
behavior in accordance with their awareness of it or ignorantly
(or foolishly) fail to. The science by which one discovers the
principle, however, is related to but distinct from the science
that guides adjustment of conduct.

Mr. Ferrara's countenancing even the *possibility* of "allowing"
the laws of economics to operate "unhindered" only reveals his
own confusion, not the alleged moral turpitude of the Austrians—
a confusion he seems determined to propagate. Principles do not
need "allowance" to operate. If they are rationally discoverable
principles, they operate willy-nilly! He continues:

---

[36] James A. Sadowsky, S.J., *The Christian Response to Poverty: Working with God's Economic Laws*, London, The Social Affairs Unit, 1986.
www.anthonyflood.com/sadowskychristianresponsetopoverty.htm With all due respect
to my late friend, I would have referred, not to entities' "obeying" but rather their *expressing*
laws in the sense of principles (or *embodying* or *participating in* them—or some other non-anthropomorphic metaphor).

Therefore, moral scrutiny of the marketplace necessarily involves individually accountable moral agents, whose freely willed acts are neither determined nor excused by the operation of any economic "law." (8)

Agreed, as we said earlier, the "field" that is the marketplace is ontologically nothing over and above the "transactions between individuals" who alone are subject to the moral law. The decisive difference between us is that I hold that the moral scrutiny of the marketplace involves those personal agents *exclusively*. That is, there *is* no collective object of moral scrutiny. Further, as we will argue, the "hindering" that Mr. Ferrara proposes violates the dignity of persons (even when committed in the name of that dignity) and that's why Austro-libertarian Catholics oppose such hindering.

Chapter 10

The State and Morals: Aquinas's Proto-Liberal Concerns

The first chapter's title, "Meet the Austrians," kindles an expectation of biographical sketches, but there are none. The reader meets only gratuitous, unsourced, atmospheric generalizations such as this:

> The Austrians, citing economic "laws," propose not merely a "pure market" for its own sake, but a "market principle" of legally unhindered interpersonal exchanges that is the *ethical foundation* of a "market society" and fixes the moral limits of public authority as to *all* spheres of social interaction, even if "private" morals might be Christian. No matter how this is dressed up, this is nothing other than the classic false liberal disjunction between "public" and "private" morality. (8)

Note that Mr. Ferrara continues to "dress up" his sentences with scare quotes, which only impede our understanding of his intention.

As gratuitous as it is complicated, his first assertion merits only gratuitous denial. No Austrians have proposed a pure market (or "pure market") "for its own sake." Neither have they ever suggested that a market principle is the *ethical* foundation of a market society. Austrians may ask whether the principles of economic causality render a certain ethical prescription or proscription redundant or counterproductive. (Since people cannot fly merely by flapping their arms, for example, it makes no sense to morally command, permit, or forbid them to do so.)

Austrians do not distinguish themselves from other thinkers by not wanting to get more of what they want less of, and less of what they want more of. Everybody wants to avoid those kinds of results![37]

No, Austrians *as economists* distinguish themselves by their unpopular and constant admonition to politicians—be they professional or amateur, secular or religious—that a coercive (e.g., statist) means to a good end may cost more than they, upon reflection, would be willing to pay by their own standard of moral accounting.

Austrians *as ethicists* might condemn a statist means to a good end on purely moral, non-utilitarian grounds. That is, they may hold that the principled commitment to voluntary exchange and peaceful cooperation, that is, the principled repudiation of the initiation of force *expresses* rather than establishes one's ethical obligation to his or her fellows.

If these Austrians ethicists are *natural law* theorists, they may formulate that ethical obligation in ontological terms: that *persons* are self-respecters and mutual respecters pertains to the substance, not the accidents, of being human. (Universal interpersonal *dis*respect leads to the negation of the disrespecters, i.e.,

---

37 It may be wise to reject anti-consequentialism in metaethics, but certainly foolish not to try to foresee *unintended* as well as intended possible consequences of one's policies. Presumably, even Mr. Ferrara is interested in getting more of what he wants and less of what he doesn't.

to human annihilation.) That is, for them, the dignity of the person "fixes moral limits" of the authority exercising responsibility for the framework of liberty (which is a common good). This is then a case of one's ethical insights inspiring the formulation of a market principle, not the reverse.

If the Austrian natural law ethicists are *Christians*, then their ontological reasoning goes much deeper: the person is a created image-bearer of the God whose *eikon* or image is the man Christ Jesus (Colossians 1:15) whose *eikon* we hope one day to bear after being transformed in and conformed to Him (1 Corinthians 15:49). Our quotidian "getting along with each other" has an everlasting context, namely, "getting along" with God. The latter "vertical" relationship anchors the "horizontal," without which the latter can be reinforced only by our syllogisms, rather than also by our experience of divine love. To define persons as self-respecters and mutual respecters is merely to express analytically the second great commandment (Matthew 22:29). The so-called "golden rule" sums up the law and the prophets (Matthew 7:12).

Anarcho-Catholics don't insist that all Catholics draw the inference they draw about the State, but they do insist on their right to draw it and to defend that inference as sound. We have addressed in a preliminary way Mr. Ferrara's concerns that a market principle might "fix the moral limits of public authority as to *all* spheres of social interaction, even if 'private' morals might be Christian." There is no cause for alarm, we argued, provided we interpret the market in terms of persons, that is, mutually respecting divine image-bearers, the living sources or "principles" of all social phenomena.

Consider this scenario: *both* (a) the dominant (not exclusive) ethos of a given territory (as large or as small as you please) is Christian *and* (b) its several classes of guardians of peaceful cooperation understand economics more or less as Austrians do and, in accordance with that understanding, deal with the

violent non-cooperators in their midst.[38] Expanding our hypothetical scenario: occurring with unwelcome regularity on that
territory are instances of non-violent moral evil (as a Christian
ethos defines moral evil). What are Christian guardians of the
framework of peaceful cooperation to do?

One answer is obvious: one ought to use every means at
one's disposal to suppress the immoral behavior by imposing
penal sanctions on the miscreants. To tolerate the evil is to give
one's sanction to it, which God forbid. Is this Mr. Ferrara's
position? We cannot validly infer that it is from words of his we
have so far quoted.

We do, however, have his so-far implicit disapproval of the
idea that Christian morals might fall outside the scope of "public
authority," but because it is implicit, it is also without nuance.
He may reject libertarian strictures on public authority when it
comes to the suppression of immoral activity, but he apparently
did not feel it necessary, at least here, to suggest what limits he
would favor.

We will, of course, charitably assume that Mr. Ferrara is
as anti-totalitarian as he is anti-liberal unless and until we have
evidence that defeats that assumption. A writer for whom
historic Christendom is a model for future social reconstruction,
however, should not leave his readers guessing about those
limits. To avoid any misunderstanding he should spell them out
soon and as explicitly as he can.

---

38 Even anarchist territories must have guardians of the consensus of the non-initiation
of force, the framework of peaceful cooperation. They include the parents of a nuclear
family, the elders of an extended one, and property owners who contract for the services
of private suppliers of defense and courts. It does not follow from this "must" that the
persons who carry out these guardianship functions devolve into criminals, macro-
parasites who live off of the wealth they systematically confiscate by force or the threat
thereof. Anarcho-Catholics will be in the vanguard of efforts to demystify, and keep
demystified, that function by withholding from those who perform it the symbolic
trappings and incantations that communicate and reinforce the suggestion of permanent
monopoly and divine right. (Especially when the *demos* plays *theos*.)

A different answer may be found in the writings of Saint Thomas Aquinas: some evils tear at the fabric of the common good, which in this case is the framework of peaceful cooperation, which tearing is an absolutely impermissible evil and therefore must not be tolerated; other evils do not rend it and therefore ought to be tolerated. Why?

Because active suppression, *would* rend it. A policy of non-toleration would benignly intend the common good while unintentionally harming it. We charitably assume that this is not what Mr. Ferrara had in mind when he referred to the "morally invalid consequentialist and utilitarian ethic the Church condemns." (8)

A socially intolerable evil: murder; a socially tolerable evil: prostitution. Prostitution is not any less evil for being socially tolerable, but it does not fall to the public authority to suppress it, for it does not have a virtue-instilling function. Its office is solely directed to protecting the framework within which persons peacefully, cooperatively pursue their diverse ends (including virtue). As Thomas put it:

> Human laws leave certain things unpunished, on account of the condition of those who are imperfect, and who would be deprived of many advantages, if all sins were strictly forbidden and punishments appointed for them.[39]

Or:

> ... it suffices for it [human law] to prohibit whatever is destructive of human intercourse, while it treats other matters as though they were lawful, *not by approving them*, but by not punishing them.[40]

---

[39] *Summa Theologiae*, 2-2, q. 78, reply to Obj. 3. Thomas is arguing against the moral licitness of charging interest on a loan. In this instance we are agreeing with him only on the narrow point of the office of human law.

[40] *Summa Theologiae*, 2-2, q. 77, reply to Obj. 1. (Emphasis added: A.F.)

Professor Richard Symanski summarized Thomas on this point as follows:

> The aim of the criminal justice system is not to impose public standards of morality upon the private acts of consenting adults, immoral though they may be by widely held social standards, but rather to protect people and property from the harmful effects of others.[41]

It would be anachronistic to describe the Angelic Doctor as a liberal. He was no libertarian. I am sensitive to Kevin Craycraft's concerns about aligning the thought of Saint Thomas with the liberal tradition. His paper "Was Aquinas a Whig? St. Thomas on Regime" documents the dangers to which loose talk can lead.[42]

I cannot follow Craycraft, however, in his suggestion that the modern liberal ideal is a lost cause, incapable of assimilation

---

41 Richard Symanski, *The Immoral Landscape: Female Prostitution in Western Societies.* Toronto, 1981, 228; as quoted in Vincent M. Dever, rich with citations from Aquinas' writings, "Aquinas on the Practice of Prostitution." *Essays in Medieval Studies,* Vol. 13, 1996. After documenting the condemnation, Professor Dever writes:

> Given this strong condemnation of fornication and prostitution, it would seem obvious that Aquinas would want to engage every force against them, especially civil law. Oddly enough he does not. Instead he notes that the state should allow fornication and prostitution to exist for the sake of the common good. Relying on the well-known passage from Augustine's *De ordine,* Aquinas advocates tolerance of prostitution by noting: "Accordingly in human government also, those who are in authority rightly tolerate certain evils, lest certain goods be lost, or certain evils be incurred: thus Augustine says [*De ordine* 2.4]: 'If you do away with harlots, the world will be convulsed with lust.'" If these social practices were to be suppressed, the public reaction might be such as to threaten the peace of society. Remember, Aquinas already maintains (1) that prostitution is a species of lust that is one of the capital vices that wreak the greatest havoc on the human soul and leads to other sins; (2) that it is a mortal sin that threatens the proper rearing of children and by extension threatens the common good of society; and (3) that it violates the natural law and matrimonial union. How then could one tolerate such an evil, particularly a natural law thinker such as Aquinas? Is Aquinas compromising on his principles or playing utilitarian?"

Readers who find the suspense intolerable should read Professor Dever's paper.

42 Kevin Craycraft, "Was Aquinas a Whig? St. Thomas on Regime" *Faith and Reason,* Fall 1994.

into the Catholic worldview with its realist epistemology just because the first thinkers to articulate that ideal were nominalists or skeptics.

By one contingency of history Locke and other Protestant empiricists retrieved and formulated an ideal consonant with a truth about the dignity of persons as divine image-bearers. *They did so in a world extricating itself from the nightmare of royal absolutism, which was, by another contingency of history, all too Catholic.*

Liberty is the political expression of that Biblical insight.[43] That is, liberty is not merely logically consistent with the insight into the dignity of persons, but it also illuminates that insight: person A may not initiate force against person B, *regardless of the identities of A and B*, and regardless of the fact that many Christians have initiated, or rationalized the initiation of, force against others. The claim of the anarcho-Catholic is that *that* insight ought to govern.[44]

On the basis of passages cited in the Dever paper (or which may be found directly in Thomas' *Summa Theologica*, I-II, Question 96), however, we would argue that Thomas Aquinas was a *proto-liberal.*

Aquinas was proto-*liberal* in that he maintained that *the scope of human law is not total.* His was a political liberty-honoring stance that presaged more robust limitations of the State to be articulated in a later century.

---

[43] Later I will address the danger of equivocation Christians face when using the word "liberty." Unless otherwise noted, I use "liberty" in the political sense, that is, with regard to the morally licit use of interpersonal force, *without prejudice to the traditional theological context of spiritual slavery to sin and liberation therefrom* (*eleutheria*, e.g., Galatians 5:1, 5:13). The two senses are related, not opposed as "true" and "false" as Mr. Ferrara's propaganda suggests.

[44] It governs my reading of Aquinas, whom I read with great admiration and reverence, but not uncritically. I cite Aquinas against Mr. Ferrara, not because I believe that whatever Aquinas wrote is *ipso facto* true, but because the saint cared whether a given morally inspired state repression might harm the common good, and Mr. Ferrara ignorantly dubs that sort of reasoning "consequentialist." I have no problem with critically determining my proximity to and distance from the Angelic Doctor. I suspect Ferrara's appropriation of him is less nuanced.

He was only *proto*-liberal, however, in that he argued for a much larger role for the force-monopolizing public authority than can sensibly be called "liberal" (let alone "libertarian") without fatal qualification.

Significantly, by "proto-liberalism" I do not mean merely the insistence, which unites virtually all Catholics, that the State's reach stops at the Church's door. No, I mean the further restriction upon the State (or whatever is functioning as the "public authority") that it may not penalize a behavior merely because Catholic theology condemns it as immoral; that what is immoral ought not *ipso facto* be illegal.

The class of behaviors Aquinas deems morally illicit is not identical to the class of behaviors he says should be prohibited by law; and neither is the morally licit identical with the legally permissible. His interests in (a) demarcating what is destructive of interpersonal cooperation ("human intercourse") from what is not and (b) confining the scope of the public authority to the former are arguably *liberal* interests, even though there were no liberals in his day.

This dual interest is not any less liberal (or "proto-liberal") because the framework of Thomas' political thought was a Catholic cosmology (in which human cooperation is a divine intention as well as a human project). Aquinas' restricted proto-liberal point may be a conclusion that he draws from his cosmology, but it is not to be regarded as trivial: *it is common ground with those who reach that conclusion by another worldview.* The conceit of liberalism (and its further elaboration, libertarianism) is, after all, that disagreement over cosmology might be regrettable, even remediable, without also being an obstacle to social peace.

Is that to be despised? Or celebrated? Do Catholics not want the Muslim, the Jew, the Buddhist, et al., to conclude, *each integrally from his or her own worldview*, that cooperation is the cosmologically sound option? Or, until all are converted to

Catholicism, are we to be embroiled in a long *bellum omnia contra omnes*, a war to the knife, *in saecula saeculorum?*

The anarcho-Catholic argues that the State *per se* (properly defined) is destructive of human intercourse and that *only institutions that honor human dignity ought to administer justice.* The State *per se* offends human dignity. Error may have no rights, but erring persons have dignity.

I agree with Aquinas that there is no coherence to the idea of having "a right to be wrong." That truth, however, does not offer the slightest warrant to individuals calling themselves "the public authority" to rob, kidnap, imprison, enslave, or kill the one who is wrong.[45]

The anarcho-Catholic and the Thomist would, I argue, agree about the terms of the discussion—"Where does one draw the line between what furthers and what impedes human cooperation?"—while disagreeing about where to draw that line (or about what institutional forms the line-drawing takes). One wonders whether Mr. Ferrara accepts the terms of the discussion.

While it has been more than two decades since the fall of the Berlin Wall, it is not too soon to recall that not only Catholics like Mr. Ferrara, but also totalitarians have disparaged "the classic false liberal disjunction between 'public' and 'private' morality."

---

[45] Michael Novak faced the limits of the Angelic Doctor's proto-liberalism at this point in "Aquinas and the Heretics," *First Things,* December 1995, 33-38. www.firstthings.com/article/1995/12/aquinas-and-the-heretics.

Christendom's fatal embrace of the State underlay Thomas's willingness to have that public authority engage in those offenses against human dignity: a heretic's error struck at what he thought was indispensable to human cooperation, namely, the medieval monistic State: "Once the integrity of the social fabric had been made to rest on key Christian beliefs (and the power of legitimate rulers on ecclesiastical approbation)," Novak writes, "criticisms of Christian practice that spilled over into criticism of underlying interpretations of the gospels were easily taken as acts of treason against the state. In short, by allowing Christian faith to be the consensual foundation of the political and social order, as it were the form of political life, Christendom confounded the things of Caesar with the things of God."

You would think he'd be anxious to distinguish his non-liberalism from theirs.

There may be a liberal disjunction between the private and the public, and it may be false, but merely *calling* it false, as Mr. Ferrara does, does not *make* it so. (Yes, he may later offer arguments for calling it false, but then why did he not postpone the generalization until then?) Since Mr. Ferrara has use for the idea of "public" authority, he must have his own take on the public-private duality, but this was the place to be explicit about it and to assure his readers that there is a norm of privacy that he does respect.

There is no important difference that I can see between the *public* and the *common* or *shared*. Common to whom? Shared by whom? Why, individuals, the only agents there are. The *private* therefore pertains to the individual *as* individual. It rests on a logical contrast between the specific, concrete individual who one is and the generalized, abstract "others" with whom one interacts. There are goods that, irrespective of who each of us is an individual, we value at least implicitly and ought to explicitly. One common good is liberty, the framework of peaceful cooperation, a necessary condition of our pursuits of diverse ends and worthy object of attention, evaluation, and protection.

* * *

Quoting from a publication or two of the Ludwig von Mises Institute that summarizes its educational mission, Mr. Ferrara notes that in "recent years Austrians have allied themselves with libertarians and are now promoting a complete political philosophy and theory of human liberty." (8) A bad thing, one surmises.

The Mises Institute, he notes, believes that it has achieved the status of "*the* research and education center of classical liberalism, libertarian political theory, and the Austrian School of economics."[46] (8). More putatively damning evidence comes from the mouth of the accused, in this instance, Mises Institute founder and Chairman, Lew Rockwell. The Institute supports

> the tradition of thought represented by Ludwig von Mises and the school of thought he enlivened . . . which has now blossomed into *a massive international movement* of students, professors, professionals, and people in all walks of life. It seeks *a radical shift* in the intellectual climate as the foundation for a renewal of the free and prosperous commonwealth.[47] (8)

So, Mr. Ferrara suggests that there is a danger emanating from a global movement of people who wish to achieve a free and prosperous commonwealth *via* a radical shift in the intellectual climate, that is, by writing, reading, and teaching from books. Now, what in that movement is *verboten* to a faithful Catholic? Certainly not the intellectual life *per se* or its international scope. Surely not the radical shift away from the current climate of opinion.

Does not Mr. Ferrara's traditionalist Catholic Distributism offer just such a thing? That is the impression one gets from the book's last chapters. So, what's the problem?

Here's the problem.

> This [Mr. Ferrara writes] is clearly a movement whose intellectual pretensions have carried it far beyond mere economics into areas governed by the teaching of the Magisterium. "We have long known," boasts Mises head Llewellyn H. Rockwell, Jr., a professing Catholic, "that Austro-Libertarianism is

---

[46] This is the brief quotation to which he appends a significant reference note, buried 319 pages later, wherein he whispers in 9-point font that all the emphases that readers find in all subsequent citations are *not* as in the original "unless otherwise indicated."

[47] From Lew Rockwell, "More Powerful than Armies," April 16, 2010. Italics courtesy of Mr. Ferrara.

https://www.lewrockwell.com/2010/04/lew-rockwell/more-powerful-than-any-government/

the only truly international economic-political movement outside Marxism . . . . This is a worldwide struggle, and now especially, we must work together, in the tradition of Mises and Rothbard for the good of all."[48] (8-9)

There it is. This is what drove the writing of TCATL. Across its pages Mr. Ferrara elaborates upon this accusation of illicit rivalry between what Austro-libertarians (especially Catholics among them) teach and what Christ taught his Apostles, which, Catholics believe, has been apostolically transmitted to and preserved for us today. And we will rebut that case—which in most instances will amount to vacuuming a smoke-filled room. The detail of our rebuttals will vary directly with that of the charges.

Like so much else in this mistitled first chapter, Mr. Ferrara's words merely generate suspicion in the minds of those already disposed to trust him, so our immediate response is correspondingly brief, aimed only at dispelling that poisonous atmosphere.

The first thing to note is his phrase "far beyond mere economics into areas governed by the Magisterium." Given the gravity of the accusation, it is hard to imagine a less responsible use of language. If one wants to show that a Catholic is teaching something not consistent with the Deposit of Faith, or indeed dissenting from it, and by extension contradicting Christ Himself, one must do more than mumble about "areas governed by." One must specify both what one means by "area" and what it means for the Magisterium to "govern" it. And until one is prepared to do more than mumble, as Mr. Ferrara apparently is in later chapters, one ought not poison the well of debate with insinuations of heresy.

---

[48] More italics to help penetrate the skulls of dull readers.

The second thing to note is his implicit admission that "mere" economics is not so "governed." No, it is not. I appreciate his discovery of common ground. I return the favor: like faith, morals *does* fall under the care of the Magisterium.

Together those two notes inspire the question we look forward to exploring, once Mr. Ferrara clarifies his lingo: to what extent, if any, does the meaning of certain Magisterium-"governed" sentences logically depend upon the meaning of economics-"governed" sentences? Totally? To some degree? Not at all? Everything, as we shall see in due course, hangs on the answer.

Chapter 11

An Inconvenient Anarcho-Catholic

According to Mr. Ferrara, the sort of praise one finds in a tribute marking the departure (or anniversary thereof) of a notable and affectionately remembered figure can count as *prima facie* evidence that a *cult* has formed around that person.

Excuse me, dear reader, Mr. Ferrara didn't put things so directly. He wrote: "The [Austro-libertarian] movement has taken on *the aspect of* a cult" and "clearly *savors of* a cultic *dulia.*" (Emphasis added.) Perhaps clearly to Mr. Ferrara, but not to anyone who knew Murray Rothbard (and knew what he thought of political cults of personality). I grant Mr. Ferrara's claim that the "word 'cult' is not used lightly" (9): I'm sure he gave it all the thought of which he is capable.

His evidence for his bizarrely counter-intuitive charge? "Rothbard's innumerable 'anarcho-capitalist' tomes, tracts, articles and speeches are foundation stone of Austro-Libertarianism. . . ." And the connection between literary production and cultic *dulia*? That's apparently for him to know and for the reader to figure out.

Mr. Ferrara then mentions an implication of Rothbard's political philosophy that has nothing to do with supporting the specific charge under review: there is "a legal right to allow unwanted children to starve to death." (9) Now, in his reference note, Mr. Ferrara quotes Rothbard to the effect that he distinguished the question of the *moral* obligation one has to feed one's children from that of the justification a third party may have to use legally organized violence to force one to do so. He argued that there was no such justification. The implications of ignoring or denying that distinction go far beyond ensuring that a child's natural protectors carry out their moral duty.

Mr. Ferrara does not put that distinction into the body of the text, let alone discuss it, for doing so would digress from his *dulia* charge, intolerably so even by his standards of literary composition. In accordance, therefore, with our policy of dealing with Mr. Ferrara's charges serially, but only on a level of detail corresponding to the level on which he makes them, we must postpone our scrutiny of his distortion of Rothbard's argument until we get to that section of TCATL (about sixty pages from our present context). For now we can only bring to the reader's attention yet another symptom of Mr. Ferrara's propagandistic style: the out-of-left-field, *"Let-'em-starve!"* insinuation has one purpose: to poison the well (a fallacy given its name, we are happy to note, by Blessed John Henry Newman.) Now, back to the matter at hand.

In 2005, on the tenth anniversary of Rothbard's death, the Mises Institute published a mostly prosaic summary of his life, work, and influence. One may judge its purpose and tone by reading it in its entirety here. Of its nearly two thousand words, Mr. Ferrara cites the last paragraph as though it were suggestive of *dulia*:

> And so, to dear Murray, our friend and mentor, the
> vice president of the Mises Institute, the scholar who
> gave us guidance and the gentleman who showed us

how to find joy in confronting the enemy and advancing truth, the staff and scholars of the Institute offer this tribute, alongside the millions who have been drawn to his ideas. May his works always be available to all who care to learn about liberty and do their part to fight for the cornerstone of civilization itself. May his legacy endure and may we all become happy warriors for the cause of liberty.

This would be the first cult to my knowledge that regards the object of its veneration or *dulia* as a friend and addresses him by his first name (even prefacing that by "Dear"). There is no basis for his smear. I wonder what he thinks of these words:

> And may God also bless the Ludwig von Mises Institute, which for 20 years now has been promoting freedom without compromise. I make it my habit to start the day by reading its excellent website, lewrockwell.com. Congratulations to Lew Rockwell for carrying on the work of von Mises and the late, great Murray Rothbard, both of whom would be justly proud of their brilliant, dauntless disciple.

Well, there you have it: Rockwell was the "great" Rothbard's "disciple," and upon his "excellent" work God's blessings should be poured out. How many readers would guess that they have read the words of Joseph Sobran, R.I.P., arguably America's greatest Catholic social commentator and wordsmith? They were published in the November 2002 issue of *Sobran's*.

It is hard to imagine anyone less likely to join anything redolent of a cult than Sobran, whose credentials as a faithful and courageous Catholic I hope are beyond doubt. Sobran was intellectually converted to Rothbardian anarcho-capitalism, as many years earlier he had spiritually converted to Roman Catholicism. I hope my readers will read his *apologia* in "The Reluctant Anarchist" (first published in his newsletter's December

2002 issue; posted on www.lewrockwell.com/2009/03/joseph-sobran/the-reluctant-anarchist/)

No one to my knowledge ever thought him any less a Catholic for his public, eyes-wide-open intellectual conversion to anarcho-capitalism.

I am only one of many who learned of Joe's painful last days through the reports of his friend, literature professor David Allen White in *Catholic Family News* and kindred traditionalist Catholic organs. One looks in vain through all the obituaries in that genre of journalism for any mention of what, to them, must have been at best a serious lapse in judgment on his part, at worst an accommodation of evil. (*Nil nisi bonum . . .?*)

The fact of Sobran's conversion to anarchocapitalism does not, of course, constitute a formal argument in its justification, or even a premise in such an argument. For those who admired him, however, and who subscribe to Aristotle's approach to virtue (namely, that we learn what virtue is, not from reading books, but by observing the habits of men deemed virtuous), it is, I submit, a strong *suasive consideration*. For if his fellows regard a man as good independently of his assent to a controversial thesis, the principle of charity counsels us to presume that the assent is a *reflection*, not a betrayal, of that goodness until evidence to the contrary defeats that presumption.

Sobran's "high favorable" rating among traditionalist Catholics like Mr. Ferrara (and, of course, not only them) does not cohere with the "strong unfavorable" rating they give Austro-libertarians. As he was a member of that class, however, they are impaled on the horns of a dilemma: either Austro-Libertarianism is not as evil as they say it is, or Joe Sobran was not as good a man as they say he was. So far, they have refused to enter the arena occupied by that horned bull (who evaporates upon the sacrifice of either of those opinions).

Now to let some sunshine in on this otherwise gloomy dialectical business.

Sobran wrote at least three characteristically perceptive tributes to Murray Rothbard. One of them, published originally in *The Washington Times,* January 14, 1995, is available online as part of *In Memoriam,* 38-39. It begins: "It wasn't like Murray Rothbard to die. Nothing he ever did was more out of character, more difficult to reconcile with everything we knew of him, more downright inconceivable. Murray dead is a contradiction in terms."[49] (More *dulia,* I suppose.)

Another obit by Sobran is available online.[50] I envy those of you who will be reading it for the first time. May readers who incline to Mr. Ferrara's point of view be willing to experience a little cognitive dissonance, in the interest of a charitable, Catholic reception of the legacy of Murray Rothbard as well as Joe Sobran. Allow the words of this great anarcho-Catholic to disinfect the well of discourse that Mr. Ferrara's propaganda has turned into a septic tank.

[49] Joseph Sobran, contribution to *Murray N. Rothbard: In Memoriam.* Edited by Llewellyn H. Rockwell, Jr. 38-39. Freely available on mises.org.

[50] Joseph Sobran, "Murray," *The Rothbard-Rockwell Report,* March 1995, 2-3. Reprinted from *The Washington Times,* January 14, 1995; www.unz.org/Pub/RothbardRockwellReport-1995mar-00002?View=PDF

Chapter 12

Doctorates, "Dummies," and Defamation

L et us now examine the departure from good argumentative form that characterizes TCATL entitled "digressive appeal to unqualified expert opinion." Mr. Ferrara says the Austro-libertarian movement is "of particular concern" to him because "the very founder and head of the Mises Institute, Lew Rockwell, and its leading polemicist, Thomas E. Woods, Jr., are both Catholics." (9) Unless Austro-Libertarianism is an intrinsically anti-Catholic movement, however, there is no cause for concern that Catholics are among its leaders.

Given that the libertarian movement in the United States once had a secular, even atheistic, cast, it is a welcome development that today a significant segment of it boasts many Catholic writers and even leaders *unless*, again, Mr. Ferrara can show that it is essentially anti-Catholic. He will attempt to show it in later chapters, especially chapters 3 through 12, but he apparently cannot resist the urge to create an atmosphere of suspicion in the chapter ostensibly devoted to identifying Austrians and summarizing their tenets.

... Woods's copious writings over the years against
the social teaching of the Church as enunciated in
papal encyclicals have provoked numerous Catholic
commentators to accuse him of what one, the world-
renowned Catholic economist Rupert J. Ederer,
called "objective dissent from moral teachings by the
Catholic Church." As early as 2002, Thomas J.
Fleming, editor of the respected journal *Chronicles*,
had dubbed Woods's position "the Austrian heresy,"
and ... *Chronicles* has recently [early 2010] completed
publication of a series critiquing Woods's "Austro-
Libertarianism" under the title "Is Tom Woods a
Dissenter?" (9)

The method of the propagandist is on display here. As Mr.
Ferrara's emphasis is on Thomas Woods as a "leading polemicist"
for a movement opposed to "the social teaching of the Church," it
was not opportune for him to note that Dr. Woods, a Columbia
University-trained historian, is the author of *The Church
Confronts Modernity: Catholic Intellectuals and the Progressive Era*
(based on his dissertation), *How the Catholic Church Built Western
Civilization*, and *Sacred Then, Sacred Now: The Return of the Old
Latin Mass*, to name just three books that might open a window
or two on his grasp of and commitment to Catholicism.[51]

Mr. Ferrara will eventually refer to Dr. Woods's intellectual
conversion to Austrian economics and its effect on his reception
of what is called "the social teaching of the Church," but not until
pages 119-120. Meanwhile, Mr. Ferrara's words imply that the
opinions of the editor of *Chronicles* and of a commentator on the
writings of Father Pesch bear on the matter of Dr. Woods's
fidelity to Catholicism. To bandy about terms like "heresy" and

---

[51] *The Church Confronts Modernity: Catholic Intellectuals and the Progressive Era*, Columbia
University Press, 2004; *How the Catholic Church Built Western Civilization*, Regnery Publishing,
2005; and *Sacred Then, Sacred Now: The Return of the Old Latin Mass*, Roman Catholic Books,
2007.

"dissent" is to disrespect the discipline of theology and the faith upon which it reflects. Mr. Ferrara favors the opinions of Ederer and Fleming who think little of Woods. So what?[52]

* * *

As a Catholic layman, Dr. Woods has responsibly defended a position at the interface of economics with Catholic theology. Reasonable disagreement with that defense cannot rest on fact that Dr. Woods's doctorate is in history rather than in economics or theology. The critic must show the *relevance* of that lack of expertise to Dr. Woods's defense. That is to say, the non-Austrian economist with a Ph.D.—Rudolph Ederer, for instance— may not simply lord it over Dr. Woods, but rather show him that his lack of one accounts for his alleged *economic* errors. To the discernment of any *theological* errors by Dr. Woods, a non-Austrian economist's Ph.D. (or a classicist's, like Dr. Thomas Fleming's) is utterly irrelevant. (When one is dismantling a work of propaganda, one sometimes has to belabor the obvious.)

Aware that his interpretation of those documents expresses a minority viewpoint within the Church, Dr. Woods has always assumed responsibility for delineating and clarifying that viewpoint in order to address the concerns Catholics may have. Mr. Ferrara has not only read these efforts uncharitably, but also, and more importantly, misrepresented the situation that Catholics are in when something that a pope has written about a matter *not* of faith strikes them as erroneous (and also harmful when admixed with matters that *are* of faith). Mr. Ferrara presupposes that the situation is one way when it is in fact quite another. (He also claims that such a response is evasion and bugaboo. We shall see.) If we do nothing else in this book, we will expose that presupposition as groundless.

---

[52] Yes, unlike Dr. Woods, Dr. Ederer "has academic degrees in economics" (327, n. 10), but that does not confer theological competency. Neither does Dr. Fleming's expertise in Attic poetry.

Referring to the "seemingly endless series of writings by Woods against the teaching of the Popes on justice in the marketplace" (9), Mr. Ferrara surmises that

> Woods has been "revisiting" this subject so often as to suggest a personal campaign to demonstrate that the Popes are wrong. The campaign has included an entire book on the subject, *The Church and the Market* (2005), wherein Woods contend that constant papal teaching on such matters as the just wage is "fraught with error" . . . . The controversy over "Austro-libertarian" among Catholics has become so closely identified with Woods's writings and speeches as to become impossible to address without mentioning and quoting him extensively, which will be done here." (10)

Some readers may have smiled upon reading Mr. Ferrara's reference to someone else's "seemingly endless series of writings." In any case, for all he has shown to the contrary, the list of Dr. Woods's germane writings is *appropriately* long. Notice how quickly Mr. Ferrara's personal impression of a "campaign" is promoted to a fact upon which one may confidently build.

The ellipsis in our quotation hides a citation of Dr. Ederer, the Heinrich Pesch scholar. Those words impute to Dr. Woods's evaluation of papal economic competency a mocking tone that his words do not carry. According to Dr. Ederer, *as Mr. Ferrara cites him*, Dr. Woods's book *The Church and the Market* portrays a "host of some of the most impressive and saintly Popes . . . as 'dummies' . . . and out of their depth."

The reference is to a 2005 review entitled "Economics for Dummies." The word "dummies" appears once in the body of the review in quotation marks, but *it is not a quotation from Dr. Woods*. It is as though Dr. Ederer had written, "as it were, dummies."

Let us be clear: in his review Dr. Ederer was *interpreting* Dr. Woods's evaluation of the popes' economic competency, *not* quoting Woods. In fairness to Dr. Ederer, we stress that he did *not* say that *Dr. Woods* referred to the popes as dummies, no more than he referred to their being out of their depth.

Because "dummies" appears in quotation marks inside Mr. Ferrara's quote of Dr. Ederer, however, readers may be forgiven if they get the false impression that Dr. Woods actually called certain popes dummies (which, if true, would be to Mr. Ferrara's polemical advantage). This is the sort of behavior we expect of desperate lawyers. Or propagandists.

If the citation of my words had the effect of putting another man's reputation in a bad light, I would regard not only him but also myself defamed. Mr. Ferrara was apparently not overly concerned about the risk of defaming Dr. Ederer, his ally in the war against Austro-Libertarianism. Mere collateral damage, I suppose. I will charitably assume that the defamation was unintended.

We will have occasion to consider the expert witness (qualified in economics, not in theology) whom Mr. Ferrara repaid so poorly.

Chapter 13

On Not Seeing the Forest for the Woods

In clarifying the Austro-libertarian option for Catholics, we happily acknowledge the service that the writings of Thomas E. Woods have rendered. It is not our primary purpose, however, to critically evaluate his ongoing contribution to that end. Each time Dr. Woods's words surface in TCATL, of course, we will have to consider whether Mr. Ferrara's construction of them is charitable or not, his interpretation comprehending or not, his criticism sound or not. But we do not want to create the impression that the case for that Austro-libertarian option depends on the success of Dr. Woods's efforts.

This book therefore does not reflect Mr. Ferrara's strong, if not unbalanced, focus on Dr. Woods, especially given the failure of the chapter (still) under review to fulfill the promise of its title (i.e. "Meet the Austrians"). Specifically, we do not presume to *defend* Dr. Woods against Mr. Ferrara, as though he were not capable of self-defense or has not demonstrated that capability. In some cases, we will refer the reader to those published responses. What concerns us is the truth of the matter that Dr. Woods and Mr. Ferrara address.

Having said that, we now present his explanation of his focus:

> The controversy over "Austro-Libertarianism" among Catholics has become so closely identified with Woods's writings and speeches as to become impossible to address without mentioning and quoting him extensively, which will be done here. (10)

To which this footnote is appended 318 pages later:

> In the interest of full disclosure, I must note that Woods and I were once colleagues and even co-authors of a book: *The Great Façade* (2002), a study of changes in the Catholic Church after Vatican II. We have since had a public parting of the ways over Woods's public attacks on the Church's social teaching, which, unlike the changes discussed in *The Great Façade*, has been explicitly imposed on the faithful as binding Catholic doctrine by Pope after Pope since Leo XIII. Thus far Woods has chosen to attribute my criticisms of his position to personal animus, even though other Catholics had subjected his views to severe public criticism for some seven years before I first mentioned him by name in my own writings on the controversy he has provoked. (328 n. 16)

If other Catholics had subjected Dr. Woods's views to severe public criticism for seven years without his attributing it to personal animus, one possible explanation is that such animus is a distinguishing mark of Mr. Ferrara's style of criticism. (Mr. Ferrara asserts, but does not here document, the alleged attribution.) Until we can compare the cogency and tone of those criticisms to those leveled by Mr. Ferrara, we cannot tell.

In any case, the issue is not whether Dr. Woods has received severe criticism over the years, but whether he has successfully rebutted it. It is also relevant to review the *support*, not just criticism, with which Catholic scholars have greeted his writings on Church and market. Dr. Woods is not the first anarcho-Catholic, but he is the first to have a significant impact on the culture beyond "niche" audiences, and this has moved some traditionalist Catholics to challenge him in their "respected journals," thus engendering what Mr. Ferrara dramatically dubs a controversy.

Contrary to Mr. Ferrara, it *is* possible to address the phenomenon of Austro-libertarian Catholics without focusing on Dr. Woods as he does, as though he were a dangerously influential but isolated representative.[53] There is no call for such emphasis at the price of overlooking contemporary but "pre-Woodsian" anarcho-Catholics like James A. Sadowsky, S.J., who befriended Murray Rothbard in the early 1960s and published in 1983 a critical examination of "Classical Catholic Social Doctrine"; or the widely read Joseph Sobran, who "anarched" in 2002, the year Dr. Woods debunked Vatican II with Mr. Ferrara.

Mr. Ferrara's reference to "Woods's public attacks on the Church's social teaching" (foreshadowing the middle section of TCATL) assumes what is in dispute, i.e., *whether a teaching of a pope, or even of a series of popes, is by the fact that a pope taught it, part of the deposit of faith binding on Catholics.* Mr. Ferrara begs that question, to which begging we respond: if a teaching is not found in the deposit or implied by what is found there, then it's not binding on Catholics. Period. The contrary assumption

---

53 To name two Austro-libertarian Catholic professors whom Mr. Ferrara neglected:

(1) Jörg Guido Hülsmann, Professor of Economics, University of Angers (France), author of *Mises: The Last Knight of Liberalism*. Freely available on mises.org. As Hülsmann confessed: "Once a pagan interventionist, I first saw the truths of libertarian political theory, and eventually I started to realize that the light of these truths was but a reflection of the encompassing and eternal light that radiates from God through His Son and the Holy Spirit. This realization has been a slow process and I could not say now when and where it will end."

(2) Jésus Huerta de Soto, Professor of Political Economy, Rey Juan Carlos University (Madrid), and author of *Money, Bank Credit, and Economic Cycles* , mises.org/books/desoto.pdf and (to cite only one of his articles) "The Ethics of Capitalism." Freely available on acton.org. Huerta de Soto's anti-consequentialist point of departure is a passage from Pope John Paul II's 1993 encyclical, *Veritatis Splendor*.

presupposes a certain model of church government which is also not *de fide.*

The monarcho-papalist is one such model. It displaced the conciliarist model and influenced the way the faithful heard the news that the Pope wrote an encyclical; or desired to convoke an ecumenical council; or intended to displace an ancient liturgy (with little more than a reverential tip of the hat to the equally firm intentions of his predecessor papal-monarch, an intention expressed in an Apostolic Constitution); or insisted on fast-tracking a canonization process.

An argument can be made for the choice of monarcho-papalism over conciliarism, but if it underlies one's reception of a series of papal encyclicals—being at issue in a debate over part of the content of those circulars—then that argument must be *made,* not presupposed. (Incidentally, unlike St. Pius V's *Quo Primum* of 1570, which intended the permanence of the Tridentine Rite, none of those encyclicals is an Apostolic Constitution.)

To put things with vulnerable polemical directness: Catholic traditionalists presuppose the monarcho-papalist model. For them, of course, it not a "model" at all, for that implies alternatives: monarchy just conforms to the way things metaphysically *are!* By the implementation of that model, the Tridentine Rite could be

a) established forever with a stroke of one monarch's pen, but then
b) effectively suppressed for (what seemed like) forever with the stroke of another's, and then
c) re-established, albeit with second-class status (the status of the "usurper" rite being simultaneously secured), with the stroke of a third's.

For Traditionalists, the model is not to be questioned, but rather implemented and manned by one's own personnel.

According to Mr. Ferrara, as we said in our review of Dr. Woods's *The Church and the Market* (see Appendix B) "a faithful Catholic may withstand Paul VI to his face on *Novus Ordo Missae,* but not on the living wage, or John Paul II on episcopal consecration, but not on 'consumerism.'" Mr. Ferrara's polemic trades on an overstated (if not chimerical) division between liturgical "changes" one may legitimately protest and allegedly sacrosanct "teachings."

As for "teaching," if Jesus' words at Matthew 23 on the scandal of disparity between preaching and practice have meaning, Popes have *taught* by the good they have done, but also by the evil they have acquiesced in, blessed, and ordered—including imperial conquest and attendant man-stealing and the wresting of a liturgy from the faithful—no less than by the propositions they commit to writing and would have Christ's flock take to heart. If what any pope taught, however, whether by word or deed, explicitly or implicitly, was not among the truths Christ deposited with His Apostles, then divine protection from error does not extend to it. We have to examine such implied or stated propositions on a case-by-case basis.

On what coherent grounds, then, harmonious with Matthew 23's censure, does a Catholic strenuously oppose the implementation of an Apostolic Constitution regarding the sacred liturgy (i.e., Paul VI's *Missale Romanum*) while no less zealously sealing off from criticism a papal encyclical on economic justice? There are, I submit, none. *Both* are imperfect products of fallible men and are to be respectfully examined in order to locate the evidence not only of fruits of the Spirit but also of that fallibility.[54]

---

54 Apostolic Constitution or no, I regard the *de facto* suppression and displacement over forty years ago of the ("never abrogated") Tridentine Rite and the verbal engineering that has accompanied its phased-in rehabilitation ("ordinary rite" vs. "extraordinary rite")—to amount to a scandal from which it may take longer to recover than from the one more frequently mentioned in the news.

Part Two

Main Course

Chapter 14

Capitalism: a Post-Christian Structure?

We have addressed every issue relevant to the title of Chapter 1, "Meet the Austrians," yet we are not quite finished with it. Its shabby treatment of the Austrians, which had precious little to do with history or biography, consumed all of three-and-a-half pages. That being apparently too skimpy even for Mr. Ferrara, however, he appended another page-and-a-half of material whose topics relate more clearly either to TCATL's introduction or to the second chapter (or even, by his own account, to the twenty-first!).

He distributed that material across two sections subtitled "caveats."[55] Posited ahead of Chapter 2 ("The Illusory 'Free' Market"), wherein Mr. Ferrara will offer justification of some

---

[55] In Mr. Ferrara's lexicon, an author may issue "caveats" about one's own book to one's readers. The Latin admonition, *Caveat emptor* ("Let the buyer beware") is the warning of a third party to prospective customers, not a vendor's friendly invitation to them to enter his or her store. *Caveat lector* ("Let the reader beware") is one writer's warning about the work of another that he's about to introduce. One may regard this book as one, big *Caveat lector* about another.

his assertions, his "caveats" are nothing but assertions presented for assimilation into his readers' mental innards.

One express concern of Mr. Ferrara's is that his criticism of Austro-Libertarianism may give the false impression that he is a socialistic enemy of private property, an impression that purveyors of bugaboo among the Austro-libertarians will promote. Despite its odd location (and redundancy in the light of later chapters), we deem it worthwhile to examine his self-representation on this score.

A theme of Mr. Ferrara's anti-market polemics, within and without TCATL, is that Catholic Austro-libertarians either (a) systematically misunderstand his straightforward points of criticism, or (b) do understand, but cloak their sin in rhetorical misdirection. A cursory reply will allow us to present the gist of our answer to his charge of incomprehension or culpable evasion, to the bare bones of which rebuttal we will add meat in ensuing posts. In his own words:

> . . . the more free enterprise in the morally correct *Catholic* sense expounded by the Popes, the better.
>
> As the Church teaches, nothing conduces to true social freedom better than a society in which as many people own property sufficient for the support of themselves and their families, as opposed to toiling for the wealthy in the cubicles of large corporations while living under a mountain of credit card and mortgage debt that also redounds to the benefit of a capitalist oligarchy. (*See* chapter 21) Nor is this book in any way, shape or form an argument for socialism—the bugaboo Austrians and other "conservative liberals" always invoke in response to any critique of injustices within the capitalist status quo. The Church opposes socialism as firmly as she does unrestrained laissez-faire capitalism and, as already suggested . . . it is laissez-faire capitalism itself that has encouraged the rise of

"soft" socialism in Western nations. (10. Emphasis in the original.)

As a way of framing the question, this is as confusing as it is tendentious. Mr. Ferrara contrasts *unrestrained laissez-faire capitalism* to *free enterprise*—in the papally expounded sense, of course. In order to comment on this contrast, however, we will need to determine answers to several questions:

1. Does *free* mean *unrestrained?*
2. Does the phrase *morally correct Catholic sense expounded by the popes* qualify to death the meaning of *free?*
3. Does *unrestrained laissez-faire capitalism* refer to something that exists or existed in history?
4. Does *free market* refer to something that exists or existed in history?

1. In the politico-economic context, "free" *does* mean nothing more or less than "unrestrained." That is, it has a wholly *negative* meaning. A person is politically free if he or she is not restrained, prevented, hampered, or hindered in the use of his or her property by force or the threat of force by others. Political-economic freedom is not to be confused with the *positive* spiritual grace to resist temptation to sin and instead "do the right thing," with which Christians (among others) are concerned (Galatians 4:31-5:1), indeed, for which they pray. That concern is no warrant for unfavorably comparing that freedom to that grace. They are distinct, but not rival dimensions of human living, related as interior to exterior, as it were.

The words *free* and *unrestrained*, however, while denoting the same thing, differ in connotation. Mr. Ferrara uses *free* before *markets*, but *unrestrained* before *laissez-faire capitalism.* A person is free, but a wild animal is unrestrained. Mr. Ferrara favors free, *but not unrestrained* markets. He very much wants papally guided moral rules to restrain the wild animals that roam in markets seeking whom they may devour. To put it in such terms would, however, only expose the equivocation at the heart of his propaganda.

2. Our answer to the first question yielded one to the second. The phrase *morally correct Catholic sense expounded by the Popes* qualifies the meaning of *free* to death only if *free* means *unrestrained*. But by *free* Mr. Ferrara does not at all mean *unrestrained*. Like most illiberals, he will not commit political suicide by mounting a frontal assault on the symbol of *freedom* or *liberty*. He prefers to keep the symbol but pour into it alien content.

3. Mr. Ferrara's claim that laissez-faire capitalism "has encouraged the rise of 'soft' socialism in Western nations" implies an affirmative answer: if it never existed, it couldn't "encourage" the rise of anything. But has laissez-faire capitalism ever been *unrestrained* and, if so, does that restraint continue? That is, does *unrestrained laissez-faire capitalism* describe anything real? If it does, then given the staggering growth of regulation, taxation, war and conscription in the West in just the last century—we frankly admit that we have no idea what meaning Mr. Ferrara attaches to *unrestrained*. If it doesn't—that is, if private enterprises *are* regulated in the above-enumerated ways—then Mr. Ferrara's criticism has no real target. (On the next page, however, he will identify his target to be "actually existing capitalism.")

4. For Mr. Ferrara, *a free market is a morally restrained and guided one.* The way he relates political freedom to morality illuminates neither, and keeping them related but distinct will occupy us later.[56]

---

[56] We remind our readers of St. Thomas Aquinas' concerns, explored in the first chapter, that despite one's good intentions, one might succeed in "morally" restraining markets to the point of destroying the common good, that is the framework of peaceful cooperation.

In any case, if Mr. Ferrara favors what he calls a morally restrained market, but not the current politico-economic establishment, which he wishes to transform along Distributist lines, he must hold that free markets either don't exist or exist only to the degree that the Distributist ideal is implemented.

We have a long way to go before arriving at Mr. Ferrara's exposition and defense of Distributism, but for now we may safely say that Distributism is what *he* means by *free market society,* or at least one that best "conduces to true social freedom."[57] (10)

Mr. Ferrara rejects socialism without giving a reason or even defining that term. Of course, Pope Pius XI declared in *Quadrogesimo Anno* that "No one can be at the same time a sincere Catholic and a true socialist," and perhaps that is reason enough for him. But what did His Holiness mean by "socialist"? He might not have meant what Mr. Ferrara's Austro-libertarian adversaries mean.

Socialism, according to them, is intrinsically unrealizable, because without markets for capital goods, the latter cannot be rationally allocated, and consequently no production of any commodity can be rationally directed. If they are right, then socialist parties cannot genuinely offer socialism, but only plans whose implementation would destroy production.[58]

We differ with the Angelic Doctor over how little moralistically inspired restraint it takes to do that.

[57] According to Mr. Ferrara in this video interview,

www.youtube.com/watch?v=ymtCyf8XvLQ Distributism virtually surrounds him as he dines *al fresco* in Lake Garda, Italy, "which is Distributism in action" [at 5:37]. Shortly thereafter he refers to "their [Austro-libertarians'] indefatigable defense of the corporate status quo," which is either evidence of slander or a symptom of hallucination. We recommend this video to readers who would like audiovisual images to go with Mr. Ferrara's sustained literary sneer.

[58] It is impossible for human beings to fly by flapping their arms. It is also impossible to avoid the dire consequences of so trying. (*Trying* to fly by flapping one's arms is not impossible.) The best short introduction to the theoretical and historical issues is, in my opinion, Murray Rothbard, "The End of Socialism and the Calculation Debate Revisited." *The Review of Austrian Economic,* Vol. 5, No. 2, 1991, 51-76

http://png.cdn.mises.org.468elmp01.blackmesh.com/sites/default/files/rae5_2_3_2.pdf

"All right," some of you may be thinking. "So what?" Simply this: the achievement of Mr. Ferrara's desired "society in which as many people own property sufficient for the support of themselves and their families" presupposes a certain understanding of production and exchange, which Mr. Ferrara nowhere offers *and, as we shall see, doesn't intend to.*

If we assume that the denizens of Mr. Ferrara's morally restrained free market society use money, then all the things that household A needs for "support"—its "basket of goods," so to speak—must be for sale at money prices and then bought from the vendors of the products households B, C, . . . *n*. This situation holds for each of the other households. The totality of these situations is a vast interlocking network of interdependency.

Goods must therefore be priced "just right" so that the *expenditures* of households A, B, C, . . . *n* (i.e., their purchase of their baskets) *equate*, day after day, with of *incomes* of those same households. If expenditures are too high or (what amounts to the same thing) if incomes are too low, the result is *injustice* (by Mr. Ferrara's standard).

Markets (individuals making and responding to offers) improve the situation for each market participant, but they are never so obliging as to guarantee the continual balancing those expenditures and income for all households. For the contents of those baskets change, creating imbalances. In the name of justice, according to that notion of justice, something would have to be done to correct the alleged imbalance.

If one's concept of justice demands balance, however, then, barring a miraculously continual coincidence of expenditures and revenues, those charged with the responsibility of administering justice would have to intervene in markets to ensure that each household can afford its basket. Who's going to bell that cat of minimizing expenditures and maximizing revenues? Central planners cannot solve for any variable without solving for all, which is impossible. They will irrationally allocate as far as they can, and then leave a mess for their successors to clean up.

At some point it begins to dawn on some planners that one can cut the Gordian knot by abolishing money and money prices with it. This would "free" those in charge of administering justice to command, directly and centrally, the production process, thus ensuring (or so they think) the just distribution of the contents of household baskets. Of course, eliminating money prices does nothing to meet the challenge of allocating resources.

If Mr. Ferrara believes that such allocation ought to be left to markets rather than to central planners—and I take him at his word that he does—then he must accept that allocation's uncertain import for individual incomes and expenditures. One of those consequences is the very acquisition of "property sufficient for the support of themselves and their families." In any case, how does the mere holding of property, unless it consists wholly of immediately consumable goods, "support" anybody? Genuine *support* presupposes the above-noted network of interdependency.

Every act of intervention weakens the fabric of interpersonal cooperation, which St. Thomas regarded as a common good. The logic of interventionism leads to totalitarianism, which all but destroys that good. Mr. Ferrara says he rejects socialism in favor of free markets, but adheres to a notion of *freedom* that seems to warrant such intervention.

* * *

"When I use a word it means just what I choose it to mean—neither more nor less."

Humpty Dumpty in Lewis Carroll's *Alice in Wonderland*

We have discerned that by *free* Mr. Ferrara means—without irony—*morally restrained.* He now asks the reader to entertain another symbol, a potential source of confusion because used in the same context, that is, *"free" market*:

> ... as used through this book, the term "free" market refers not to private property or free enterprise as such, but to the post-Christian structures of "actually existing capitalism," which (*see* Chapter 2) is anything but a free market in the Catholic sense of freedom as a moral faculty exercised in conformity with the divine and natural law. (11)

That is, he apparently thinks it good form to stipulate the meaning of a term one of whose words is in scare quotes.

Mr. Ferrara borrows the phrase "actually existing capitalism" from Kevin Carson, the left-libertarian theoretician from whose critique of "mainstream" libertarianism he borrows heavily (even though Catholics "cannot possibly go where left libertarians will take them" [14]).

Let's drop the redundant "actually." Mr. Ferrara's object is extant or "existing capitalism." But whether extant or extinct, what does *capitalism* itself mean? The history of the usage of *capital* or *capitalism* by socialists or anti-socialists will not help us here. Perhaps "post-Christian structures" is a clue.

The prefix *post-* implies a timeline: the temporal structures dubbed *Christian* came into being (implying pre-Christian structures), had their day in the sun, and then passed away (to be resurrected one day in a glorified Distributist body?). *That*, according to Mr. Ferrara's lexicon, is *capitalism*. In any case, when those "structures" prevailed in the West—in unspecified centuries and countries, under unspecified rulers—there allegedly were free markets "in the Catholic sense of freedom as a moral faculty exercised in conformity with the divine and natural law."

We suppose that the "faculty" in question is the human will. We accept *arguendo* Mr. Ferrara's faculty psychology, whose validity he presupposes as though everyone knows what he's talking about. Even if the mind is a network of interacting "faculties" (or "modules" or "organs"), one cannot sensibly be said to exercises one's free will only when one conforms to the law. One also exercises it when one transgresses the law. That is a necessary condition of culpability.

If the word *free* and its cognates were to pertain only to the decision to conform to the law, we would need another word to refer to the decision to transgress the law. We therefore couldn't say that one ever *chooses* to transgress, for choosing presupposes freedom, and freedom—"true freedom"—is ordered only to conformity to the law. A *reductio ad absurdum* if there ever was one.

Equivocation once again mars Mr. Ferrara's argument: in a kind of analogy to Gresham's law, *freedom* as the positive spiritual strength, virtue, or power (*dunamis*, cf. 2 Timothy 1:7; 2 Timothy 2:1-2; Ephesians 3:16-17) to do the good and avoid evil crowds out the meaning of *freedom* as the negative condition of *not* being restrained, prevented, hampered, or hindered in the use of one's property by force or the threat of force. Markets may be free in the latter sense regardless of how free or unfree market participants are spiritually. Mr. Ferrara's confusion prevents him from considering how knowledge of markets is a factor in moral deliberation.

There is also his equivocation on the word *law*. As we have discussed, *law* may refer either to *legislation* or to *principle*. Divine law is a kind of legislation; natural law (with God as its source) a kind of principle. *The choice to conform is possible in the former case, but not in the latter.* One does not sanely entertain the option of not conforming one's behavior to a law of logic, to a physical law or, as we will elaborate in due course, to an economic law.

According to Mr. Ferrara, the masses "[toil] for the wealthy in the cubicles of large corporations while living under a mountain of credit card and mortgage debt that also redounds to the benefit of a capitalist oligarchy" (10). Indeed, they do, but not under *unrestrained* capitalism, but rather under a mercantilist welfare-warfare bureaucratic state, which Austro-libertarians would dismantle root and branch.

Commitment to an unhampered free market order does *not* entail rule by a few but, if anything, a radical "consumerocracy." Mises wrote:

> The consumers patronize those shops in which they can buy what they want at the cheapest price. Their buying and their abstention from buying decides who should own and run the plants and the farms. They make poor people rich and rich people poor. They determine precisely what should be produced, in what quality, and in what quantities. They are merciless bosses, full of whims and fancies, changeable and unpredictable. For them nothing counts other than their own satisfaction. They do not care a whit for past merit and vested interests. If something is offered to them that they like better or that is cheaper, they desert their old purveyors. In their capacity as buyers and consumers they are hard-hearted and callous, without consideration for other people.[59]

Before Mr. Ferrara can judge whether "consumer sovereignty" so described is good or bad, to be promoted or opposed, he has to ascertain whether or not markets, to the extent that they are free, tend to establish it. This he will not do.

---

[59] Ludwig von Mises, *Human Action,* Ch. XV, Section 4, "The Sovereignty of the Consumers."

Chapter 15

Conflating Science and Ethics

A nother Caveat," Mr. Ferrara's second and final postscript to his book's meager first chapter, consist of two paragraphs in which he

a. mocks as a "diversionary tactic" any (so far unexamined) rebuttal to his charges based on economics (as that word has been understood post-Xenophon);

b. imputes evasiveness to any Austro-libertarian critic who maintains that questions of justice have a value-free economic dimension which we must consider apart from the value-laden dimension (to which the other cannot be reduced) and then

c. exempts himself from his own anti-theoretical proviso.

We confine our comments to a few characteristic sentences. (In this section, all quotations from TCATL are from page 11 unless otherwise indicated.)

> . . . this book [TCATL] is not concerned with "economics" as an academic discipline involving such technical matters as supply and demand curves and schedules.

This express lack of concern, odd in a book subtitled "the Catholic Church's Teaching on Man, Economy, and State," has consequences for one's thinking on ethical matters, consequences we will itemize.

Rather, it is concerned with economics in the classical sense of the word . . . . [Mr. Ferrara here appends a note on the derivation of "economics" from the Greek οἰκονομικός [oikonomikos], which he might have further analyzed into οἶκος [oikos, household) and [νόμος, nomos, law]].)

Here's what Mr. Ferrara means by "economics," which must not be confused with the "academic discipline" on pain of misunderstanding the mischief Austro-libertarians are allegedly up to:

. . . a practical ethical science whose aim is commutative and distributive justice among men in their dealings concerning the bounty of the earth—but men first and foremost as members of families, the fundamental units of society. . . . [Economics is] a branch of ethics—moral philosophy . . . .

Now, if economics is a branch of moral philosophy, Mr. Ferrara argues, then every faithful Catholic must regard economics as "lying within the domain of moral theology and thus subject to the teaching authority of the Church, as pope after pope has insisted (contrary to the opinion of Austrians)."

But if it isn't, then it doesn't. And, to belabor what should be obvious, papal insistence is not, contrary to Mr. Ferrara's opinion, a criterion of logical demarcation of one kind of question from another.

In the history of every science there occurs an intellectual breakthrough that enables scientific community to advance from an understanding of things in their relationship to the inquirers (e.g., our observation of falling apples) to an understanding of things as they relate to each other (e.g., $f = ma$). That is, an explicit theoretical interest emerges out of the practical and ethical interest, and that emergence entails a shift in horizon. The theorist doesn't deny but merely prescinds from the practical or ethical or moral dimension of the object.

An earlier, "classical" stage in the history of a scientific inquiry is not necessarily nobler, truer, more innocent, less corrupt than its "modern" offspring. One may as well claim that geometry lost its way when it ceased to be the measuring of land and began to be a study of the properties of shapes; or insist that physics, the science of motion, space, time, force, and mass, has not been faithful to its origins as the study of things that grow. The more abstract understanding encompasses the more concrete, but liberates our understanding of the concrete from its contingent circumstances. Reasonable people may argue about whether this kind of abstraction enriches or impoverishes our understanding of reality, but for Mr. Ferrara there is no debate.

The phrase "bounty of the earth" diverts attention from the salient fact that virtually all material goods, between the Garden of Eden and Paradise, are scarce (non-abundant). That reality anchors the economic question. "Scarcity," however, is a word we never encounter in his book. It apparently has no relevance for him to the formulation of practical problems.

To the satisfaction of which of several competing wants does a parent, landlord, capitalist, pirate, gangster, or finance minister first employ a unit of a given resource? What opportunity costs do their choices entail? The answers to both questions (to list no others) require us to think about the *logical* (not psychological) parameters of human action. To differentiate such questions from "What morally ought I do with that unit?" is to take a significant step in one's intellectual development. Mr. Ferrara shows no sign that he grasps this differentiation, let alone its significance.

Austrian praxeologists claim that among the many objects of scientific inquiry is human action, formally considered: the human effort to substitute a less satisfactory with a more satisfactory state of affairs.[60]

We cannot stress enough the word *formally*. The claim is that human action may be fruitfully examined *apart from the ethical motivations and consequences of those efforts*. That is, human beings act purposively, and acting on purpose has its own logic, to which moral judgment of purpose is irrelevant.[61] It is an abstraction that illuminates the concrete from which it is abstracted, and such illumination is its sole justification. That is, it is an enriching rather than an impoverishing abstraction, or so praxeologists claim.

Reasonable people can and do debate whether we may profitably and responsibly consider human action apart from the moral quality of the ends of human action. Not so for Mr. Ferrara: his *ipse dixit* is that economics it is an ethical science, and therefore one may *not* prescind from the moral quality of either the means or the ends pursued.

Mr. Ferrara's preference for an antiquarian definition of "economics"[62] would not merit such extensive criticism had he not expressed it with disrespect for those with whom he disagrees. It is the glory of the human mind to analyze and synthesize, to differentiate what is compact in their experience

---

[60] "We call contentment or satisfaction that state of a human being which does not and cannot result in any action. Acting man is eager to substitute a more satisfactory state of affairs for a less satisfactory." Ludwig von Mises, *Human Action,* Chapter 1, Section 2.

[61] "On the formal fact that man uses means to attain ends we ground the science of *praxeology*, or economics; *psychology* is the study of how and why man chooses the contents of his ends; *technology* tells what concrete means will lead to various ends; and *ethics* employs all the data of the various sciences to guide man toward the ends he should seek to attain, and therefore, by imputation, toward his proper means." Murray Rothbard, *The Mantle of Science*, 1960. Freely available on mises.org.

[62] Ultimately, nothing hangs on a word, everything on what we mean by our words. The Austrian Nobelist Friedrich Hayek proposed to replace "economics" with "catallaxy" or the science of exchange.
www.catallaxy.org/1.2.aspx Were that usage to catch on and displace "economics," Ferrara and other advocates of (empirical) Catholic Social Teaching could keep the term. *The problem of how knowledge of man's catallactic situation informs ethical reasoning would remain.*

and then reflectively reintegrate those features, aspects, or dimensions into a systematic cognition of the object.

The claim of the praxeologists is that each human action has not only a particular *telos* or purpose, but that human action *as such* has a universal *logos* or intelligibility that we can grasp intelligently and affirm reasonably. From our knowledge of that *logos* we can deduce historically invariant principles. We invite the reader to engage in such self-reflection and logical analysis as we examine Mr. Ferrara's distortion of a school of thought whose writings more than meet the standard of intelligent, reasonable, and responsible discourse. Unfortunately, however, the road to that examination is littered with sentences like this:

> We will examine the Austrians' attempt to *disguise* as technical economics, with the aid of "praxeology," a pseudo-science of human behavior based on subjective utility theory, what are really *a priori* value judgments underlying a "philosophy of liberty" that stands in direct conflict with Catholic doctrine and even the simple rational recognition of man's nature as an ensouled creature of God. (Emphasis as in the original.—A.F.)

We will ignore Mr. Ferrara's imputation of bad motive ("attempt to disguise") and the scare-quotes—par for the course in his "fraternal appeal" to fellow Catholics. Much more interesting is his ironic failure—given his professed subscription to what he will later refer to as "the Aristotelian-Thomistic system" (50)—to recognize that praxeological reflection and deduction qualify as *episteme* or science in the Aristotelian sense.

Praxeology, far from being *based* on marginal utility theory, is its theoretical *ground.*[63] As we shall see, there is no evidence that he understands the whole any more than he does the part. As for *a priori* value judgments, they are inevitable,

---

63 In *Human Action*, marginal utility is defined in the seventh chapter; praxeology, the first.

even for Mr. Ferrara. (Or did he discover *empirically* that murder is morally objectionable?) The germane question is whether, and how, they can be justified. One method of justifying one's claim to have discovered an *a priori* truth is retortion, whereby the very attempt to deny the putative truth depends on its being true. (In this chapter he fails to specify the *a priori* value judgments Austrians allegedly make, so we cannot yet test their rational undeniability.)

In any case praxeology, the subject of Chapter 6, only presupposes that human beings act, that is, *move their bodies with conscious purpose in order to enact causal scenarios for realizing their purposes, scenarios they envision and from among which they freely choose.*

But that is not a value judgment (except in the sense that every act of judgments presupposes the value of truth). It is a *wertfrei* claim about reality.

We postpone a full answer to the charge of "direct conflict" between the philosophy of liberty and Catholic doctrine. Like so much else in his "caveats," it is a gratuitous assertion, which we are within our rights to gratuitously deny. By way of promissory note, however: we will show a harmony between the two.

That is, we are not content to argue that the libertarian philosophy and the Gospel are merely logically compatible. We rather hold that the philosophy—its essence, not every conclusion of every adherent of that philosophy—illuminates an aspect of the Gospel of Jesus Christ and has implications for living and implementing the Gospel by believers. We will go further and argue that only on the basis of the Gospel can libertarianism be justified.

Catholic doctrine is nothing without the Gospel, which can be discerned in its essence (but not in its fullness) apart from the former, by "a simple rational recognition," to borrow Mr. Ferrara's phrase. That is, a person hears or reads the Gospel and is immediately attracted to it. Catholic doctrine offers an explanation of that attraction and builds on it, which it subserves. Our distinctive claim is that the Gospel is essentially libertarian, spiritually, ethically, and politically.

If Catholics can learn from Aristotle, who thought some human beings were slaves from the moment they are born[64], while others ought to be killed before they are born[65], perhaps they can also learn from a libertarian admirer of the Church like Murray Rothbard, despite his own grave blunder regarding abortion. How Catholics may learn from this or that non-Catholic is to be decided only by reflection on what the latter wrote, not *a priori*. As we quoted Mr. Ferrara in our last post:

> . . . this book [TCATL] is not concerned with "economics" as an academic discipline involving such technical matters as supply and demand curves and schedules. (11)

You can bet he's not concerned with such things. Unfortunately, they're interwoven into the things with which he professes to be concerned.

> Thus, there will be no discussion of the purely technical economics in Austrian economics. The focus, rather, will be on the Austrian School's ventures into areas in which it can have no claim to special competence: human action, philosophy, ethics, politics, liberty and justice. (11)

The consideration of evidence of the Austrians' allegedly unqualified venturing lies in the future. In the meantime, it is good to remember that an expert in one field can, and usually does, have broad knowledge in areas beyond that of his or her expertise. Provided he or she qualifies his or her labors in another's vineyard and is willing to defer to qualified experts, there is no problem. If there were, then *ipso facto* Mr. Ferrara

---

[64] *Politics*, Bk. 1, V-VI.

[65] *Politics*, Bk. 7, XVI.

was unqualified to have written TCATL (although I'm not sure pointing that out to him would have had any effect).

Finally, here's what we meant when we said he "exempts himself from his own anti-theoretical proviso." (11)

> One seemingly technical matter, however, will come under examination: the role of Austrian utility theory in Austrian arguments in favor of a "market society" and against Catholic social teaching on the errors of economic liberalism. (11)

Let's see . . . no discussion of purely technical economics of the Austrian school . . . except for one of the technical doctrines for which it is best known (which is, after all, only *seemingly* technical). We decline to dilute with comment the impact of Mr. Ferrara's self-exemption.

Chapter 16

Disparaging Imaginary Constructions as Illusions

M r. Ferrara begins Part I's only substantial chapter with a conclusory statement of his position. What he calls an "essential preliminary" to the ensuing "discussion" (his word for the rest of his book) is the reader's "understanding of the insuperable problem that undermines the entire Austro-libertarian defense of what they call the 'free' market: that it does not exist in the real world, as they themselves admit." (12)

To claim to understand something is to imply that it is actual, for one cannot understand what is not there to be understood. What Mr. Ferrara intends for his readers to "understand," however, is nothing more than the uncharitable construction that he puts upon his Austro-libertarian opponents' words, an interpretation he apparently cannot trust his reads to arrive at on their own after he puts the evidence in front of them. The only thing he leaves for them to decide is whether Austro-libertarians are too stupid to notice that the free market doesn't exist (even though they admit it doesn't), too dishonest to call attention to this cognitive dissonance, or too schizophrenic to care how they're perceived.

After this tendentious start, Mr. Ferrara quotes Ludwig von Mises to the effect that the free market is an imaginary construction. Unfortunately, however, he never explains what Mises meant by "imaginary construction." Had Mr. Ferrara done that, his reader would understand that this effort of the imagination serves a theoretical, not an historical, purpose. The debate would then be over the effort's success or failure. Parties to the debate would be armed with competing philosophies of theory and practice. Mr. Ferrara expresses no interest in such a debate.

The Austro-libertarians' theoretical or scientific intention, once recognized, would undermine the defamation, implied in the chapter's title (and repeated at the head of its every odd-numbered page), that they suffer from an *illusion*. An imaginary construction might illuminate reality, but illusions can only occlude it. One who suffers from an illusion is disqualified from serving in a scientific capacity.

Let's see who's shutting out reality. Mr. Ferrara quotes *Human Action* from the opening paragraph of the third section of Chapter XIV, "The Scope and Method of Catallactics," the section's title being "The Pure Market Economy." As the words his ellipsis obscure are relevant for assessing his diagnosis of a cognitive break with reality by Austro-libertarians, and as the words that follow give a fuller sense of Mises' theoretical interest, we will italicize them:

> The imaginary construction of a pure or unhampered market economy assumes that *there is division of labor and private ownership (control) of the means of production and that consequently there is market exchange of goods and services. It assumes that the operation of the market is not obstructed by institutional factors. It assumes that the* government, *the social apparatus of compulsion and coercion,* is intent upon preserving the operation of

the market system, abstains from hindering its functioning, and protects it against encroachments on the part of other people. The market is free; there is no interference of factors, foreign to the market, with prices, wage rates, and interest rates. *Starting from these assumptions economics tries to elucidate the operation of a pure market economy. Only at a later stage, having exhausted everything which can be learned from the study of this imaginary construction, does it turn to the study of the various problems raised by interference with the market on the part of governments and other agencies employing coercion and compulsion.*

This is a window into Mises' theoretical context, with which Mr. Ferrara announced in the previous chapter that he has no interest (except when it suits him). As we can see, however, Mr. Ferrara's several omissions are arguably germane to his topic:

1) *The ontology of the market*, namely, the division of labor, private property in capital goods, and market exchanges, which flesh out the meaning of the "operation of the market," which "institutional factors" might obstruct.

2) *Mises' view of government* as that agency of coercion that allegedly confines its tender mercies to protecting market actors from other forms. Anarcho-capitalist students of Mises like Murray Rothbard deny that the government *can* "abstain from hindering its [the market's] function": governments can *only* supply instances of the "hindering" and "encroachment" which the imaginary construction must bracket out. We understand that Mr. Ferrara may not be interested in whether Mises' "minarchism" is less grounded in reality or coherent with his own theoretical strictures than is anarchism. We fail to see, however, how he can avoid the question of coercion in any responsible "discussion" of free markets.

3) The *theoretical* (not historical) purpose of Mises' imaginary construction: it "elucidates" market operations by (a) distinguishing *categorically* between peaceful exchange and violent interference therewith, (b) considering the logic of the former apart from the latter, and then (c) studying the effects of the latter on the former.

Notably, Mises does not lump peaceful exchange and violent interference together as "human behavior." The former is the norm, the latter subversive of it. This categorical demarcation is ethical, in a Kantian way: it is possible to universalize peaceful exchange; it is not possible to universalize violence without destroying the human race (and *a fortiori* all possible subjects and objects of economics).

More significantly, Mr. Ferrara fails to disclose that the preceding section of this chapter of *Human Action*, that is, Section 2 of Chapter XIV, is devoted to justifying the imaginary theoretical construction that he would have his readers confuse with an illusion.

Mr. Ferrara was off to a good start when he quoted Ludwig von Mises. Unfortunately, however, quotation *per se* doesn't satisfy all of one's obligations. The purpose of the quoted author matters, as does the relevance of the quoted material to one's thesis. So, we wonder how that passage on the theoretical role of imaginary construction triggered this:

> One of the principal reasons the "pure or unhampered" market has never existed (except in the imagination of Austrians) is that *capitalist entrepreneurs themselves* have militated against its [the free market's] existence from the very inception of the capitalist eras by obtaining special favors, protections and exemptions from the post-Catholic and then post-Christian nation-states that replaced the decentralized structures of political authority in Christendom. (12) (Italics in the original.—A.F.)

Now, who is asking the historical question Mr. Ferrara was moved to answer with such gusto? Mises was not. In the section of *Human Action* just before the one from which Mr. Ferrara quoted, that is, Section 2, "The Method of Imaginary Constructions," Mises justifies the product of theoretical creativity that Mr. Ferrara would have his readers regard as an illusion.[66] The free market, so defined, "has never existed" for the simple reason that it is the fruit of a thought experiment (*Gedankenexperiment*).

Of course imaginary constructions don't exist! The question is whether they illuminate what *does* exist, including events that occur. Such concepts focus attention on different factors, holding all but one of them constant, permitting the theorist to conjecture what the effect of changing one of them might be. One may say just as obtusely that subatomic particles exist only in the imagination of theoretical physicists, and perhaps that is Mr. Ferrara's view of their field as well.

Unlike those particles, however, which are only objects for us, we human beings can test what *Human Action* says about us by reflecting on what we are doing when we are acting and see whether Mises' articulation squares with that reflection. Because Mr. Ferrara is in such a hurry to hold Austrians up to ridicule, however, he misdirects his readers' attention away from Mises' theoretical interest to a gratuitously asserted thesis of historical causation.

---

66 One may read Mises' discussion here: http://mises.org/humanaction/chap14sec2.asp

Chapter 17

"Statism" versus "Greed"

Mr. Ferrara continues his practice of frontloading his presentation of Austro-Libertarianism with his own biases:

> Austro-libertarians are prepared to admit the long historical development of "corporate welfare" and "crony capitalism," while attributing it entirely to "statism" rather than the sheer greed of the entrepreneurs who demanded favors from the State. (12)

Mr. Ferrara does not cite any writers dumb enough to attribute the rise of this phenomenon entirely to one factor, like "statism" (undefined). But then, we do not expect him to make his adversaries case intelligible before mocking it. We expect him to exaggerate and put his adversaries in the worst possible light. He does not disappoint.

He opposes the Austrians of his imagination, not over the silliness of assigning one cause for a complex historical phenomenon, but only over the identity of that fictive sole cause. They allegedly indict an ideology ("statism"), whereas Mr. Ferrara unabashedly imputes it to a grave moral defect, indeed, one of the seven Cardinal Sins ("greed"), thereby betraying a narrow understanding of the ways sinners can express their various moral defects.

Greedy persons do indeed transact on the marketplace, whose norm is peaceful cooperation. There is no shortage of them at any time in history. They also, however, walk the corridors of power where, unlike in the marketplace, they are in their element. Statism, which Mr. Ferrara characteristically holds up for ridicule in scare quotes, is the modern rationalization of the *libido dominandi*, the perverse desire for the power to coerce others (a topic of Saint Augustine's *The City of God*, Book I). Those who wield great coercive power can influence the scope of greed by removing natural checks on its expression, like fear (e.g., by central bank credit expansion encouraging unsound investment).

Jesus commanded his disciples to resist the temptation to push others around (Matthew 20:25). This warrants a serious examination, rather than a contemptuous dismissal, of the anarcho-Catholic's claim that the State *per se* as a moral hazard. If the market can supply all the goods and services that the marketplace's peaceful cooperators need, including the means of dealing with violent non-cooperators, then there is no need for a State of which sheerly greedy capitalists can demand any favors.

Chapter 18

Confusion or Calumny?

Austro-libertarians proudly document how capitalists were heavily involved in the creation of the modern state (in both its welfare and warfare dimensions, we might add) and continue to be in its maintenance, from which they profit. But Mr. Ferrara does not wish to leave his readers with an impression of significant factual agreement between himself and his Austro-libertarian adversaries. His words *prepared to admit* poison that common ground, insinuating that they "concede" it, reluctantly, as it were, against self-interest:

> . . . they do so with a very convenient inconsistency that allows them to condemn any kind of government intervention in favor of employees or consumers because it would interfere with the processes of the "unhampered market," when they have already conceded that the market is not "unhampered" in the first place precisely because of massive government interventions in *favor* of big business among other factors. (12-13; emphasis in original.—A.F.)

As we argued before, the "unhampered market" was an object in the theoretical space of Ludwig von Mises (and that of many other economists, Misesian and non-Misesian). Theoretical constructs or "models" enable one to analyze otherwise unmanageable complexities, whether generated by, say, subatomic particle collision or interpersonal property exchange. Models are not intended to account for historical contingencies or to help assign historical praise or blame any more than they are to account for why a particular physical, chemical, or biological event occurs.

Now, it is hard to tell whether Mr. Ferrara's repeated confusion on this point, on which most of his case against Austro-Libertarianism rests, is due to his intellectual inability to grasp it, which would be morally innocent; or due to his refusal to do so, which is not so innocent. Our commitment to norms of charitable construction inclines us to the former alternative.

Working against that, however, is his suggestion that a "very convenient inconsistency" warps Austro-libertarian discourse. By what warrant does Mr. Ferrara impute ill motive to them? Intellectual confusion could account for his seeing a non-existent "inconsistency" in another's thought, but he gives the game away when he describes as "very convenient."

The theoretical model of the unhampered market illuminates the non-theoretical transactions of real persons with their flesh-and-blood divergences from that model. At least that is what Austro-libertarians claim for it, nothing more, nothing less. They have never conducted their researches in an ivory tower: the author of *Human Action* was, after all, a Gestapo target.

Human persons, even in their fallen state, can be intellectually converted to a standpoint informed by a true economic model; having grasped the certain consequences of disregarding that model, they may, by a further moral conversion, freely decide to attempt to realize that model as far as is humanly possible this side of the New Heavens and New Earth. The undeniable reality of human persons is the ontological ground of intelligent, reasonable, and responsible reference to free markets.

Chapter 19

The Kevin Carson (Side-)Show

r. Ferrara makes something like a charge we can
sink our teeth into on page 13. Oddly, he does so by
invoking someone else's authority, which invocation
he qualifies, because that person is no authority in the area of
Catholic controversy. But he provides a stick that looks useful
for beating up on Austro-libertarians, and that is too good an
opportunity for Mr. Ferrara to pass up.

His mode of attack continues along the lines suggested in
the first dozen pages of TCATL, that is, to insinuate, to create
an "atmosphere," to assert promiscuously and gratuitously, and
occasionally to mimic the art of providing warrant for one's
assertions by citing anyone who anywhere has published an
opinion concordant with his.

The forensic antic of the hour is: digressive appeal to
unqualified expert opinion. The unqualified expert whose opinion
is adduced: Kevin A. Carson, self-described "free market anti-
capitalist" libertarian theoretician, antagonist in an intramural
libertarian squabble that has arisen over the last half-decade
(and which has pretty much settled down). Mr. Carson's
expertise in the historical, political, and economic areas on

which he has written is at least debatable, and Mr. Ferrara cites that debate (of which more in due course). His expertise touching the Catholic reception of Austro-Libertarianism, however, is not debatable: it is non-existent.

The charge of "convenient inconsistency," applied with a broad brush to an undefined population of Austro-libertarian writers, gratuitously leveled on page 12 is treated as proven by page 13. On such a platform Mr. Ferrara will proceed to build. He now seeks to amplify its rhetorical force by appeal to another writer, whose side he will take in the dialectic (wherein Mr. Ferrara is the unqualified non-expert witness). He begins by employing another epithet for the "inconsistency":

> No one has been more adept at exposing this Austro-libertarian tap dance than Kevin A. Carson, a left-libertarian "anarcho-distributist" whose brilliant written commentaries have attracted a great deal of hostile attention in "right-libertarian" circles. Citing Thomas Woods and others as examples of what he calls "vulgar libertarianism," Carson encapsulates the vulgar libertarian polemic in a single scathing paragraph.[67] (13)

We'll review the scathing paragraph presently, but we observe that all we have so far is Mr. Ferrara's opinion of Mr. Carson's "written commentaries" ("brilliant") and of the kind of attention they have attracted (not critical but "hostile").

We also note that Mr. Ferrara used quotation marks correctly when indicating that he's citing Mr. Carson's description of the ideas of certain libertarian writers. But thereafter Mr. Ferrara never uses his favorite punctuation device for that term

---

[67] Mr. Ferrara, a Distributist, provides no warrant from Mr. Carson's (or anyone else's) writings for suggesting some sort of distributist commonality between their two positions, and I could find none. Perhaps some reader will inform me of the source. It doesn't really matter, however, for after all, the descriptor appears between scare quotes. *"I never said Kevin Carson was an anarcho-distributist! I said he was an 'anarcho-distributist'"!*

again. He'll never refer to *so-called* "vulgar libertarians," but simply to vulgar libertarians.

We remind the reader that this book is about TCATL and about the thought of others only to the degree that it bears on our task. It is therefore *not* about Kevin Carson's distinctive economic, political, and organizational doctrines, which he has expounded in many publications, each of them resting on a large body of literature.

And now for that single paragraph of Kevin Carson's that Mr. Ferrara's finds "scathing" which, because Mr. Ferrara assigns such weight to it, is worth quoting in full:

> Vulgar libertarian apologists for capitalism use the term "free market" in an equivocal sense: they seem to have trouble remembering, from one moment to the next, whether they're defending actually existing capitalism or free market principles. So we get the standard boilerplate article arguing that the rich can't get rich at the expense of the poor, because "that's not how the free market works"—implicitly assuming that this is a free market. When prodded, they'll grudgingly admit that the present system is not a free market, and that it includes a lot of state intervention on behalf of the rich. But as soon as they think they can get away with it, they go right back to defending the wealth of existing corporations on the basis of "free market principles."[68]

Mr. Ferrara thought this paragraph "scathing." Perhaps it is—to Mr. Carson's reputation as a writer. I do not wish to prejudice my readers against his scholarly efforts, but I wouldn't

---

[68] Kevin Carson, *Studies in Mutualist Political Economy* [2007], 115-116. The 2004 edition is available for free download. The words "the standard boilerplate article" are followed by "in *The Freeman*." He deleted that phrase for the revised edition, published the year *The Freeman* began to publish his presumably non-boilerplate articles.

www.mutualist.org/sitebuildercontent/sitebuilderfiles/MPE.pdf

blame them if this first impression, courtesy of Mr. Ferrara, left a bad taste in their mouth. He seems to be a graduate of Mr. Ferrara's literary finishing school.

Mr. Ferrara apparently approves of Mr. Carson's diagnosis of impaired memory ("they seem to have trouble remembering, from one moment to the next . . . .). It is not long before that is replaced by a suggestion of intellectual shadiness ("they'll grudgingly admit . . . [b]ut as soon as they think they can get away with it . . . .").

So which is it? Are "vulgar libertarians" doddering fools? Or sneaky-petes? And is this merely a postulated definition of "vulgar libertarian apologists for capitalism" that no one writer fully instantiates? Or is this a blanket smear against a whole class of writers, i.e., Austro-libertarians, as Mr. Ferrara's use of Mr. Carson's epithet seems to suggest? What are we to think about an ostensibly serious writer who belittles his equally serious adversaries that way?

And what are we to think of a Catholic writer who overlooks that want of charity in another in order to "admir[e] his intellectual honesty"? (14)

It is not surprising that Mr. Ferrara, a connoisseur of the rhetorical slap-in-the-face, fancies Mr. Carson's coinage of "vulgar libertarianism,"[69] which refers to the habit (allegedly widespread in popular libertarian literature) of defending politically hampered markets in the name of free markets, and turning a blind eye to the sordid historical tale of the hampering. Mr. Ferrara intends to exploit Mr. Carson's insult, but fails to show the empirical fit of that critique to Austro-libertarians.

---

[69] Mr. Carson's discourteous tag, "vulgar libertarian," now circulating in Mr. Ferrara's "fraternal" overture to fellow Catholics, is of Marxist vintage (i.e., Karl Marx's contempt for the "vulgar economists" who succeeded the "classical" economists, e.g., Adam Smith). As one who, we presume, respects the *versio vulgata* of the Bible, rendered largely by Saint Jerome into Latin, the common language of Western Europe in the Fourth Century, Mr. Ferrara might have taken pains to distinguish his sense of "vulgar" or "common" from Mr. Carson's (and Marx's).

Whatever the verdict on Mr. Carson's distinctive contributions to libertarian discourse—including his (in our opinion) quixotic attempt to meld the labor theory of value with Austrian subjectivism—he is to be commended for his efforts to broaden and deepen the historical context of the libertarian critique of the statist order. He has extended what is essentially a Rothbardian program of revisionism, and has creatively envisioned ways for "getting out from under" Leviathan.

It is unfortunate, however, that Mr. Carson went about furthering that purpose, at least in part, by holding certain other libertarian writers up to ridicule, going so far as to suggest that they are slightly demented, rather than asking them to assess the historical narrative that he favors, which was decidedly *not* the topic of their articles. It is a performance that had the unintended consequence of encouraging an illiberal propagandist who has no interest in improving the prospects for liberty as Mr. Carson and we understand the term.

In a book of Mr. Carson's that Mr. Ferrara cites, the words of certain writers are quoted to illustrate "vulgar libertarianism." Unfortunately for Mr. Carson's (and Mr. Ferrara's) rhetorical gambit, those writers were concerned *in those articles* to confute myths confabulated to justify further interference with free exchanges between property owners. Their purpose was *not* to morally evaluate the relationship of certain classes of property owners (e.g., multinational corporations) to any state and to its subjects. To say that Mr. Ferrara does not make this distinction is to understate things.

Specifically, Mr. Carson presents no evidence to the effect that these writers defend either the existing *level* of hampering of markets or the historical *evolution* of such interference. There's evidence to the contrary:

> . . . [T]he [anti-capitalist] activists, among others, will demand—on behalf of the union workers—government restrictions on the importation of bananas from

Ecuador, while the economist will denounce those restrictions as harmful to everyone."—Barry Loberfield[70]

If we closed our borders to avoid "exploiting" the poorer nations of the world, we would face higher prices and have a lower standard of living. . . . You can see the difference by imagining more and more severe forms of protectionism in the United States.— Russell Roberts[71]

The Harvard students wanted to force multinational corporations of the West to pay a "living wage" to foreign workers in the developing world, just as they were demanding of the university with respect to its custodians. . . . activists like the Harvard students who believe their protests help the world's poorest workers actually harm them by pricing them out of the market and denying them the opportunity to develop their skills and economies.—Stephen Spath[72]

That is, there is no evidence that they subscribe to what Mr. Carson mockingly refers to as a "nursery tale" of the evolution of capitalism. Their common point is that those who call for *further* state interference in the name of achieving a better outcome for one class of market players unwittingly work

[70] Barry Lorber, "A Race to the Bottom: Who Benefits from High Prices and Low Supplies?," *The Freeman,* July 2001, an article cited in Carson, *Studies in Mutualist Political Economy,* 2004 online edition, 140. www.fee.org/the_freeman/detail/a-race-to-the-bottom/ The article opposes further governmental restriction on trade. It does not comment on such restriction as already exists.

[71] Russell Roberts, "Does Trade Exploit the Poorest of the Poor? Both Parties Benefit from Trade Even When There Are Gross Inequalities of Skill and Productivity," *The Freeman,* September 2001, an article cited in Carson, 140. www.thefreemanonline.org/columns/the-pursuit-of-happiness-does-trade-exploit-the-poorest-of-the-poor/ The article opposes protectionism. It does not celebrate any kind of privilege that multinational corporations enjoy at the expense of any group of taxpayers.

[72] Stefan Spath, "The Virtues of Sweatshops: The Law of Comparative Advantage Directs the Production of Goods," *The Freeman,* March 2002, an article cited in Carson, 141. www.fee.org/the_freeman/detail/the-virtues-of-sweatshops/ The article opposes third-party forcible interference in trade. It does not deny, or applaud the fact, that such interference is business-as-usual in most countries most of the time.

for the opposite result and thereby tend to harm the very persons their interference was intended to help.

Mr. Ferrara—and for that matter, Mr. Carson—should have charitably assumed that those writers share his moral outrage against State-facilitated robbery of the many to the advantage of the politically connected few until one has evidence that defeats that assumption. Murray Rothbard, for example, is hardly one of Mr. Carson's "vulgar libertarians," and that he liberally draws upon the work of that veritable anti-Christ of Mr. Ferrara's nightmares is something else you would never know from reading Mr. Ferrara's rendition of Mr. Carson's thought.

And then, as luck would have it, there's Dr. Woods's *Freeman* article:

> Does capitalism, when left undisturbed, tend to increase everyone's well-being, or is government intervention necessary to prevent widespread impoverishment? This is what is at stake in the ongoing debate over the Industrial Revolution, and in this undertaking F. A. Hayek and Ludwig von Mises were noticeably ahead of their time.[73]

One doesn't have to champion "consequentialist ethics" to assert the relevance of increased standards of living when evaluating calls for *further* departures from the norm of voluntary exchange. There are no grounds for insinuating, rather uncharitably, that Dr. Woods is insensitive to any injustice that may condition, accompany, precede, or succeed the voluntary exchanges that bring that material improvement about. Both parties to a voluntary exchange must, *logically* must, expect to benefit from it or they would not enter into it. A third party has no business making light of that benefit.

---

[73] Thomas E. Woods, Jr., "A Myth Shattered: Mises, Hayek, and the Industrial Revolution," *The Freeman* November 2001, an article cited in Carson, *Studies in Mutualist Political Economy*, 2004 online edition, p. 140.

The crucial point, against which Mr. Ferrara offers invective but no argument, is that while the result of a voluntary exchange may yet leave much to be desired from the perspective of charity, that exchange *per se* cannot be deemed *unjust.* What would be unjust, that is, a violation of the dignity of the persons involved, is a third party's forceful interference either with that exchange, or with future exchanges in any effort to "rectify" the result of the original exchange.

(Mr. Ferrara does not explicitly support such interference, but as we shall see, he does claim that the result of a voluntary exchange can be unjust, and a claim of injustice opens the door to the use of force to [re-]establish justice.)

The desire, born of humaneness and compassion, that one party to a voluntary exchange be in a stronger negotiating position, that it have options other than what the other is offering, is logically irrelevant to deciding whether a given exchange is voluntary and therefore just.

So that there is no misunderstanding: a voluntary exchange need not be a test of the virtue of charity. It would be, of course, morally praiseworthy were each party to exercise charity toward the other, but while one may enforce justice, one cannot, *logically* cannot, enforce charity. Justice requires that each gives the other his or her due, but charity is due no one. (To regard charity, which springs from the heart, so to speak, as something that one *owes* another is to misconceive, if not offend against, charity.) Both parties may exercise charity, but their failure to do so is not evidence of injustice.

In the Winter 2006 issue of the *Journal of Libertarian Studies* (JLS), several leading libertarian scholars examined Kevin Carson's distinctive economic, political, and historical theses and invited him to respond to their criticisms on its pages, which he did. Here is Mr. Ferrara's tendentious description of this symposium:

Carson's devastatingly effective critique of "vulgar
libertarianism" . . . has provoked a barrage of articles
against him the *Journal of Libertarian Studies* by no
fewer than two "Senior Scholars" and two "Adjunct
Scholars" of the Mises Institute (13-14)

The gentlemen alluded to are Walter Block, Roderick
Long, Robert Murphy, and George Reisman.[74] As they really
are senior and adjunct scholars, Mr. Ferrara's use of scare quotes
here is (once again) uncalled for, but par for his propagandistic
course. And since they were not among the Austrians Mr. Ferrara
wanted us to "meet" in Chapter 1, we will cite evidence of their
scholarly productivity.

Professor Long, then-editor of now-defunct JLS (reincarnated
as the online *Libertarian Papers*) introduced the alleged "barrage"
of "attacks" in this editorial:

Individualist anarchist Kevin A. Carson's recent
book *Studies in Mutualist Political Economy* seeks to
revive and defend the mutualist position on these
topics, while incorporating some Austro-libertarian
concepts along the way. For example, Carson defends
the labor theory of value—but in an "Austrianized"
version that, unlike its Marxist counterpart, attempts
to incorporate both subjectivism and time-preference;
and Carson's account of the historical role of the
corporate power elite draws on the work of radical

---

[74] Block's curriculum vitae:

www.walterblock.com/wp-content/uploads/cv/block_cv.pdf
Long's:

media.cla.auburn.edu/philosophy/bio/bio_display.cfm?PersonID=1024
Murphy's:

http://consultingbyrpm.com/resumecv
Reisman's:

web.archive.org/web/20060531150909/http:/bschool.pepperdine.edu/programs/facult
y/vitae.html?Name=Reisman,+G.

Austro-libertarians like Murray Rothbard and Joseph Stromberg.

Yet while Carson's mutualist version of libertarianism has much in common with the Austrian version, Carson—like his mutualist forebears, but unlike most Austrians—indicts as unjust the separation of workers from ownership of the means of production. His brief against "capitalism" (in this sense of the term) is interdisciplinary in character, deploying economic arguments as to the dependence of such separation on state interference with the market, historical arguments as to the process by which this separation actually came about, and philosophical arguments as to the proper principles of justice governing the acquisition and transfer of property rights.

The assessment of Carson's arguments must likewise be an interdisciplinary enterprise. Carson's provocative claims deserve a hearing to whatever extent they are right, and require a refutation to whatever extent they are wrong. Accordingly, the present issue of the *Journal of Libertarian Studies* is devoted to an appraisal of Carson's book from an Austro-libertarian standpoint (or rather from several Austro-libertarian stand-points). Articles by Robert Murphy, Walter Block, George Reisman, and myself critically examine the various aspects of Carson's thesis—economic, historical, and philosophical; a reply by Carson follows.[75]

A rather different, calmer impression from the one Mr. Ferrara's language creates. An appraisal, not a "barrage." Let's sample another of his gratuitous assertions:

It is remarkable that four holders of doctorates, considered "heavyweights" of the "Austrian School,"

---

[75] "Editorial," *Journal of Libertarian Studies,* Vol. 20, No. 1, Winter 2006, 3-4. Freely available on mises.org.

felt compelled to answer a self-published work by Carson, who describes himself as a "health care worker." But it is easy to see why: Carson's rejoinders completely outclassed his professional academic critics in scholarship, critical reasoning, and polemical style. (14)

Ah, yes, polemical style, right up there with scholarship and critical reasoning. In Mr. Ferrara's world, it is remarkable that scholars would engage serious criticism if it originates from a non-academic source. We think that speaks highly of their integrity. There's certainly no danger of TCATL's attracting such interest. As for who "outclassed" whom ("completely," no less), we will not ask our readers to take our word for it: they are in for a treat if they examine that issue of the JLS—online, no access fees—for critiques of Mr. Carson's thought by Walter Block[76], Roderick Long[77], Robert Murphy[78], and George Reisman[79], followed by Mr. Carson's rejoinders thereto. We leave it to them to discover whether Mr. Carson "outclassed" those who invited him into their forum or merely held his own.

Mr. Ferrara's sideshow featuring Kevin Carson is nearing an end. Unfortunately we must subject ourselves to more of the former's innuendo and hand-waving.

Even if Catholics cannot possibly go where left-libertarians would take them, one must admire Carson's intellectual honesty. (14)

---

[76] Walter Block, "Kevin Carson as Dr. Jekyl and Mr. Hyde," *Journal of Libertarian Studies,* Vol. 20, No. 1, Winter 2006, 35-46. Freely available on mises.org.

[77] Roderick T. Long, "Land-Locked: A Critique of Carson on Property Rights," *Journal of Libertarian Studies,* Vol. 20, No. 1, Winter 2006, 87-95. Freely available on mises.org.

[78] Robert P. Murphy, "The Labor Theory of Value: A Critique of Carson's *Studies in Mutualist Political Economy,*" *Journal of Libertarian Studies,* Vol. 20, No. 1, Winter 2006, 17-33. Freely available on mises.org.

[79] George Reisman, "Freedom Is Slavery: Laissez-Faire Capitalism Is Government Interventionism: A Critique of Kevin Carson's *Studies in Mutualist Political Economy,*" *Journal of Libertarian Studies,* Vol. 20, No. 1, Winter 2006, 47-86. Freely available on mises.org.

Pray, where would left-libertarians take Catholics, for whom Mr. Ferrara presumes to speak, where they cannot follow? Would the implementation of Mr. Carson's version of the good society pose an obstacle to that of Mr. Ferrara's? We are given not a hint of an answer, just innuendo.

We charitably presume that his own Distributist arrangements will be peacefully established and maintained, that they will pose neither obstacle nor threat to other peaceful arrangements, even those animated by non-Catholic ideologies, that they would be, in effect, anarchist communities (regardless of what they call themselves). That is, no permanent monopoly of force and violence would be established within Distributist territory.

Realistically, we conjecture that while the state has no redeeming value in the eyes of Mr. Carson, Mr. Ferrara feels compelled to provide permanent employment for the civil magistrate, who would enjoy such a monopoly. But why does Mr. Ferrara leave it to our powers of conjecture? He had just praised Mr. Carson for his intellectual honesty. Why didn't exercise a bit of it here? That is, why didn't Mr. Ferrara just spell out what evil allegedly lurks in the hearts of left libertarians? Doing so would have saved him from the appearance of uncharitably provoking unwarranted suspicion.

We wonder whether the following sentence is TCATL's longest:

> For the truth he recognizes (not unsympathetically to the Catholic Church, by the way) is that from the time of the Protestant revolt to the "Glorious Revolution" of 1688, to the American and French Revolutions, and down to the present day, proto-capitalists and their capitalist descendants have done everything in their power to skew the "free" market their way in an alliance with secular nation states whose unprecedented centralized governments have

wielded power no Christian king could even have imagined. (14)

A few observations.

Mr. Carson's pro-Catholic sympathies, expressed *en passant*, count for something on Ferrara's balance sheet, while Murray Rothbard's positive appraisals of the Church as a libertarian force in the history of the West, more centrally and frequently expressed in his writings, do not.

Obviously, except perhaps to Mr. Ferrara, markets, to the degree that they are "skewed" by political forces, are to that degree not free. If the skewers were and are capitalists, then by libertarian standards—Austro-libertarian, left-libertarian, and garden variety—those capitalists stand condemned. We shall infer that Mr. Ferrara condemns all such historical skewing of markets for political reasons whenever he discovers an instance of it, no matter whose ox is being gored, and hold him to that standard.

We shall also defer to Mr. Ferrara's insight into the imaginative poverty of Christian kings of yore. It seems that the difference is chiefly technological: we shudder to imagine, for example, Louis XIV of France, that ostentatiously pious Catholic "Sun King," who cordially resented the presence of heretics among his subjects, with modern weapons and surveillance technology.

Mr. Ferrara respects Mr. Carson's intellectual honesty yet fails to realize an implication of one of his chief concerns, namely, the "subsidy of history." By that phrase he refers to the role of state coercion in the historical genesis of the mutually convenient arrangement between throne room and boardroom. "The extent to which present-day concentrations of wealth and corporate power are the legacy of past injustice," he writes, "I call the subsidy of history."

Mr. Ferrara broadcasts Mr. Carson's indictment, yet arbitrarily keeps from his readers' notice those instances in which the Church was the indirect beneficiary of such subsidies.

That is, Mr. Ferrara expresses no interest in how certain kings who professed Christ acquired the land they then magnanimously donated to the Church, some of which was then "redistributed" by modern editions of the State. Those beneficent monarchs did not originally homestead the land in good Lockean fashion. They took it by force or inherited it from those who did. The land had blood on it when it was donated. Such circumstances nullify justice in title.

The forcible loss of what was never properly one's to begin with may be experienced as a misfortune, but it entails no violation of rights beyond that of the stolen land's original owners, who had worked it. Justice demands that title be reassigned to their descendants, *ceteris paribus*, if they can be identified.

Chapter 20

What Is "The Free Market"?

Before continuing with the critique of Chapter 2, "The Illusory 'Free' Market," we must pause for a conceptual interlude. We need to explain just how "real" modifies "free market" in the title of the current series of posts.

After all, we have claimed that "free market" refers to an abstraction, a non-actual theoretical construct, and that the hampered markets of economic history and political commentary are, to the degree they are hampered, not free.

This philosophical excursus will not only explain how we relate the theoretical to the practical, but also inform our subsequent evaluation of the gallery of historical "sketches" on display in the rest of the chapter.

By "real" we mean the logical contrast of the illusory, the delusional, the fictional, the artificial, etc. When we know or suspect that we are in the presence of the latter, we appeal to some notion of the real to negotiate our encounter with it. A good analogy is found in the contrast between the true and the false: the notion of truth emerges only through the experience of falsehood. (If we could never experience being in error, or being deceived or lied to, we'd have no use for a notion of truth.)

Whatever is a function of real entities is also real. A market is a network of exchanges that persons, according to their human nature, spontaneously form. (That is, they do not engage in exchange because they read in some book that that's what they must do.) Markets are functions of persons, and persons are real. (Persons are entities with causal efficacy, however, markets are not.)

The market is an *order*—specifically, a network of exchanges—that persons naturally create in pursuit of their flourishing (which exceeds in value their mere biological sustenance and continuance).

Since persons generate that order by acting in accordance with their nature, it is a *natural order*, one level, aspect, or dimension of several that make up the universal natural order. Violations of that order, which tend toward human self-destruction, is not to be put on the same ontological level as that which contributes to human flourishing.

Persons are the network's "nodes" out of whom radiate catallactic "ties" (as distinct from, say, familial, ecclesiastical, or military ties). And so, the reality of free markets is the reality of persons who, in order to achieve their goals freely make, accept, and decline offers of goods and services that are within their natural right to make, accept, or decline. (What A offers to B can only be title to scarce resource R that A has justly acquired.)

The reality of the free market is a function of the natural desire of real persons for a good life or happiness (human flourishing) to which free markets are conducive. A person may, of course, have desires that are not conducive to that end, which are therefore not even implicitly a desire for free markets. Further, the existence of free markets may be a necessary but is by no means a sufficient condition for human flourishing.

The desire for human flourishing—εὐδαιμονία, *eudaimonia*, "living and doing well"—is real, and that reality extends to the network it generates, despite any failure to eliminate all forcible interference with voluntary exchanges. *Eudaimonia* is not, however, the concern of economics (catallactics) *per se*. The pursuit of economic knowledge—the logic of human action and interpersonal exchange—can only *presuppose* an interest in it on the part of those who pursue it.

But there is no necessary connection between the two. Malevolent people can join their analytical knowledge of the laws of supply and demand, for example, to their empirical knowledge of the supply and demand for a particular commodity and act to effect human misery.

This holds true for the knowledge of any other kind of causal laws. Economics, however, does not judge the malefactors. Only a eudaimonistic ethics, which affirms that the end of man is *eudaimonia* or happiness and that end ought to be pursued and misery and extinction avoided, can so judge them.

Catholic ethics shares its commitment to eudaimonistic ethics with many non-Catholic schools of thought, including some that self-identify as libertarian. It is a point of connection among them. They will differ, of course, over how they conceive of the cosmos within which the flourishing is pursued and the means by which it is attained.

The free market is a *good of order*, as distinct from *goods of immediate satisfaction*. The regular enjoyment of such goods requires that persons explicitly regard the good of order as worthy of attainment and protection. (Not just, for example, "This meal for me now," but also "Good meals for me and my family several times a day, every day.")

Persons face a *moral* challenge when they realize that they can enjoy a good of immediate satisfaction only by rending the fabric of the good of order. In the name of *eudaimonia*, they must at times forfeit particular satisfactions.

Human beings enjoy *essential freedom*. They are free by nature. They can conceive of alternative futures, prefer one of them, understand the causal path to it, and act so as to set that causal chain in motion.

But although it is natural for them to honor the good of order, they are perfectly capable of perversely, self-destructively, dishonoring and undermining it. That is, they can perceive a conflict between the good of order and a satisfaction attainable only at the cost of that order and still subordinate the order to the satisfaction.

That is, although they are naturally ordered to pursue a good life, which depends upon the good of order, human beings can, through their exercise of essential freedom, irrationally act to undermine that good.

One consequence is the diminution and even loss of their *effective freedom*, a constriction of the range of choice. The smoker, for example, has less effective freedom to quit smoking than he or she had to start, even if his or her essential freedom to conceive of a smoke-free life has not diminished.

Human beings can, and do, inject the surd of sin into the historical equation, effectively "throwing a spanner in the works." Sin is not just immoral: it is also irrational, absurd. There may be non-rational causes, but never a *reason* for it.

One way to describe history is as the story of pro-market and anti-market choices and their consequences. By counterfactual praxeological analysis, we can understand the logic of market exchange. By eudaimonistic criteria, we can morally approve of the pro-market side (peaceful offers of exchange of justly acquired property and responses thereto) because it favors human flourishing; anti-market choices (violent interference with peaceful offers and responses thereto) invite only deterioration, poverty, enslavement and other miseries, and which can logically terminate only in human extinction. And if *that* most unnatural *telos* is programmed, so to speak, into the anti-eudaimonistic ethic of anti-market ideologies, then they have no ethics worthy of the name.

Freedom and the attempt to suppress it are not onto-logically on the same footing, any more than are natural living shoots and the artificial concrete slabs that, although tempo-rarily stronger, will crack and crumble as the burgeoning tree slowly but surely pushes through. One is in accord with man's nature, for it promotes his flourishing; the other, unnatural and potentially fatal to him. The free market that human beings generate, however imperfectly and inconsistently, is therefore as real as they are, and attempts to hamper it are only as real as sin, surds for which there are no reasons and which enjoy no permanent abode.

It is not favorable to Mr. Ferrara's reputation as a writer that he employs Kevin Carson's writings in his propaganda war against Austro-Libertarianism, especially its Rothbardian founda-tion. For the aspect of those writings that Mr. Ferrara high-lights only develops a thesis that Murray Rothbard pressed for over forty years, as even a cursory glance at Mr. Carson's reference notes confirm. Rothbard encapsulated his view, expressed in many studies from the early 1950s until his death in 1995, in this passage:

> For some time, I have come to the conclusion that the grave deficiency in the current output and thinking of our libertarians and classical liberals is an enormous blind spot when it comes to big business. There is a tendency to worship Big Business *per se* . . . and a corollary tendency to fail to realize that while big business would indeed merit praise if they won that bigness on the purely free market, that in the contemporary world of total neo-mercantilism and what is essentially a neo-fascist corporate state, bigness is *a priori* highly suspect, because Big Business most likely got that way through an intricate and decisive

network of subsidies, privileges, and direct and indirect grants of monopoly protection.[80]

Mr. Carson's complaint, uncritically repeated by Mr. Ferrara, may be fairly directed at some libertarians, but not at Austro-libertarians to the degree that they identify with Rothbard's thought, which on this point, if on no other, Mr. Carson does.

That concurrence notwithstanding, Mr. Ferrara ridicules Austro-libertarians for explaining so much of modern history, including the development of "crony capitalism," in terms of "statism," or more precisely, the political struggle over control of society's central apparatus of coercion, "rather than the sheer greed of the entrepreneurs who demanded favors from the state." (12) Mr. Ferrara offers not one suasive consideration, let alone an argument, in favor of such a simplistic etiology. (Oh, he will, as we shall see, treat his readers to a gallery of historical sketches, but offer no theory that makes sense of history.)

Perhaps Austro-libertarians don't favor his causal hypothesis, assuming they give it any thought, because greed, (φιλαργυρία, *avaricia*) is a constant in human history (as is every other deadly, capital, or cardinal sin). What is present all the time, however, distinguishes no time from any other.

The ability to resist the temptation to commit a deadly sin varies from person to person, but we can generalize to say that no one is immune from being "within range" of an occasion of sin. We can imagine how the ways of being within its "gravitational pull" can vary in number and intensity from territory to territory and from era to era. But by what conceivable warrant might one propose that in the general European population in, say, 2008, there was more (or less) latent greed—the inherent capacity

---

[80] Murray Rothbard to Peter Klein, 1966. Published on Dr. Klein's blog, "Rothbard on Big Business," August 6. 2008.

organizationsandmarkets.com/2008/08/06/rothbard-on-big-business/

to act on a greedy impulse—than there was in 1917, 1848, 1776, 1688, 1517, 1492, 1378, or 1204?

As we said, we can contrast one period of history with other in terms of the occasions it makes available for the expression of a given vice, but human nature's fallen state is not an historical variable, at least not for Catholics. The advent of photography, for example, brought with it more opportunities to excite lust (πορνεία, *fornicatio*) than existed in the age of oils, graphite, ink, and charcoal; the age of film brought even more; then came home video, and now the Internet. But is there a good reason to believe that this technological progress corresponds to or reflects an increase in the level of latent lust? We can think of none.

The moral hazard that is the State offers many occasions for the expression of greed (to name no other sin), and they vary with the power of the particular state. A state with a central counterfeiting agency, more politely called the central bank, creates many more opportunities for greed to express itself than does a state without one.

And while many people may wish they could exercise their influence over the state's personnel in order to create, through the implicit violence of state edicts, non-market advantages for themselves, only a few will be able to, and historical investigation is necessary to ascertain the identity of those criminal conspirators.

Just as advances in technology decreased the fear of "getting caught" consuming pornography, so did the central bank in the financial markets decreased the fear of suffering losses for making bad loans. As Peter Schiff put it regarding the 2008-2009 Meltdown:

> Just as prices in a free market are set by supply and demand, financial and real estate markets are governed by the opposing tension between greed and fear. Everyone wants to make money, but everyone is also afraid of losing what he has. Although few

would ascribe their desire for prosperity to greed, it is simply a rose by another name. Greed is the elemental motivation for the economic risk-taking and hard work that are essential to a vibrant economy[81]

But over the past generation, government has removed the necessary counterbalance of fear from the equation. Policies enacted by the Federal Reserve, the Federal Housing Administration, Fannie Mae and Freddie Mac (which were always government entities in disguise), and others created advantages for home-buying and -selling and removed disincentives for lending and borrowing. The result was a credit and real estate bubble that could only grow—until it could grow no more.

While it is unfortunate that Schiff conflates the combination of entrepreneurial foresight and the virtue of industry with the cardinal sin of greed, his point holds even if foresight and virtue were wholly absent from the marketplace and only avarice ruled (which Schiff is *not* saying). For his point is that *fear checks vice*, and taking fear out of the equation removes a barrier to the commission of vice.

The central bank is to the cardinal sin of greed as the Internet is to the cardinal sin of lust, except the Fed is morally worse: the Internet has more, and more morally acceptable, uses than facilitating the discreet consumption of pornography, whereas the Fed has but one evil purpose: to defy the divine injunction regarding honest weights and measures. (Leviticus 19:36, Deuteronomy 25:13-16)

Mr. Ferrara writes as one with authority:

A library full of books has been written on this subject [that is, the previously cited market-skewing by anti-Catholic capitalists] but within the constraints

[81] Peter Schiff, "Don't Blame Capitalism," *The Washington Post,* October 16, 2008. www.washingtonpost.com/wp-dyn/content/article/2008/10/15/AR2008101503166.html

of this book the following examples will have to suffice to sketch the immense picture of the history of "political capitalism" and its effects upon both the illusory "free" market and social order at large. (14)

They will have to suffice because Mr. Ferrara has not mastered the books in that library. By training and profession he is a lawyer, not an historian. He delivers nothing more to his readers than an *opinion,* one that selective readings from secondary sources superficially support, and which some masters of the primary sources have contested. Never once pausing to address the question of his competency, Mr. Ferrara nevertheless proceeds to "document" his vendetta against Austro-Libertarianism.

Before evaluating his support for his eighteen claims, spread out over twenty-five pages, and about whose bearing on the Catholic reception of Austro-Libertarianism the reader may rightly wonder, we list them together without comment for his or her convenience.

1. The post-Catholic State's massive seizure of Church property and its enclosure by the new "owners." (14-17)
2. Early capitalist laws imposing the creation of an industrial economy. (17-21)
3. The widespread use of slave and convict labor in capitalist enterprises. (21-22)
4. The protection for creditors and slave-owners built in the United States Constitution. (22-23)
5. The rise of the limited liability, publicly held corporation. (23-27)
6. The government-subsidized transportation network. (27)
7. The use of State power to impose the legal and social uniformity required for "efficient" large-scale commerce. (27-28)
8. Corporate cost externalization: the "nanny state." (28-29)
9. Fractional reserve banking. (29-30)

10. The Federal Reserve System. (30-32)
11. The international credit system: usury unchained by government. (32-33)
12. Government-Sponsored Monopoly. (33-34)
13. The use of patent and trademark laws to bar entry into the market by competitors. (34-35)
14. The use of the compulsory public school system to skew education away from the liberal arts and toward technical or scientific skills. (35)
15. The creation of a vast cartelized defense industry. (35-37)
16. Government subsidies that reward overproduction, even non-production, and price small local producers out of the market. (37-38)
17. The skewing of the "free" market toward goods and services related to the social outcomes of government-subsidized industries. (38)
18. Government protection and subsidy of the "free" market's promotion of cultural and moral degeneracy. (38-39)

In tabloid-style Mr. Ferrara wraps his conflation of the complex topics of land seizure and land enclosure in an insinuation of guilt by association.

> The theft and later enclosure of former Church properties in England, the cradle of capitalism and the Industrial Revolution (roughly 1760-1830), is pre-eminently illustrative of the process. (14)

Mr. Ferrara's propagandistic approach to history is on display here. His reference to "capitalism and the Industrial Revolution" is a muddle: England may have been the "cradle" of the latter, but certainly not the former. "Capitalism" has a broader reference, one that expands or contracts depending on one's theoretical framework, scientific purpose, or ideological interest.

Capital accumulated on more or less free markets in Catholic Europe for centuries before the Industrial Revolution. That the Catholic worldview was a vital, indispensable spiritual component of the success of markets in Europe. (Their having been stymied everywhere else in the world is the thesis of Rodney Stark's *The Victory of Reason: How Christianity Led to Freedom, Capitalism, and Western Science.* We encourage our readers to read Tom Woods's review.[82])

Ontologically, markets are networks, which consist of nodes and ties. The nodes of the market are Good Life-seeking persons, and their mutual ties are offers of goods and services and responses thereto. Free persons—strictly speaking, persons to the degree that they are free from the coercion of others—spontaneously generate markets, which are as real as they are. This is the reality Mr. Ferrara obscures with his baseless suggestion that Austro-libertarians are apologists for mercantilism and its variants. Mr. Ferrara's failure to show that Austro-libertarians support such interference renders his gallery of "illustrations" utterly off-topic and useless to his polemical purpose.

His omission of evidence of explicit and long-standing Austro-libertarian opposition to mercantilism, however, is a more serious ethical lapse. We are merely pointing this out over and over. We are under no illusion, however, that our efforts will have any effect on Mr. Ferrara's future writings.

Austro-libertarians—that is, supporters or practitioners of Austrian economics on their anti-political side—are morally opposed to interference in markets wherever or by whose agency it has occurred. Contemplated interference with markets, however, with or without the assistance of the state, presupposes markets that are already in operation.

Markets form the natural order of producers offering goods and customers responding to those offers; the exploitation of market participants, unnatural disorder. Historically those traders were from different countries, speaking different languages,

---

[82] *The Independent Review*, Spring 2007.

www.independent.org/publications/tir/article.asp?a=637

using different currencies, and taking varying amounts of time to fulfill contracts. These flesh-and-blood historical actors generated the distinctive ethical problems (the just price, the charging of interest on a loan, etc.) that Catholic casuists, preeminently the scholastics of the School of Salamanca, addressed.[83]

In the eighth chapter of his *How the Catholic Church Built Western Civilization*, Tom Woods traces theoretical differences in economic understanding, from the fourteenth to the eighteenth centuries, to divergent theological ideas of the nature and purpose of human labor.[84] Unfortunately for Mr. Ferrara's project, they divide along Catholic and Protestant lines, with his own labor-glorifying emphasis clearly aligned with the latter. But let us not get ahead of our story.

Mr. Ferrara adds color to his narrative by alluding to (and sourcing in a reference note) William Blake's "dark Satanic Mills" which appears in *Milton, a Poem*. (Blake used capitals in the original.[85])

> The English Civil War (1641-51) and the "Glorious Revolution" of 1688 had made England into a capitalist nation of Whig oligarchs long before the "dark satanic mills" of the Industrial Revolution began to operate." (15)

He elaborates:

> The famous phrase from an untitled poem by William Blake (now known as "Jerusalem") and generally interpreted as a comment upon the Industrial Revolution in light of a legend that Jesus

---

[83] Murray N. Rothbard, "New Light on the History of the Austrian School," in *The Foundations of Modern Austrian Economics*, edited by Edwin Dolan (Kansas City: Sheed and Ward, 1976), pp. 52–74. mises.org/daily/2357

[84] Thomas E. Woods, Jr., *How the Catholic Church Built Western Civilization*, Regnery Publishing, 2005

www.tomwoods.com/books/how-the-catholic-church-built-western-civilization/

[85] See en.wikipedia.org/wiki/File:Milton_preface.jpg

once visited England and will return to rebuild a new Jerusalem there. (329 n. 8)

His invocation of the visionary poet is itself poetic, for there is as much evidence for the thesis that Jesus once visited England as there is for the opinion that "dark Satanic Mills" truthfully symbolizes the import of "capitalism" for the masses. As for that much-abused label, let us hear Hayek:

> In many ways it is misleading to speak of "capitalism" as though this had been a new and altogether different system which suddenly came into being toward the end of the eighteenth century; we use this term here because it is the most familiar name, but only with great reluctance, since with its modern connotations it is itself largely a creation of that socialist interpretation of economic history with which we are concerned. The term is especially misleading when, as it often the case, it is connected with the idea of the rise of the propertyless proletariat, which by some devious process have been deprived of their rightful ownership of the tools for their work.[86]

Satan is the enemy of life and liberty, yet with the help of those mills and kindred inventions, these blessings increased unprecedentedly in this period, and rained on the just and the unjust alike, whether that is what "Whig oligarchs" intended or not. Like E. J. Hobsbawm's *Captain Swing*, E. P. Thompson's *The Making of the English Working Class* and other superceded Marxist accounts, Mr. Ferrara's tale (which relies more on the obsolete work of the Hammonds' 1911 *The Village Labourer*) suffers from ideologically inspired oversights. As W. A. Armstrong wrote:

---

[86] F. A. Hayek, "History and Politics," in *Capitalism and the Historians,* Hayek, ed., The University of Chicago Press, 1954, pp. 14-15. We concur with Hayek: we're stuck with the term "capitalism," coined in the mid-nineteenth century by various socialists, e.g., Douai, Proudhon, Blanc, and decisively given currency by, of course, Marx and Engels.

Many years have elapsed since the standard histories of the agricultural labourer first saw the light of day, and they are decidedly outdated. It is true, several valuable contributions seeking to examine aspects of the labourer's position have appeared in academic journals and elsewhere, written by scholars with a specialist knowledge of agrarian or demographic change. *Yet until they are satisfactorily integrated, popular impressions will continue to be shaped by writers who follow the tradition, set by the Hammonds, of giving excessive emphasis to institutional influences and concentrating upon colourful episodes such as the Swing riots which seem capable of being explained to a large extend by short-period influences.* Innocently or not, such historians serve to cloud rather than illuminate the underlying factors affecting the situation of the labourer, by neglecting or misinterpreting the more fundamental economic, technological and especially the demographic determinants of his standard of life and position in society. [87]

Of course, what was written thirty years ago can hardly be considered the last word, but it is the burden of those who wish to promote "popular impressions" to inquire whether the studies Armstrong refers to have been "satisfactorily integrated" and whether the results restore confidence in those impressions and reverse his judgment.[88]

Mr. Ferrara's first thesis is expressed in a characteristic run-on sentence:

---

[87] W. A. Armstrong, "The Influence of Demographic Factors on the Position of the Agricultural Labourer in England and Wales, *c*1750-1914," *The Agricultural Historical Review*, Vol. 29, 1981, pp. 71-82. Emphasis added.

[88] A cursory glance indicates otherwise. As of 2000, at least, Armstrong's research is cited in E. J. T. Collins' *The Agrarian History of England and Wales*, the long "missing" seventh volume of the eight-volume definitive study (General Editor: Joan Thirsk), which the Cambridge University Press began publishing in 1967.

The pauperization [allegedly "resulting" from the "theft and later enclosure of former Church properties in England"] of English commoners gave rise to the regime of the Poor Laws of four centuries' duration, making post-Henrican England the first "welfare state" in Western history—a development unknown during all the centuries of Christendom, with its vast network of charitable institutions. (14-15)

Let's see . . . swift, violent, and uncompensated royal theft is lumped together in one breath with protracted, partially compensated parliamentary enclosure . . . and this compound crime "results" in a pauperization in England that "gives rise to" four hundred years (which four hundred?) of a Poor Law-codified welfare state (excuse me, "welfare state") . . . and the latter compares unfavorably with Christendom's charitable institutions. Such talking-in-one's-sleep hardly rises to the dignity of an historical "sketch."

Again, lest we be misunderstood: whether legally compensated or not, whether royally decreed or legislated by parliament, confiscation is a case of the initiation of force and is therefore unjust. Period. No monetary payment retroactively justifies theft.[89] The victims of outright theft and of enclosure had different experiences, however, and no narrative should conflate them. Mr. Ferrara's hyperbole will come under scrutiny again when we turn to his quasi-Marxist condemnation of "wage slavery."

That the poor were starting to live long enough to fall under Poor Law consideration is another salient point Mr. Ferrara

---

[89] One dimension missing from Mr. Ferrara's picture is the role of popes in legitimizing "Henrican England." There were, for example, the intertwined geopolitical machinations of one lord of Christendom, Pope Julius II (of "Holy League" fame), with those of Henry VIII, the totalitarian Tudor to whom His Holiness had granted a dispensation to marry his brother's widow (at the urging of her mother, Christendom's Isabella I of Castile!). Another Vicar of Christ, Julius' Medici-born successor, Leo X, had dubbed that same tyrant *Defensor Fidei* for repudiating Martin Luther, whom Henry would soon rival in expression of anti-Catholic ferocity.

fails to notice. More on that aspect presently. He once again draws upon the writings of mutualist libertarian Kevin Carson :

> . . . [T]he State's theft of Church lands [Mr. Ferrara writes] in favor of early English capitalists began at the very time abuses of the "feudal" system were "in the process of being remedied." Western Europe [according to Mr. Carson] "was evolving toward a system in which the peasant was a de facto owner, required, required to pay only a nominal quit-rent set by custom; after that nominal rent was paid, he could treat the land in practice as his own. Had that system been allowed to develop without violence, Europe today might be a continent of small proprietors." [15. Mr. Ferrara italicizes the last nine words without telling the reader *there* that he has done so.—A. F.]

Yes, imagine how Europe might have developed without State violence. Thank you, Mr. Carson.

To belabor what should be obvious: Anarcho-Catholics categorically deplore all State theft, including Henry's theft of monastic lands. Who doubts that? How statist thieves reward their friends and punish their enemies is both an ancient and contemporary theme. So is the vexed question of restitution (or reparations) based on the discovery of just title and unjust holdings.

They bear not at all, however, on the empirical question of whether free markets—that is, *markets in their catallactic, non-politically perverted dimension*—have improved the lives of all whom they touch. And by "improve" we emphatically include, "increase the quantity as well as quality of." Markets manage to do this regardless of the interference of political interest. The desideratum is always to eliminate the interference.

Mr. Ferrara's reference to Blake immediately followed a telling quote from Distributism's godfather, Hilaire Belloc:

... [T]he end result of Henry's theft from the Church [Mr. Ferrara writes] was that the beneficiaries of his theft became "a powerful oligarchy of large owners, overshadowing dwindled monarchy." [15. The quote is from Belloc's *The Servile State.*—A. F.]

Insofar as the Gospel slowly but surely influenced the *ethos* of Europe, from the eighth through the tenth centuries, it was no doubt a factor in the progressive correction of Mr. Carson's "abuses of the feudal system," the evolution of the *de facto* slave into a less "servile" serf. Mr. Ferrara's Bellockian thesis, however, is that "capitalism" derailed this progress to the serf's harm by devolving him into a "servile" factory worker, who is a virtual slave with no means of production of his own that would enable him to assert his independence.[90]

In the light of that devolution, we find it ironic to sense Belloc's implicit shedding of a tear for a "dwindled" monarchy, suggesting that an "undwindled monarchy" would have been the champion of the interests of the progressively evolving serf. In fact, raw, unbridled power in the hands of a tyrant initiated the theft that set the catastrophe in motion, as Belloc defined catastrophe. Or have we forgotten so soon about those hapless English monks?

Even though the parliamentarians who "overshadowed" the dwindled monarch were mostly anti-Catholic heirs of stolen Catholic lands, Anarcho-Catholics remind the reader that Henry no more *intended* to benefit those Whig heirs than Whigs *intended* to benefit the masses who worked for them. And given that the theft cannot be undone, what transpired afterwards?

Mr. Ferrara continues:

---

[90] On the point, and in preparation for our discussion of Distributism, we cannot recommend too highly Marcus Epstein, Walter Block, and Thomas Woods, "Chesterton and Belloc: A Critique," *The Independent Review*, XI: 2, Fall 2007, pp. 579-594. www.independent.org/pdf/tir/tir_11_04_07_epstein.pdf.

By the turn of the 18th century, "more than half of the English were dispossessed of capital and land. Not one man in two . . . inhabited a house of which he was the secure possessor, or tilled land from which he could not be turned off." (Quoting from Belloc, *The Servile State.*)

And turned off he was. By means of thousands of privately initiated parliamentary acts of enclosure in the 18th century, the heirs of the new "owners" of the stolen lands of the Church converted them into "private property" in the modern sense, thereby creating a vast dispossessed class of propertyless paupers whose only means of survival was wage labor in factories for the able-bodied, including women and children. The few tenants remaining on the land, and thus in possession of means of production, suffered the imposition of "rack rents" more burdensome than any feudal levies. (15)

The parliamentary acts of enclosure were initiated at the behest of private interests, but facilitated by the State, without which it would have happened, if it did, very differently. (How "secure" were the Catholic monks who were unceremoniously "turned off" their lands by an "undwindled" monarch?)

The "dispossessed" class was vast because the death rate dropped and so many more ordinary people than ever lived to have children of their own. How does Mr. Ferrara account for that demographic effect, assuming he is aware of it? We charitably assume it matters to a pro-life lawyer which conditions are conducive to human fecundity and which are not. As the historian T. S. Aston put the question:

Whether it is good or ill that more human beings should experience the happiness and misery, the hopes and anxieties, the ambitions and frustrations of life, may be left for the philosopher or the theologian to determine. But the increase in number was the result not of a rise of the birth rate but of a fall of the death rate, and it might be thought that this was indicative of an improved quality of life.[91]

"Be fruitful and multiply," anyone? (Genesis 1:28) It was only until the much-maligned period of the Industrial Revolution and freer markets that God's image-bearers could, in effect, fulfill this Edenic imperative. That pagan environmentalists curse capitalism is understandable. Catholics have good reason not to join them.

Because Mr. Ferrara has bound himself to Hilaire Belloc's century-old historiography, he cannot countenance research that puts the origin of the enclosure movement in England (a) a full century *earlier* (and therefore before the Industrial Revolution that allegedly evacuated the fields and pauperized their former proprietors) and (b) in a *common law* context of private agreements predating the statist parliamentarian process that popular writers traditionally focused on. And so, the authors of that paper write:

> J. R. Wordie [in a 1983 paper published in a peer reviewed journal] has concluded that by 1760 some 75 percent of English land was already enclosed and that contrary to the earlier [but superceded scholarly] consensus [which Mr. Ferrara & Co. presuppose to be true], it was not during the eighteenth century but during the seventeenth that "England swung over from being mainly an open-field country to being a mainly enclosed one." Thus, the bulk of enclosure had long since been accomplished by the time Belloc and other distributists seem to have thought it was busy creating the industrial proletariat.

---

[91] T. S. Ashton, "The Standard of Life of the Workers in England, 1790-1830," in *Capitalism and the Historians,* F. A. Hayek, ed., The University of Chicago Press, 1954, p. 127.

Moreover, the tenants themselves often initiated the enclosure, again contrary to the impression Belloc left, and even parliamentary enclosure operated on the basis of consensus.

Thomas Woods neatly summarizes Mr. Ferrara's epistemological state:

> The enclosure movement was in fact not a single movement and was in some cases not a "capitalist" phenomenon at all, so it's not clear what Ferrara would have proven by citing it even if he had gotten the history right. But, as usually happens when you ignore the past 50 years of scholarship, he got it dreadfully wrong. (I guess those PhD's who blurbed the book hadn't read much about this, either.)[92]

---

[92] Thomas E. Woods, "Propaganda, Meet Modern Research," July 16, 2011. www.tomwoods.com/blog/anti-capitalist-propaganda-meet-modern-research/

Chapter 21

If I Had a Hammer:
Hayek on Tool-Ownership

Now, about the "propertyless paupers" of Mr. Ferrara's solicitude, Hayek wrote in his own contribution to the previously cited volume:

Discussions of the effects of the rise of modern industry on the working classes refer almost always to the conditions in England in the first half of the nineteenth century; yet the great change to which they refer had commenced much earlier and by then had quite a long history and had spread far beyond England. The freedom of economic activity which in England had provide so favorable to the rapid growth of wealth was probably in the first instance an almost accidental by-product of the limitations which the revolution of the seventeenth century had placed on the powers of government; and only after its beneficial effects had come to be widely noticed did the economists later undertake to explain the connection and to argue for the removal of the remaining barriers to commercial freedom.[93]

Self-interested lords may have intended only to assert their own interests against the monarch, but they unleashed a wave of "beneficial effects" that many beyond them enjoyed. The prescient among them, including some economists, thought it would be good to "roll out" the idea of limited government even further. But Mr. Ferrara's emphasis on tool-ownership—"the few . . . in possession of the means of production"—is a Distributist "tell" that merits a comment.

We know there are environmentalists who prefer fewer human beings enduring a subsistence-level (but environmentally "sustainable") standard of living to more people enjoying better and longer lives at the "expense" of nature. Can it be that Distributists prefer numerically fewer serfs who at least owned their own tools, to many factory workers, if they had to choose between these two scenarios? But what about those tools? Hayek again:

> The actual history of the connection between capitalism and the rise of the proletariat is almost the opposite of that which these theories of the expropriation of the masses suggest. The truth is that, for the greater part of history, for most men the possession of the tools for their work was an essential condition for survival or at least for being able to rear a family. The number of those who could maintain themselves by working for others, although they did not themselves possess the necessary equipment, was limited to a small proportion of the population. The amount of arable land and of tools handed down from one generation to the next limited the total number who could survive. To be left without them meant in

93 "History and Politics," F. A. Hayek, ed., *Capitalism and the Historians,* The University of Chicago Press, 1954, 14.

most instances death by starvation or at least the impossibility of procreation.

In short, there is an intimate connection between human economic productivity and human biological "reproductivity," if you will: one is a function of another. Hayek continues:

There was little incentive and little possibility for one generation to accumulate the additional tools which would have made possible the survival of a large number of the next, so long as the advantage of employing additional hands was limited mainly to the instances where the division of the tasks increased the efficiency of the work of the owner of the tools. It was only when the larger gains from the employment of machinery provided both the means and the opportunity for their investment that what in the past had been a recurring surplus of population doomed to early death was in an increasing measure given the possibility of survival.

It is hard not to hear in Hayek's reference to "a recurring surplus of population" an implicit answer to Scrooge's unwanted Christmas Eve visitor who informed the miser that many poor men "would rather die" than avail themselves of whatever assistance could be gotten from the "prisons" and the "workshops." Dickens's protagonist coldly rebuffs him with "If they would rather die, they'd better do it, and decrease the surplus population."

Ironically, what members of Scrooge's class had been doing for the previous century, whether they intended to or not, whether their moral character mirrored or diverged from Scrooge's, was effectively ensuring that great numbers of human beings, once deemed "surplus," would no longer be "doomed to an early death." Hayek elaborates upon the pro-life import of this development:

Numbers which had been practically stationary for many centuries began to increase rapidly. The proletariat which capitalism can be said to have "created" was thus not a proportion of the population which would have existed without it and which it had degraded to a lower level; it was an additional population which was enabled to grow up by the new opportunities for employment which capitalism provided. An historical movement that enhanced human fruitfulness, enabling a heretofore doomed "surplus" of human beings to "grow up," may be called "Satanic" only in propaganda that trades on the ignorance of its target audience.

In so far as it is true that the growth of capital made the appearance of the proletariat possible, it was in the sense that it raised the productivity of labor so that a much larger number of those who had not been equipped by their parents with tools were enabled to maintain themselves by their labor alone; but the capital had to be supplied first before those were enabled to survive who afterward claimed as a right a share in its ownership.

Although it was certainly not from charitable motives, it still was the first time in history that one group of people found it in their interest to use their earnings on a large scale to provide new instruments of production to be operated by those who without them could not have produced their own sustenance.

But everyone knows that capitalism is nothing but the concentration of wealth in the hand of a few to the detriment of the many . . . or so goes the Marxist-Distributist fractured fairytale. That's their story, and they're sticking to it.

Chapter 22

Rothbard on Enclosure

Before considering Mr. Ferrara's next historical sketch of an "immense picture" culled from "a large library of books," we'd like to call upon one more witness for our pro-life defense of the rise of capitalism. Our witness is none other than Murray Rothbard. The following is from his review of Karl Polanyi's *The Great Transformation*. It highlights a basic truth about which Mr. Ferrara and his sources have virtually nothing to say:

> It was population growth . . . that was wrecking mercantilist Europe. Population growth was the reason for the rise of able-bodied beggars and thieves in eighteenth-century England. There was no work for them to do. It was the rise of capitalism—the advance of capital to provide them with jobs, the expansion of the market to produce cheap goods for the masses—that not only enormously increased the standard of living of the masses but also provided jobs for these increasingly "excess" people.
>
> Furthermore, Polanyi continues the old anti-capitalist canard that the Industrial Revolution was made

possible by the enclosure movement, which supposedly drove sturdy yeomen off their lands and into the cities.

This is nonsense; not only did the enclosure movement enclose the "commons" and not people, and by the great increase in agricultural productivity provide the wherewithal in resources and income for the Industrial Revolution, but also the enclosures did not drive people off the land. The surplus population in the rural areas was a consequence of population growth; it was this increase in rural population that drove these desperate people into the cities to look for work.

Capitalism did *not*, therefore, tragically disrupt, as Polanyi would have it, the warm, loving, "social" relations of pre-capitalist era. Capitalism took the outcasts of society—the beggars, the highwaymen, the rural overpopulated, the Irish immigrants—and gave them the jobs and wages that moved them from destitution to a far higher standard of living and of work.

It is easy enough to wring one's hands at the child labor in the new British factories; it is, apparently, even easier to forget what the child population of rural England was doing before the Industrial Revolution—and during the Industrial Revolution, in those numerous areas of England where it and the new capitalism had not yet penetrated: these children were dying like flies and living in infinitely more miserable conditions.[94]

On the matter of dying like flies: we need to consider a story, germane to the case we are progressively making, that

94 Murray Rothbard, "On Polanyi's *The Great Transformation*," Memo to the William Volker Fund, dated June 1961, published in *Rothbard vs. The Philosophers*, Roberta Modugno, ed., 2009, 121-139. Freely available on mises.org. Our citation is from 127-128.

predates the Industrial Revolution by over a century. If ever there were an anti-life phenomenon in the history of Europe, it was the mid-Fourteenth Century bubonic plague pandemic, often referred to as the Black Death, which more or less halved that continent's population. Earlier in that century, however, another anti-life force had lowered the European standard of living, thus facilitating, among other things, the proliferation of the *Yersinia pestis* microparasite.

We refer to the incipient modern nation-state, embodied most notably in Philip the Fair of France, who more than any other "civil magistrate" (the Theologically Correct euphemism for Plunderer-in-Chief) up-ended the balance that had hitherto obtained between Church and State. (Inevitable, in our opinion, whenever one attempts to strike a "balance" with an intrinsically evil institution.) The result was the subsequent subordination of Church to State, papal bulls to the contrary notwithstanding. And all this was in full swing long before Henry VIII, Martin Luther, John Locke, and the other usual suspects of Mr. Ferrara's anti-capitalist propaganda. Indeed, Fourteenth-century France was the heyday of those guilds of Bellockian romance (or *corps de métiers*, as they were called there).

Philip the Macroparasite's edicts—imperialistic, anti-trade (specifically against the international Fairs of Champagne), direct and indirect (*via* inflation) taxation, combined with outright confiscations too numerous to list here—contributed decisively to the secular decline that had substantially decreased the population long before the arrival of the Asiatic microparasites that finished the job.[95]

---

[95] No one has told this story more compellingly and concisely than did Rothbard in his *An Austrian Perspective on the History of Economic Thought, Vol. 1, Economic Thought Before Adam Smith*, 68-69. Freely available on mises.org.

Chapter 23

The Hammonds, T. S. Ashton and Emily Litella

We pass over quickly Mr. Ferrara's reliance on the Hammonds's long-superseded *The Village Labourer, 1760-1832* (1911), which he refers to as "a Protestant source with no Catholic axe to grind" (16), the latter phrase being one he should perhaps not mention aloud. He apparently never cared to see whether they maintained their uniformly gloomy assessment of period:

> [S]tatisticians tell us that when they have put in order such data as they can find, they are satisfied that earnings increased and that most men and women were less poor when this discontent was loud and active that they were when the eighteenth century was beginning to grow old in a silence like that of autumn. The evidence, of course, is scanty,

and its interpretation not too simple, but this general view is probably more or less correct.[96]

Mr. Ferrara's distortion of T. S. Ashton's perspective is more serious. He introduces his quotation of the historian with: "Even that sturdy Protestant defender of the Industrial Revolution, T. S. Ashton, was constrained to admit the truth." (16) It is uncharitable to suggest that Ashton, a master of the period, would feel "constrained" to "admit" any facts, as though he were afraid of their effect on his prejudice. On the contrary, it is Mr. Ferrara who has reason to fear the effect of what Ashton actually wrote on Mr. Ferrara's reputation as a writer.

In the very paragraph from which Mr. Ferrara took his quotation, Ashton—having just noted that enclosure "had been taking place almost continuously from at least as early as the thirteenth century," that most of these enclosures "were made by private arrangement between the proprietors concerned," and that "enclosure by Act [of Parliament against unwilling tenants] did not play an important part until after 1760"— writes sympathetically of:

> . . . humbler classes of people who received little or no consideration. The cottagers who had cultivated a few strips in the open fields, and supplemented their incomes by part-time work on those of their wealthier neighbours, might, indeed, be given a small holding when the land was re-divided. But it was less easy to graze a cow, keep fowls, or gather fuel, when the greater part of the waste [land] had been allotted to the squire or the larger cultivators. On the fringe of most open-field villages, there were many squatters who obtained a precarious living, either by primitive husbandry on tiny intakes, or by wage-earning, poaching, begging, thieving, or the receipt

---

[96] J. L. and Barbara Hammond, *The Bleak Age,* revised edition, London: Pelican Books, [1934] 1947, 15. Cited in F. A. Hayek, "History and Politics," Hayek, ed., *Capitalism and the Historians*, The University of Chicago Press, 1954, 14.

of poor relief. Taking little part in the life of the community, they had been tolerated by the easy-going, open-field cultivators. But the enclosed village had little use for such people: their presence was an obstacle to the full utilization of the land, and their poverty laid a burden of parish rates on the tenant farmers.[97]

It is hard to see how Mr. Ferrara could introduce to his readers parts of that paragraph and the next in terms of what Ashton would be "constrained to admit" *unless* he was confident that they probably did not have Ashton's immediately preceding words at hand. Here are those parts in Mr. Ferrara's rendition:

Evicted from their cottages, which were afterwards razed to the ground, they [the dispossessed peasants] crowded to areas where the fields were still open, or took to vagrancy. They and their descendants must have contributed largely to the body of semi-employed, inefficient labour that was to trouble the peace of politicians and poor-law administrators until 1834 and beyond . . . . [I]t was precisely because enclosure released [!] (or drove) [Ashton's embarrassed parentheses] men from the land that it is to be counted among the processes that led to the industrial revolution. (16-17)

Mr. Ferrara's exclamatory sound effect and suggestion that the facts that Ashton had just recounted "embarrassed" him express only insolence. Men *were* mainly released from the land by voluntary agreement for centuries *before* the violent seizure of Church lands by Henry VIII (with whose violent images Mr. Ferrara is determined to associate enclosure in the minds of his readers) and *before* the industrial revolution. In *some* cases they were evicted unjustly. Ashton's non-embarrassing, parenthetical

97 T. S. Ashton, *The Industrial Revolution* [1961]. With a new preface and bibliography by Pat Hudson. Oxford University Press, 1997, 20.

reference to those who were driven out expresses proportion. What Mr. Ferrara's ellipses hid from the reader we will italicize:

Evicted from their cottages, which were afterwards razed to the ground, they crowded to areas where the fields were still open, or took to vagrancy. They and their descendants must have contributed largely to the body of semi-employed, inefficient labour that was to trouble the peace of politicians and poor-law administrators until 1834 and beyond.

Some writers who have dwelt at length on the fate of those who were forced to leave the land have tended to overlook the constructive activities that were being carried on inside the fences. The essential fact about enclosure is that it brought about an increase in the productivity of the soil. There has been much discussion as to whether it led to a decline in the number of cultivators, and some who hold that it did write as though this were a consequence to be deplored. It is a truism, however, that the standard of life of a nation is raised when fewer people are needed to provide the mean of subsistence. Many of those who were divorced from the soil (as the stereotyped phrase goes) were free to devote themselves to other activities: it was precisely because enclosure released (or drove) from the land that it is to be counted among the processes that led to the industrial revolution, with the higher standards of consumption this brought with it.[98]

One unjust eviction is one too many, but Ashton is interested in what else was going forward besides eviction, just as we would ask despisers of the Catholic Church whether they are interested in knowing anything else about Her besides pedophile priests and their episcopal protectors. Ashton argued that much else went on during the period we call the industrial

---

[98] Ashton, 20-21.

revolution, and much of that redounded to the benefit of the "humbler classes of people."

Mr. Ferrara, who apparently knows how to use an ellipsis when it suits him, appended a full stop after "revolution," even though there is more to the last sentence. Unless higher standards of consumption embarrass him, why not refer to it, or have the decency to cover mention of it with three dots? Again, we are not so naïve as to think that pointing out lapse after lapse from standards of controversy has any effect on him. His obduracy in error may be the rhetorical equivalent of Emily Litella's hearing deficit, but even she would eventually face the camera and say "Never mind!"[99]

---

[99] For the identity of Emily Litella, see en.wikipedia.org/wiki/Emily_Litella

Chapter 24

Grand Theft Monastery

We decline to cross-examine Albert Jay Nock, "that great hero of contemporary libertarians" (17), whom Mr. Ferrara called to the witness stand. Nock's many literary services to libertarianism cannot save an opinion overthrown by scholarship, which Nock's generalization (at least as Mr. Ferrara represents it—not a negligible modifier) unfortunately is.

In any case, the fortunes of Austro-Libertarianism do not depend on Nock's implicit endorsement of Dickensian fable that makes *The Village Labourer* look up-to-date by comparison.

It should not be thought, however, that Mr. Ferrara endorses Nock's interpretation of the alleged facts, because he "lays the blame for early capitalist depredations entirely upon government intervention rather than rugged individualism and laissez-faire" (17), presumably Mr. Ferrara's preferred explanation.

How individualism (of whatever texture) or a policy of limited governmental intervention could be morally responsible for "depredations," that is, the unethical behavior of *some* owners of capital, he leaves to his reader's imagination, which he is happy to excite with facile generalizations:

... the historical truth is that the State and capitalism partnered in the grand theft that caused the destruction of Catholic social order, the loss of village life and the independence of the cottager with his small plot of land, and finally the creation of capitalist social order with all its abuses. (17)

A necessary, if not sufficient, condition of our recognizing a proposition's being true is its being coherent. A thesis that treats "capitalism" as both cause and effect of the same thing, however, does not satisfy that condition. If "capitalist social order" is the result of the grand theft, "capitalism" cannot also be behind it. Mr. Ferrara has not even suggested that any individual capitalists were, only that some of them later benefited from that prior State action with which they had nothing to do. What beneficiaries of crime or their heirs ought to do with their property, once they realize how it was acquired, is a separate moral question, one that does not bear on that of the moral goodness of a social order comprised wholly of free markets.

In the period in question the only event that qualifies as "grand theft" is the dissolution of the monasteries consequent to Henry VIII's edicts (i.e., Act of Supremacy, and the First and Second Suppression Acts). Mr. Ferrara's prose habitually conflates those confiscatory acts with the enclosure of the commons that took place over centuries, by fair means and foul. Enclosure was not achieved by grand theft. Nor can one sensibly impute such State crimes to owners of capital (the only stable meaning of "capitalists") or even a concerted move by them to seize power.

Of course, some believe that the theological issues ostensibly presenting themselves to students of the period were mere ideological "superstructure" erected upon the "base" of the means of production, and that changes in the nature of those means and the struggle over their control hold the Key to History. On this view, Henry VIII and his minions were merely agents (conscious or not) of the nascent English bourgeoisie, incarnating, willy-nilly, the dialectic of history. Such writers may be politely referred to as historical materialists or, more frankly, Marxists among whom, of course, Mr. Ferrara is not to be numbered.

At least, however, we understand what the Marxist is suggesting. By contrast we do not know what Mr. Ferrara meant when he wrote that the State, in the person of Henry, "partnered [conspired?] with capitalism" (A social order? An ideological movement?) to displace one social order with another. If he meant to say that a grand conspiracy overthrew the Catholic social order, then he should have done so, and plainly. But the transition from one social order into another is not the sort of thing that has a unitary cause like "grand theft." But the propagandist must resort to such facile narratives to hold his audience.

Chapter 25

Dismissive of the New, Evasive of the Old

When Thomas Woods cited two books by G. E. Mingay, he showed us, as only a trained historian who keeps abreast of the literature could, where we could supplement our knowledge.[100] We have not read Mingay, but doing so is not a condition of exposing the inadequacy of Mr. Ferrara's awareness of what had been written *before* Mingay. When we provided an excerpt from a review by Murray Rothbard on enclosure, we omitted a reference note of his that Roberta Modugno had included in her edition of Rothbard's unpublished reviews, *Rothbard vs. The Philosophers:*

> For a refutation of the enclosure myth and a recognition of the key being increase of population, see W. H. B. Court, *A Concise Economic History of*

---

[100] The books by Mingay are: *Enclosure and the Small Farmer in the Age of the Industrial Revolution* and *Parliamentary Enclosure in England.* The paper that cites them is: Marcus Epstein, Walter Block, and Thomas Woods, "Chesterton and Belloc: A Critique," *The Independent Review,* XI: 2, Fall 2007, 579-594.

Britain from 1750 to Recent Times (Cambridge:
Cambridge University Press, 1954).

That book, more than fifty years old—and therefore falling
within Mr. Ferrara's chronological ambit of possible interest—
shows in its first two chapters that the coffin of Received Opinion
on the Industrial Revolution and enclosure, if only nailed shut
by Mingay's day, was at least closed by Court's. We now cite
parts of Court's narrative that bear on Mr. Ferrara's promotion of
Dickensian tragedy, *which makes incomprehensible the pro-life story
that was unfolding during this period,* including an increase in
living standards, most centrally the dramatic increase in the
numbers of Britons who were born and lived to have children of
their own:

> In eighteenth-century Britain we are watching the
> gradual rise of the large average size of family which
> prevailed in this country in Victorian times.... To put
> the matter more exactly, the large surviving family
> was, so far as can be seen on imperfect evidence, mainly
> the result of forces which diminished mortality, but
> which had as their secondary effect the increase of
> fertility, meaning by fertility the number of children
> born to a family. The saving of children at birth or in
> the first years of life and the lengthening in the
> expectation of life among mothers may account for
> the greater part of the advance of population in the
> eighteenth century.... (Court, 10-11)
>
> The general fall in the death-rate was due to many
> things. An improvement of medical services was one
> of them. Medical knowledge in the eighteenth
> century was beginning to show what it could do,
> although much of the knowledge was empirical
> rather than scientific in the strict sense.... Knowledge
> of the rules of health, however, could not have helped
> very much, if the slow improvement in the water-

supply, paving and sanitation of English towns had not made it possible to apply them. (Court, 11)

. . . Taking the country as a whole, the rate of deaths per thousand of population began to fall, as far as we can tell, after the first quarter of the century and declined markedly from 1780 onwards, despite the rapid growth of town life. Between the end of the French wars in 1815 and the cholera epidemic of 1831-2, the death-rate rose sharply, but it never regained the old levels. (Court, 12)

. . . Every increment in the productivity of British agriculture and industry, from the end of the Civil War [1642–1651—A.F.] onwards, had a bearing on the increase in numbers in the subsequent century and a half. The population of Tudor [1485-1603] and Stuart [1603-1714] England had lived a hard life. Every change for the better, however small, in their food, clothes or housing, must have affected the chances of survival. Many changes of this kind took place in the late seventeenth and early eighteenth century, not least owing to improvements in agriculture. . . . (Court, 12)

Industrial production provided cheaper and cleaner underwear, cotton and soap and greater cleanliness increased the resistance to disease. . . . (Court, 12)

There were, therefore, powerful forces playing in the eighteenth and early nineteenth century upon the old high mortality which British population had suffered along with that of other countries, and they brought it down. . . . The saving of lives among young children and child-bearing women promoted a high birth-rate; but as more children were born and survived, the greater proportion of young people in the population may be assumed to have brought the average death-rate down, for an old population dies faster. These interactions must have been important, but they cannot with the surviving material be easily traced and weighed. (Court, 13)

The picture presented by the British population after 1750 is therefore one of a land in which the old conditions of life had been sufficiently modified to permit a rapid increase of numbers. (Court, 13)

Mr. Ferrara ignores all of this and instead bemoans "the loss of village life, and the independence of the cottager with his small plot of land" (17), that is, what Court summarily referred to as "the old conditions of life," redolent in its anti-human implications of the most chilling of today's "green" propaganda.

Chapter 26

Lie, Rinse, Repeat

So far, we have explained what we mean by the reality of the free market, namely, the norm-guided, ontologically real (i.e., extra-mental) network of persons who, by trading their property, actualize the market's "ties" and "nodes."

As long as there are human beings, the free market principle will be operative. That is, free markets will perdure through the ethical deformations that persons who forcibly interfere with trade introduce into those networks. (The logical consequence of *total* deformation is the abolition of man, deformers not excluded.)

We have claimed that there is no basis for imputing to any Austro-libertarian writer any approval of such interference in any form it has taken in history, and Mr. Ferrara has shown none. His accusatory strategy trades exclusively on Kevin Carson's polemics-driven diagnosis of the "forgetfulness" of the "vulgar libertarian."

On the subject of illusions, perhaps the biggest is the one that Mr. Ferrara seems to labor under, namely, that the repetition of easily refuted propaganda, coupled with equally gratuitous denials of the refutation, is a winning strategy. The operative propaganda repeated *ad nauseam* throughout these historical "sketches" may be rendered by this syllogism:

1. Austro-libertarians say they support the free market.

2. But "free market" refers to an illusion, for capitalists who inordinately influence state policy systematically distort the only markets that have existed. (Exhibit A: theft of Church lands; Exhibit B: enclosure of the English field; Exhibit C: England's Poor Laws; Exhibit D: John Locke was an investor in the Royal African Company, which traded in human beings, etc.)

3. Therefore, Austro-libertarians are deluded. Q.E.D.

In every case, however, the sources on which Mr. Ferrara relies either (a) have been overthrown by more recent research and/or (b) have no bearing whatsoever on the views that Austro-libertarians hold.[101] He keeps asking how come it's taking us so long to get to (what he thinks) insists is the "substance" of his book, i.e., the just wage, usury, etc. It takes time to correct historical narratives and deconstruct fallacies; that's how come. *As Mr. Ferrara implicitly defines "capitalistic," Austro-libertarians are anti-capitalistic.*

At last we turn to Sketchy Story Number 2: "Early capitalist laws imposing the creation of an industrial economy." (17) Here Mr. Ferrara repeats his Hammonds-dependent tale, but not before drawing upon (but without citing in the main text) that nemesis of "vulgar libertarians," Kevin Carson, whom we met earlier.

Before Mr. Ferrara cites the Hammonds, however, he highlights the miserable failure, by anyone's standards, that were the implementation of the Poor Laws and the Laws of Settlement and their draconian provisions—*all of them statist*

---

[101] Mr. Ferrara has recently wondered out loud, and apparently without embarrassment, why one should, *ceteris paribus*, favor more recent over older historical research. distributistreview.com/mag/2011/07/the-austrian-version-of-the-english-enclosures/ For an historian's answer, see Tom Woods's July 27, 2011 column, "Keep Digging that Hole." www.tomwoods.com/blog/keep-digging-that-hole/

concoctions. Without fear of contradiction we affirm that all Austro-libertarians repudiate these edicts. We know that affirmation means nothing to Mr. Ferrara.

Strictly speaking, we may end our discussion of Sketchy Story Number 2 here, but it would be good to separate what his propaganda conflates, namely, the distinction between the circumstances of "free labor children" and that of "parish children." Lawrence W. Reed, in a classic article, spells out the difference: free labor children "lived at home but worked during the days in factories at the insistence of their parents or guardians," while parish children "were under the direct authority and supervision, not of their parents in a free labor market, but of government officials."[102]

> Private factory owners could not forcibly subjugate "free labour" children; they could not compel them to work in conditions their parents found unacceptable. The mass exodus from the socialist continent to increasingly capitalist, industrial Britain in the first half of the 19th century strongly suggests that people did indeed find the industrial order an attractive alternative. And no credible evidence exists that argues that parents in the early capitalist days were any less caring of their offspring than those of pre-capitalist times.
>
> The situation, however, was much different for "parish apprentice" children, and close examination reveals that it was these children on whom the critics were focusing when they spoke of the "evils" of capitalism's Industrial Revolution. . . . . Most were orphans; a few were victims of negligent parents or parents whose health or lack of skills kept them from earning sufficient

---

[102] Lawrence W. Reed, "Child Labor and the British Industrial Revolution," *The Freeman*, Vol. 41, No. 8, August 1991, 304-307.

http://www.unz.org/Pub/Freeman-1991aug?View=PDF

income to care for a family. All were in the custody of "parish authorities."

Commenting on the Hammond's culturally prestigious but superseded account, Reed notes that they

> . . . report the horrors of those [cotton] mills with descriptions like these: "crowded with overworked children," "hotbeds of putrid fever," "monotonous toil in a hell of human cruelty," and so forth. Page after page of the Hammonds' writings— as well as those of many other anticapitalist historians—deal in this manner with the condition of the parish apprentices. *Though consigned to the control of a government authority, these children are routinely held up as victims of the "capitalist order."* . . . [My emphasis.—A.F.]

> It has not been uncommon for historians, including many who lived and wrote in the 19th century, to report the travails of the apprentice children without ever realizing *they were effectively indicting government, not the economic arrangement of free exchange we call capitalism.* [My emphasis.—A.F.]

In acknowledging the desirability of improving the conditions under which people work, Reed makes this salient demographic point (which we dealt with earlier):

> Though it is inaccurate to judge capitalism guilty of the sins of parish apprenticeship, it would also be inaccurate to assume that "free labour" children worked under ideal conditions in the early days of the Industrial Revolution. By today's standards, their situation was clearly bad. Such capitalist achieve-ments as air conditioning and high levels of productivity would, in time, substantially ameliorate it, however. The evidence in favor of capitalism is thus compellingly suggestive: From 1750 to 1850, when the population of Great Britain nearly tripled,

the exclusive choice of those flocking to the country for jobs was to work for private capitalists.

Of course, Mr. Ferrara's probable rebuttal, which we now paraphrase, is at-the-ready: "But if Henry VIII didn't steal Church lands . . . if the English people weren't turned off their own land through enclosure . . . they would never have had to enter a factory and subject their children to the horrors of the industrial system! They would be independent farmers or small business proprietors, denizens of Merrie Old Distributist England!"

That is, he will repeat the charge you already answered, perhaps in the hope that you've forgotten your answer. When you refute it (again), he will change the subject to another anti-free market canard (perhaps another one you've dealt with already).

Chapter 27

Sudha Shenoy on Enclosures

In one of his posts on enclosures, Thomas Woods linked to a 2006 essay on libertarian opinion on enclosure by the late Austrian economist and historian Sudha Shenoy.[103] There we learn that Dr. Woods read Mingay's indispensable work on enclosure (cited and linked in his post) at her suggestion. We commend Shenoy's extended blog post to our readers because "specialized research gives a very complex picture" and her essay gives the reader a handle on that complexity, contrary to the impression Mr. Ferrara's sketch gives.

And now, on with the show.

As it was with enclosure, so it is with Mr. Ferrara's sketch covering the Poor Laws, the Laws of Settlement, the Combination Act (aimed at preventing free association among those who worked for politically influential capitalists), and kindred statist, anti-market edicts. More anti-libertarian legislation can hardly

---

[103] Dr. Woods cites Sudha Shenoy, "Enclosure, Libertarians, & Historians," *History News Network* (George Mason University), June 19, 2006.
http://hnn.us/blogs/entries/26982.html in "Still More on Enclosures," August 7, 2011. http://www.tomwoods.com/blog/still-more-on-enclosures/ "The Global Perspective," an enlightening interview with Dr. Shenoy, was published in the *Austrian Economics Newsletter*, Winter 2003. Freely available on mises.org.

be imagined. And yet after snarling several historical, ethical, and economic questions, Mr. Ferrara *fails to cite even one Austro-libertarian who supports such repugnant interferences in markets.* Again, since what he pillories as "capitalistic" are intrinsically anti-market phenomena, his vignettes are irrelevant to the target of his smears. Perhaps he hopes the denials will be interpreted as admission of guilt and the gunk will nevertheless stick.

In addition to the usual suspects like the Hammonds and Kevin Carson, Mr. Ferrara cites a snippet about the suppression of the home-based spinning jenny, courtesy of the neo-Luddite Kirkpatrick Sale (of SDS notoriety). His sole qualification to contribute to this discussion, *for all Mr. Ferrara has told us,* is that he expressed an opinion against mass production that Mr. Ferrara fancies he can use in his quarrel with Austro-libertarians. He does not distinguish his own Catholic Distributist worldview from Mr. Sale's rather different one, articulated over the course of about a dozen books, but simply helps himself to the latter as he sees fit.

If Mr. Ferrara doesn't hold that mass production the root of all evil, he comes awfully close to that judgment. One gets the distinct impression that he prefers home production, and that you should, too. The afterthought with which he closes out his second of eighteen points rings hollow.

> . . . of course, Catholic critics of the moral abuses of radical laissez-faire accept the reality of modern industrialization in England and every other Western nation. The issue is how to conform our industrialize world to the law of the Gospel, the moral imperative that is discussed throughout the following pages. (21)

They "accept" that realty, all right, sort of the way Hamas accepts the reality of the State of Israel.

Mr. Ferrara's reference notes and sources provide more evidence of his second-hand approach to plugging holes in his propagandistic dike. First, he cites Mr. Sale *as rendered by Mr.*

Carson (19-20) and then quotes Mr. Carson's commentary on Mr. Sale, thus reaffirming approval of the former's arguably slanderous reference to the "average vulgar libertarian" straw man:

> Apparently, the recipe for "free" market as the average vulgar libertarian uses the term, is as follows: 1) first, steal the land of the producing classes, by state fiat, and turn them into wage-laborers; 2) then, by state terror, prevent them from moving about in search of higher wages or organizing to increase their bargaining strength; 3) finally, convince them that their subsistence wages reflect the marginal productivity of labor in a free market.[104] (20-21)

A better example of Mr. Ferrara's scattershot approach to framing a question can probably not be found. (But we're only up to page 21.) It gets better: after vowing that "there will be no discussion of purely technical economics in Austrian economics" in TCATL (11), he cites an opinion that requires the one entertaining it to understand what is meant by "marginal productivity." Why mention a topic that, despite one's promise, one will deal with much later in the book? Well, the better to take another pot-shot at Thomas Woods, that's why. According to Mr. Ferrara:

> Woods provides confirmation of Carson's assessment when he defends the exploitation of labor during the Industrial Revolution on the ground that a worker was "*forced* to work 80 or more hours a week" because "his labor [was] so unproductive that 80 hours of labor is necessary for his sheer survival"—with "productivity," of course, being determined solely by factory owners who kept all the profits.[105] (21)

---

[104] Mr. Ferrara cites Carson's *Studies in Mutualist Political Economy*, 126. After Mr. Sale, Mr. Carson's next authority is Karl Marx.

[105] As the reader may have already surmised, Dr. Woods did not emphasize "forced," but you won't learn that from the reference note Mr. Ferrara associated with this passage. For

In the sentence of Dr. Woods's that Mr. Ferrara holds up for ridicule, however, he is *presupposing, not* expounding, the theory that he had defended much earlier in *The Church and the Market,* namely, that the purchasing power of wages is a function of labor's productivity. What that greater productivity, the fruit of investment by capitalists, may purchase is *leisure* in addition to food, clothing, and shelter, leisure that may be spent on the pursuit of education and others goods of civilization.

That is, the context of that sentence was a discussion of how labor's progressively greater productivity since the Industrial Revolution has enabled workers to buy time so that, if they wish, they may partake of the culturally significant activities which had been restricted to a few. Dr. Woods was not comparing rival theories of wage determination.

> Greater leisure and greater wealth are precisely what make it possible for people to spend more time doing the things in life that really matter. A man forced to work 80 or more hours per week because, as in the early Industrial Revolution, his labor is so unproductive that 80 hours of labor is necessary for his sheer survival, cannot even dream of such things. The real friend of the "higher things" in life, therefore, are the supporters of the market whose favored system makes those things readily available to more people than anyone centuries ago would have thought possible.[106]

What a difference a context makes. The suggestion that Dr. Woods was willy-nilly "confirming" the quasi-Marxist labor theory of value underpinning Mr. Carson's historical narrative is ludicrous, if not also dishonest; that he was "defending the

---

Mr. Ferrara announced early on—exactly once—that all emphasis found in his quotations has been *added* except where otherwise noted—you need to have caught it the first time and remembered it! Smaller deceptions enable greater ones.

[106] Thomas E. Woods, Jr., *The Church and the Market: A Catholic Defense of the Free Economy,* Lexington Books (Rowman & Littlefield), 2005, 166. See Appendix B for my review of it.

exploitation of labor," gratuitously insulting. The idea that factory owners determine productivity is just silly. Productivity is ever *of* goods or services that satisfy the wants of *others*, and if they fail to do that, factory owners quickly become non-owners. As difficult as conditions were for workers raising families early in the Industrial Revolution, the salient fact is that workers increasingly had more children to raise for more years, and it took time for their productivity to catch up with not only these basic demographic facts but also their non-material aspirations. But catch up with them it did.

Chapter 28

The Gnat of Enclosure, the Camel of Slavery

P art of our present effort involves showing that the meaning of "Catholic Social Teaching" on which Mr. Ferrara's propaganda trades is not stable enough to rule out Austro-Libertarianism as an option for Catholics. We will begin to explore a case in which "Catholic Social Teaching" for most of Church history failed a test that virtually everyone, including all current Catholic moral authorities, regards as a "no-brainer." You see, when it comes to *slavery*, virtually *everyone's* a libertarian.

* * *

Our examination of his third sketch will allow us to comment on his second-sketch description of John Locke as the author of an *Essay on the Poor Law* (1697), an American colonial slave-owner (i.e., an owner of slaves who worked in the American colonies), and "early Father of capitalism." (18)

> 3. The widespread use of slave and convict labor in capitalist enterprises.

The use of slave and convicts to provide labor for capitalist ventures was commonplace in post-Catholic Europe and in the American colonies and states until the mid-19th century. It should not be surprising that [John] Locke, the very author of the grand new theory of property rights that is libertarian political philosophy at its core, had investments in two slave-trading companies in the Carolinas for which he drafted the *Fundamental Constitutions of Carolina*, providing that "every freeman of Carolina shall have absolute power and authority over his negro slaves of what opinion or religion whatsoever." (21)

This is an odd opinion, even for Mr. Ferrara. It *should* be "surprising" that a theoretician of liberty was heavily invested in the slave trade, and that's because slavery is the antithesis of liberty. He who defends liberty *and* slavery is either intellectually schizophrenic or hypocritical.

It should be no less surprising, however, yea, *scandalizing*, to find professed custodians and teachers of the Gospel of Christ—Who proclaimed liberty to the captives in his inaugural sermon (Luke 4:18, citing Isaiah 61:1-2)—justifying slavery as a "natural" institution, making fine distinctions between "just slavery" and "unjust slavery" and between "primary" and "secondary" intentions of the natural law (e.g., God never intended slavery, but it is a meet punishment for Original Sin, a punishment that benefits slaveowners and penalizes children). They did this for eighteen centuries before doing an about-face, pronouncing the whole sordid business intrinsically evil, and then white-washing it, pretending the rationalizations never occurred.

And so, for instance, Pope Leo XIII, in his 1891 *Rerum Novarum* (about which we will, of course, have much more to say), regarded human labor as "personal"

> . . . since the active force inherent in the person cannot be the property of anyone other than the person who

exerts it, and its was given to him in the first place by nature for his own benefit. (*Quia vis agens adhaeret personae, atque eius omnino est propria, a quo exercetur, et cuius est utilitati nata.*)

Only about a quarter-century earlier, however, on June 20, 1866, when Leo was known as Vincenzo Cardinal Pecci, one of his predecessors, Pope Pius IX, authorized the following *Instruction* of the Holy Office:

> . . . slavery itself, considered as such in its essential nature, is not at all contrary to the natural and divine law, and there can be several just titles of slavery and these are referred to by approved theologians and commentators of the sacred canons. For the sort of ownership which a slaveowner has over a slave is understood as nothing other than the perpetual right of disposing of the work of a slave for one's own benefit—services which it is right for one human being to provide for another. From this it follows that it is not contrary to the natural and divine law for a slave to be sold, bought, exchanged or given. The purchaser should carefully examine whether the slave who is put up for sale has been justly or unjustly deprived of his liberty, and that the vendor should do nothing which might endanger the life, virtue, or Catholic faith of the slave who is to be transferred to another's possession.[107]

---

[107] *Collectanea Sacra Congregatio de Propaganda Fidei*,1907, Rome, I, n. 230, 76-77. As cited in John F. Maxwell, *Slavery and the Catholic Church: A History of Catholic Teaching concerning the Moral Legitimacy of the Institution of Slavery* (London: Barry Rose Publishers, 1975), 78-79. It is dismaying that this book has been out of print and that second-hand copies are hard to come by. Until a digitally searchable edition of this invaluable text is available—a project we may undertake if no one else does—interested readers can study the facsimile posted on my web site: anthonyflood.com/maxwell.htm

The year before his *Rerum Novarum* was published, Pope Leo XIII would have the faithful believe that

> . . . almost nothing was more venerated in the Catholic Church . . . than the fact that she looked to see a slavery eased and abolished which was oppressing so many people . . . : she undertook the neglected cause of the slaves and stood forth as a strenuous defender of liberty, although she conducted her campaign gradually and prudently so far as times and circumstances permitted. . .; nor did this effort of the Church to liberate slaves weaken in the course of time; indeed the more slavery flourished from time to time, the more zealously she strove. The clearest historical documents are evidence for this. . . and many of our predecessors including St. Gregory the Great, Hadrian I, Alexander III, Innocent III, Gregory IX, Pius II, Leo X, Paul III, Urban VIII, Benedict XIV, Pius VII and Gregory XVI, made every effort to ensure that the institution of slavery should be abolished where it existed and that its roots should not revive where it had been destroyed.[108]

Father Maxwell comments (summarizing materials documented earlier in the book):

> With the greatest respect to Pope Leo XIII this is historically inaccurate. In his earlier letter of 1888, he had made selective use of a number of documents written by these same 12 Popes to suggest that there had been a constant "anti-slavery" tradition in the Catholic Church. But a number of other conciliar and Papal documents, as well as canons of general Church Law, are simply ignored; all these 12 Popes

---

[108] Letter, *Catholicae Ecclesiae,* November 20, 1890. *Leonis Papae Allocutiones*, 1898, IV, 112. As cited in Maxwell, 117.

who are given especial commendation had only condemned what they and contemporary moral theology held to be *unjust* methods of enslavement or *unjust* titles of slave ownership. Five of the Popes mentioned were the authors of other public documents which actually authorized enslavement either as an institution or as a penalty for ecclesiastical crimes or as a consequence of war. The historical inaccuracy of writing that these five Popes "made every effort to ensure that the institution of slavery should be abolished where it existed and that its roots should not revive where it had been destroyed" is proved as follows:

Pope Alexander III with the Fathers of the Third General Council of the Lateran in 1179 authorized the penalty of enslavement for captured Christians who had assisted the Saracens, and *Pope Innocent III* did the same with the Fathers of the Fourth General Council of the Lateran in 1215, (v) (2) above; and *Pope Gregory IX* repeated this enactment in a letter to the English in 1235.

Pope Leo X in 1514 followed the example of three of his predecessors in authorizing the Kings of Portugal to invade and conquer the newly discovered territories of the New World, to reduce the non-Christian inhabitants who lived there to perpetual slavery and to expropriate their possessions, (vi) (2) above.

Finally *Pope Paul III* in 1535 sentenced King Henry VIII of England to the penalty of being exposed for capture and enslavement by the Catholic Princes of Europe, (v) (2) above, and in 1548 gave full permission for all persons, clerical and lay, to own, buy and sell slaves in the City of Rome, and abrogated the privilege of the conservators of Rome to emancipate Christian slaves, (vii) (2) above.

Finally, there was no condemnation by any of the Popes mentioned of the capture and enslavement of Moslem prisoners of war by the galleys of the Pontifical squadron in the innumerable naval actions which are well documented from about 1500 to about 1800, (vii) (3) above.

The significance of these two letters of Pope Leo XIII [in 1888] is that it was no longer individual Catholics, whether lay or clerical who were expressing "anti-slavery" sentiments, it was the Pope himself. For the Popes who were held up for especial praise were those who (whether historically accurately or not is here irrelevant) had "made every effort to ensure that the institution of slavery should be abolished where it existed and that its roots should not revive where it had been destroyed." No distinction was made between just and unjust enslavement; it was the institution as such which was equivalently condemned.

Pope Leo XIII offered no explanation for this change of theological attitude. He did not indicate in these two letters whether it was a correction of Scriptural exegesis, or the beginnings of the movement for revision of the canon law of the Church, or a correction of the philosophical analysis of the very nature of slavery, or a growing awareness that economic and social circumstances and conditions in many countries had completely changed, or a realization that rationalist humanists and Protestant Christians could have been assisted by the Holy Spirit.

Clearly, this was already about 100 years too late to be of any effective value in the anti-slavery campaigns and civil wars and revolutions of the nineteenth century; the lay reformers and abolitionists had won their campaigns without much effective help or moral leadership from the teaching authority of the Catholic Church which had hitherto consistently refused to condemn the institution of slavery or the practice of slave-trading as such.[109]

As Father Maxwell's herculean scholarship shows, the "use of slave and convict labor" for *imperial* ventures, regularly and duly rationalized by learned theologians, was a standard feature of Catholic Europe, and by no means an accidental one. Some theologians, to their credit, protested especially dehumanizing features of the peculiar institution in the name of the slave's personhood, but never the *institution* itself until the late 19th century. Manuals of instruction for seminarians offered justifications of the *institution* as in accord with nature up to the time of Second Vatican Council.[110]

It would be otiose for Mr. Ferrara or his comrades to suggest that what the highest levels of Church authority taught so consistently for so long about slavery, of all things, did not reflect "Catholic Social Teaching" in any normal sense of those words, or was regarded as anything less than an expression of the Ordinary Magisterium than are the papal encyclicals of the last 120 years. (*"No more slavery, starting . . . now!"*) This yields the following trilemma for Mr. Ferrara:

(a) *Modern* Catholic Social Teaching on the intrinsic evil of slavery is true, but previous editions of "Catholic Social Teaching," i.e., those that countenanced certain "just" forms of this intrinsic evil, were false; or

(b) Slavery *became* intrinsically evil when when "Catholic Social Teaching" declared it to be so; or

(c) There was no such thing as "Catholic Social Teaching" before the late 19th century, and therefore whatever any

---

[109] Maxwell, 117-119. Emphasis in the original. Internal references, e.g., "(v) (2) above," are to earlier sections of *Slavery and the Catholic Church*. Emphasis in last paragraph has been added.

[110] The chronologically last example that Father Maxwell cites is M. Zalba, *Theologiae Moralis Compendium*, published in 1958. Maxwell, 88, n. 173.

pope or Doctor of the Church may have written about slavery over the previous eighteen centuries does not count as "Catholic Social Teaching."

Mr. Ferrara, not content to criticize the labor policies and practices of global corporations, whose employees he deems "wage-slaves," elected to complicate his case by raising the complex, and emotionally charged, topic of genuine, non-metaphorical slavery. He has thereby invited inquiry into the Catholic theory and practice thereof—arguably germane, even without his invitation, to an assessment of the meaning of "Catholic Social Teaching"!

He has opened that door, but he will not willingly walk through it: the reality of Catholic slavers and apologists for slavery is occluded for him. He must be prodded, if not pushed. By all means, let's discuss what contemporary Catholic authorities mean by "the just wage" on its merits. Perhaps we will be forgiven, however, if we do not suffer lectures about "wage slavery" from representatives of "Catholic Social Teaching."

Chapter 29

Lock(e), Stock, and Jesuit

M r. Ferrara writes:

As Mr. Flood explains, it is not that he is trying to belabor a point. Oh no. Rather, he is seeking to "discredit the rhetorical performance of a propagandist." Once I am discredited (so the plan goes) no one will pay any attention to the book's actual subject: an exposé of the atrocious moral, philosophical and theological errors of the libertarian cult to which Woods and Flood belong and which Woods is relentlessly promoting as "eminently congenial to the Catholic mind." (Woods, *The Church and the Market*, 217).

The part he got right concerns the relationship between the exposure of the propagandistic character of a writer's treatment of evidence and the suspicion that such exposure will naturally arouse in a reader's mind regarding the writer's approach to the "actual subject." After all, *falsus in uno, falsus in omnibus.* (In Mr. Ferrara's case the antecedent should be *falsus in multis.*)

Friends and foes of our enterprise must acknowledge that TCATL does not *begin* with a discussion of usury, or the just wage, or the epistemic weight of papal encyclicals, etc. No, several dozen pages of rhetorical misdirection, as we characterize them, set the mood. We simply cannot jump into Chapter 3 without saying something about Chapter 1 and 2. And there has been so much to say.

And so we approach the third of Mr. Ferrara's historical "sketches," none of which were necessary, in our view, for a critical examination of Austro-Libertarianism. For his rhetorical purposes, however, all of them *were* necessary: bad things happened in history in the name of "capitalism," and he wants to associate those things with us.

Although he may find it "hilarious" that we are paying so much attention to his *ipsissima verba*, it should be hard even for him not to discern in what we are doing a modicum of respect. Mr. Ferrara took the time to write something, to adduce alleged example after alleged example of Austrian enormity, to cite, to quote, and to name names. We are taking all of that with utmost seriousness. That, however, entails his being made to take responsibility not only for the "what" but also the "how" of his exercise.

Reckless disregard of the standards of controversy exacts a price not only in the coin of one's reputation, but also of one's cause. This blog is all about determining the price of such carelessness.

* * *

Now, what has the foregoing to do with whether John Locke was an investor in the slave trade? If the words "actual subject of his book" have meaning, however, the question Mr. Ferrara needs to answer concerns any connection John Locke's ethical lapse (or hypocrisy or intellectual schizophrenia) has with the philosophical and theological errors that Austro-libertarians allegedly commit. There is no such connection that we can make out, except that it creates the kind of psychologically negative impression on which Mr. Ferrara's rhetorical performance trades. To be blunt: that Locke owned slaves has no logical bearing on the evaluation of his argument for self-ownership.

Mr. Ferrara touches the highly charged subject of slavery in the context of defending the "Catholic Church's Teaching on Man, Economy and State" (his book's subtitle). Her spokesmen have taught a number of contradictory things about slavery, especially the kind that Locke invested in. (Not Wal-Mart "wage slavery.") We find it disingenuous in the extreme that Mr. Ferrara mentions slavery in an apologia for empirical "Catholic Social Teaching" without having notice *in this book* the six hundred-pound gorilla squatting in his parlor.

We walk through the forensic door he has opened, not to hold our ancestors in the Faith up to shame—we shudder to think of the probability of our acquiescence in the enormity of slavery had we been in their shoes, having neither the insight to discern nor the courage to follow the Gospel's abolitionist logic, which other Christian bodies were apparently more attuned to. We do it solely to undermine (in advance of our examination of) Mr. Ferrara's criterion of "Catholic Social Teaching." For that criterion, if applied to slavery, either counsels an embrace of that institution as ordained by God or implies a self-discrediting ethical and historical relativism (i.e., *"No more slavery, starting . . . now!"*)

Not that it lessens his offense, but John Locke was an absentee slave-holder, while the Jesuits of Georgetown and Baltimore "got their hands dirty," so to speak, overseeing around 300 slaves (some estimates put it at 500) on six plantations at any one time.[111] Having interviewed scholars involved in the "Jesuit Plantation Project" of Georgetown University's American Studies Department, Kathryn Brand, writes:

> Compared to other plantation owners in the area, when it came to slavery, "The Jesuits were no better or

---

[111] Jesuit Plantation Project: Maryland's Jesuit Plantations, 1650-1838.
http://www8.georgetown.edu/departments/americanstudies/jpp/

worse," according to [University Dean Hubert] Cloke. Many of the slaves had been gifts from wealthy Catholic families to sustain the Church. The abolition of slavery was not an issue in the area until the early nineteenth century, when Georgetown's Jesuits became deeply divided over the issue of slavery. "But they were not conflicted in the way you would want," Cloke said. "They were conflicted over what to do about the threat of abolitionists."[112]

Perhaps Mr. Ferrara regards "the way you would want" as presumption on Dean Cloke's part, evidence of submission to the liberal *Zeitgeist*, which Catholics have admirably resisted longer than anyone else. In any case, by the 1680s (after the supply of indentured servants dried up), the Society of Jesus in Maryland "relied upon a fully developed slave system," and American Catholics generally regarded "abolitionism" as a cussword of Protestant heretics. Father Maxwell wrote:

> Already in 1836 the propaganda of Christian anti-slavery movement had achieved considerable force in North American and Europe, and at this date the lay editor of a Catholic journal considers that the Christian abolitionists should be regarded as a sect since they differ from all other Christians in believing that slave-holding is a sin against God.[113]

The older generation of Jesuits had long made their peace with the surrounding non-Catholic society's acceptance of slavery. Prefect-Apostolic (i.e., Bishop) John Carroll (1735-1815), for example, was kind to his slave (he also had a free servant) and

---

[112] Kathryn Brand, "The Jesuits' Slaves," *The Georgetown Voice* ["Georgetown's Blog of Record"], February 8, 2007.

http://georgetownvoice.com/2007/02/08/the-jesuits-slaves/

[113] John F. Maxwell, *Slavery and the Catholic Church: A History of Catholic Teaching concerning the Moral Legitimacy of the Institution of Slavery* (London: Barry Rose Publishers, 1975), 110. The lay editor was B. J. Webb of *Catholic Advocate*, in a piece published April 2, 1836.

generous to him in his will, but was no abolitionist. Emancipation would come gradually, and only at the initiative of slaveowners, if he had his way.

A year after Carroll died, John Hughes (1797-1864), the future first Archbishop of New York, arrived in the United States with his father, settling first in Chambersburg, Pennsylvania. Desperately in need of work, John superintended a garden for the Reverend John DuBois, future founder of Mount St. Mary's University in Emmitsburg, about fifty miles from Baltimore, in exchange for room, board, and an opportunity to enroll in St. Mary's College, which he at last was qualified to do in 1820. (A friend of Father DuBois, Saint Elizabeth Ann Seton, who had established Catholic communities in Emmitsburg, was young John's "booster.") Hughes' biographer, tells us that his "force of laborers consisted chiefly of two negroes, Timothy and Peter, well-known characters, who are still remembered by old students of the Mountain [i.e., Catoctin Mountains]," but omits to indicate the legal status of these chaps.[114] In Hughes' own hand we find an odd moral distinction between the one sold into

---

[114] John Rose Green Hassard, *Life of the Most Reverend John Hughes, D.D., First Archbishop of New York. With Extracts from His Correspondence.* D. Appleton and Company, 1866, p. 24. There is an interesting case of a Maryland slave named Peter, whom we cannot with certainty identify as one half of young John Hughes's labor force, but whose situation reveals something of the educated Catholic mentality regarding slavery. Historian Thomas Murphy, himself a Jesuit, writes:

> On May 5, 1801, when the [Corporation of] RCC [Roman Catholic Clergy] convened at Newtown [MD], there was concern about the plans of a Father Brasuis to free a slave named Peter. The corporation informed Brasuis that such a step would harm "that sublimation, which ought to be preserved among the other slaves." Therefore, they advised that Peter be required to purchase his own freedom by providing security equal to the amount for which he might otherwise have been sold. The clergy felt that if Peter managed to fulfill these conditions, he would thereby demonstrate that he had earned freedom . . . rather than received it as a right. . .
>
> . . . the priests showed a conviction that if Peter could manage to purchase his liberty, he would thereby witness to the remaining slaves that freedom had its patient price. Hopefully, his example then would guard against slave revolts and the temptation to believe that freedom could be claimed on demand. *Jesuit Slaveholding in Maryland, 1717-1838.* New York, Routledge, 2001, 75.

slavery and his or her offspring born into it. Having entertained the scenario of slavers purchasing human beings from enemies who almost certainly would have butchered them, Hughes raises what he calls the "terrific part of the question":

> . . . not only the individuals brought to the American continent or islands are themselves to be slaves, but their posterity, in like manner, for all time to come. *This is the only terrific feature about American slavery.* And yet it is not alien from the condition of mankind in general. Original sin has entailed upon the human race its consequences for time and eternity. And yet the men who are living now had no part in the commission of original sin.[115]

The view of slavery expressed here is, of course, that of the contemporaneous Instruction of the Holy Office, promulgated under the authority of *Pio Nono*, the Roman Pontiff who initiated "Dagger John's" rise through the American hierarchy.

The younger generation of Jesuits, though cordially anti-abolitionist, wanted to divest themselves of their holdings in this unseemly business as soon as possible, at least for economic reasons. Never did they entertain the notion that persons who ought never to have been considered property should simply be manumitted, let alone compensated. No, they thought, rather prosaically, that the money could be invested better, and elsewhere. In Catholic education up north, for instance.

> Although by the mid-1830s, the plantations were beginning to turn higher profits, this did not placate the younger Jesuits, because the estates were still not seen as sufficient to support the mission. These new

---

[115] Hassard, 426. Emphasis added. This is from an unsigned article in his diocesan journal in 1862. Father John Maxwell commented on this passage: "Emancipation was held to be desirable because of the existence of recognized abuses in the slave-system, not because of any intrinsic injustice in the system itself; but such emancipation should be gradual. Abolitionism without compensation of the slave-masters was condemned as an unjust denial of property-rights." Maxwell, *Slavery and the Catholic Church*, 114.

Jesuits had no moral quandaries selling their slaves downriver; they felt their investments should be moved to urban centers such as New York or Philadelphia. So, in 1838, at a time when the plantations were at their most profitable, the Jesuits decided to sell their slaves to Louisiana's ex-governor, Henry Johnson, whose son was a Georgetown student.[116]

Now, they weren't a cold, heartless bunch. Not at all.

Before the sale, the mission drafted "Conditions for Sale," a set of guidelines to protect their former slaves. They determined that the slaves could only be sold to a plantation, rather than families, "so that the purchasers may not separate them indiscriminately and sell them." In what reads like a bill of rights, the slaves were promised to be kept with their families, and those with family on other plantations were to be sold to those plantations. Those who were too old or sick to be sold were to be provided for "as justice and charity demands." Finally, the slaves were guaranteed the right to practice religion. The document also made a demand of the Maryland Jesuits, likely an addition from the new school of Jesuits. The sale's profit was not to pay off debts or purchases, but "must be invested as Capital which fructifies," specifically educational centers in New York and Philadelphia.[117]

---

[116] Brand, "The Jesuit Slaves." It was not uncommon to see a Georgetown University student in those days accompanied by his slave.

[117] Brand notes the irony of the situation: ". . . all Jesuits recognized certain basic rights for the slaves. A report from the time demanded adequate fixed rations, half of Saturday to themselves, and the promotion of morality and the administration of the sacraments. However, the report also states that for other slaves, "chastisement should not be inflicted in the house, where the priests live." That is, it was acceptable for priests to whip the slaves, as long they did not do so in their own quarters. Similarly, the document stated that pregnant women should not be whipped."

Well, guess where those funds wound up:

> [Georgetown Plantation Project Professor Edward] Curran believes that some of the older Jesuits listed their slaves on the inventory, but warned them of the sale so that they could hide in the woods when the officials came to transport them. Curran explained, "The 1840 census shows a surprisingly large number of younger slaves still on certain plantations, which supports the tradition that some slaves hid themselves then returned to the plantations once the provincial had left."
>
> With the sale [in 1838], the Jesuits of Maryland made $115,000 [about $2,780,000 today] and ended their history as a large slaveholding institution. The money from the sale was, as stipulated, invested in Xavier High School in New York and St. Joseph's in Philadelphia. Some of the funds also went to finance Fordham University, completed in 1842 .... "Much of the funding for these schools came from the ignoble sales," [Dean] Cloke said.[118]

Talk about "the subsidy of history"! Xavier, my high school and Fordham, Mr. Ferrara's *alma mater* (which was also that to several of my uncles) were seeded with profits from the sale of human beings, who should have been simply manumitted.

---

[118] Brand, "The Jesuit Slaves."

Chapter 30

Slavery, Real and Bogus

While the Sun King (r. 1643-1715) was basking in his reflected glory, Pope Urban VIII (r. 1623-1644) was in the market for 40 galley slaves to be bought for his personal squadron of *bonavoglie* (rowers). Following suit, his successor, who took the unintentionally ironic name of Innocent X (r. 1644-1655), ordered 100, as did *his* successor to the Throne of Peter, Alexander VII (r. 1655-1667).[119]

It is also worth noting that papal solicitude for the natives of the Americas vis-à-vis the Spanish empire's demand for slave labor did not officially extend to *Africans* until 1839 during the reign of Gregory XVI (1831-1846). Even at that late date, however, His Holiness was maintaining a distinction between "just" and "unjust" acquisition of slaves.

In the third historical "sketch," currently under review, Mr. Ferrara does not explain what he means by "wage slaves." (The reader is free, however, to form an emotionally charged impression from his heart-rending illustrations.) He nevertheless

---

[119] For citation of contemporary documents supporting these claims, see John F. Maxwell, *Slavery and the Catholic Church: A History of Catholic Teaching concerning the Moral Legitimacy of the Institution of Slavery* (London: Barry Rose Publishers, 1975), 76-77.

employs that term in a way that (a) fails to illuminate the true condition of employees in global corporations and (b) trades on the emotional charge that rightly attaches to the enormity of genuine slavery.

As "wage slavery" is a staple of socialist, even Marxist, propaganda, a Catholic should have strong reasons for parroting such lingo.[120] Mr. Ferrara offers none, yet irresponsibly plants this malignant seed in his reader's mind. We are merely uprooting that seed. When he returns to that ground, we will not only repeat but also elaborate upon our counterargument.

There is an additional strategic reason for our rummaging through the Church's moral dumpster: papal *apologiae* for slavery discredits in advance any simple appeal to encyclicals on behalf of empirical Catholic Social Teaching. *Rerum Novarum* is silent on the long-standing casuistic distinction between owning a person (magisterially long forbidden) and owning his labor (once magisterially permitted), a distinction that once gave slavery canonical "wiggle room."[121]

---

[120] As there is a kind of "Gresham's Law" of language whereby bad words tend to drive good words out of circulation, it is worth noting that one consequence of this linguistic corruption is the shutting out from consciousness of genuine slavery which, since it plainly does not involve working for a wage, needs a new name. And so, when a union activist, for example, targets "wage slavery" for elimination, he or she trivializes the plight of upwards of 27 million people who would gladly trade places with wage-earners. 19th century abolitionists repudiated this identification, notably former slave Frederick Douglass, who delighted in his first wage-paying job, and William Lloyd Garrison, who explicitly regarded it as involving an "abuse of language." It does not bode well for our times in general, or for the Church in particular, that such things need to be spelled out, that educated Catholic laymen are among those responsible for the currency of such a template of mental laziness. One of the insights that the study of the free market yields is that no one "works for himself." The rig operator, for example, works for its owner, but the owner works for the oil company that rents the equipment, and everyone who sits on its board of directors works for the consumers of oil. Their livelihoods depend on the desirability of their oil, and over that desire they have no control. The distortion of market behavior via the state does not invalidate that insight. Language is abused if dependency *as such* is made a sufficient condition of slavery.

[121] Leo XIII's statement that "a small number of very rich men have been able to lay upon the teeming masses of the laboring poor a yoke little better than that of slavery itself," while walking right up to the line of abusing language, does not cross it. If a condition is

Given the ordinary magisterium's track record on this issue, however, no papal condemnation of slavery *per se*—whether implicit as in *Rerum Novarum* (1891) or explicit as in *Veritatis Splendor* (1993)–suffices to command assent. We need something besides a pope's *ipse dixit*. (Again, *"No more slavery, starting . . . now!,"* simply will not do.) We need, for instance, to ponder the meaning of Jesus' inaugural sermon, recorded in Luke 4, and draw conclusions that it took 18 centuries for theologians to draw.

Mr. Ferrara, our unsung Doctor of the Church, may *wish* that the concurrence of seven consecutive (historically recent) popes is all that's needed theologically, that a modern "social" encyclical is to be received by Catholics virtually as Holy Writ, but wishing doesn't make things so.[122]

"little better than slavery," then it's *not* slavery, not even "wage slavery." *Rerum Novarum*, paragraph 3.

[122] That reasoning holds for *Ubi Arcano* no less than for *Rerum Novarum*: one cannot establish the juridical sufficiency of a papal encyclical by citing a papal encyclical, as Mr. Ferrara seems to think. (327, "Introduction," n. 2)

Chapter 31

If This Is Infallibility . . .

T he ownership of one human being by another violates the law of nature and of nature's God. Such is the teaching of Pope Leo XIII in *In Plurimus*.[123] Unfortunately for a certain view of the Church's ordinary magisterium, that teaching is inconsistent with that of many, if not most, of Leo's predecessors.

Of course, Jesus did not explicitly condemn slavery any more than he did the Roman Empire. Had He and His followers engaged in a frontal assault on the empire and its slavery, He and they would have been in violation of His prudential advice to be as wise as serpents and as harmless as doves (Matthew 10:16).

Yet, the Gospel intends the abolition of slavery in all its forms, and independently of whether its subjective and objective conditions of slavery have been fulfilled. Even if chattel slavery is but an institutional reflection of slavery to sin—that is, it presupposes the slaver's shutting out the true light given to everyone coming into the world (John 1:9)—there is no justification

[123] Pope Leo XIII, *In Plurimis*.

http://www.vatican.va/holy_father/leo_xiii/encyclicals/documents/hf_l-xiii_enc_05051888_in-plurimis_en.html for an exclusively "spiritual" reading of Jesus' inaugural sermon (Luke 4:18). He announced the liberation of captives, and not just of the men-stealers (ανδραποδισταις, andrapodistais) mentioned in 1 Timothy 1:10.

The spiritual dimension is not sealed off from the physical or the interpersonal. How we treat one another is a reliable indicator of our spiritual state, which is not knowable solely by reflection and contemplation (if at all that way [Jeremiah 17:9]). Even if for most of the Church's history it was all but impossible for Christians to have formulated abolitionism as a goal— because of, say, the hardness of their hearts (as Christ explains the Mosaic legal countenancing of divorce [Matthew 19:8])— they *ought* always to have done so. Christians ought never to have acquiesced in that institution.

Slavery itself, not just the *desire* to enslave, has no place in the Kingdom of God, which came with Christ's earthly ministry. Slavery may have been the "business-as-usual" norm under the Kingdom of Satan, but Christ announced the end of that Kingdom and the establishment of His own. Eventually the implications of the Kingdom for the institution of slavery sunk in. And some "got" it sooner than others and acted in concert to implement their insight.

Father Maxwell assured his readers that "if for over 1,400 years the Church's fallible ordinary magisterium was mistaken in its interpretation of the natural moral law concerning the institution of slavery, this in no way impugns the infallibility of the Church. For in no case were the criteria met for a statement of the magisterium on slavery to be infallible."[124] (Maxwell, *Slavery and the Catholic Church*, 13)

If we may not fairly test Church infallibility in light of the mistaken, i.e., *false*, character of the fourteen-century-long common

---

[124] John F. Maxwell, *Slavery and the Catholic Church: A History of Catholic Teaching concerning the Moral Legitimacy of the Institution of Slavery* (London: Barry Rose Publishers, 1975), 13.

teaching on slavery, just because certain technical criteria were not met, perhaps we may be permitted to wonder what purpose the notion of infallibility serves. Surely slavery was not a matter of prudence or custom, but rather one of faith and morals, touching as it does the dignity of created image-bearers.

For fourteen centuries, popes and bishops accepted slavery *as an institution* and as a just criminal penalty. They did so either explicitly or—insofar that there is no record of episcopal or papal dissent—implicitly. It does, however, call into question the "point" of a claim of infallibility when the office claiming it can fail so spectacularly. If *falsus in uno, falsus in omnibus,* does not apply, we may at least be within our cognitive rights to have reservations about the truth-value of other proclamations of that office.

The "just wage," for instance.

Part Three

Dessert and Leftovers

Chapter 32

Save Money, Live Better, Just Do It

There are only three factors of production—always land and labor, sometimes also capital—and each factor earns an income. Its income is a function of its contribution to the product. The greater the contribution of a given factor, the greater the income accruing to it. Only capital can enhance the productivity, and hence the income, of the other two factors.

And so, as even common sense should suggest, what a worker can command in wages is determined by what he offers the employer. If the latter over- or underestimates, his enterprise becomes unprofitable, or another employer bids his labor away from him. Either way he is soon out of business.

Wages, the rent-price of labor, rise with labor productivity. Labor productivity in general is not increased by workers' working "harder" or "smarter," but by capital investment. Wages are not, therefore, a function of either worker need or employer greed, to borrow George Reisman's assonant couplet.[125]

Having discussed chattel slavery, we now turn to labor conditions in the Third World—or at least to Mr. Ferrara's description thereof in all its melodramatic bluster and irresponsibility:

> Even today, in Third World countries such as China, Bangadesh and Indonesia, Wal-Mart, K-Mart, Nike and other corporate giants have been caught employing either slave labor or wage-slaves through a vast, plausibly deniable network of thousands of subcontractors and suppliers. And, thanks to the government-sponsored creation of "free-trade zones" in Central America by the United States Agency for International Development (USAID), giant American corporations can set up shop in tax-free havens (not available to small domestic competitors) where masses of impoverished people churn out products for American retail in return for near-starvation wages. (21-22)

We observe that Mr. Ferrara uses "slave" (and its cognates), if not equivocally, then at least imprecisely enough so that it is difficult to know what corporate entity he's charging with what offense. Are, for example, Wal-Mart's employees like China's prison labor? If not, what purpose does juxtaposing them serve if not a propagandistic one? (And unless "Third World" is a euphemism for "non-white," *which we doubt is Mr. Ferrara's intended sense*, it is hard to see how China may be sensibly referred to as a "Third World country.")

Mr. Ferrara shows no curiosity about whether those "masses of impoverished people" *welcome* the opportunity to avoid *actual* starvation by "churning out" those products (to be bought

---

[125] George Reisman, "Wages and the Irrelevance of Worker Need and Employer Greed," *George Reisman's Blog on Economics, Politics, Society, and Culture*, April 12, 2011. georgereismansblog.blogspot.com/2011/04/wages-and-irrelevance-of-worker-need.html

mostly by workers whose standard of living is as high as it is due to past capital investment). Relative to their pre-investment condition, the prospects of investment and their attendant employment opportunities are attractive to them. They demonstrate that by flocking to these factories as soon as they are opened.

When Mr. Ferrara explicitly defends the "just wage," he implicitly holds that there is a "zone of indeterminacy" for wages. If that were so, then suasion, moral or criminal, can be brought to bear on the interested parties as they settle on a point along that zone.

By a "just wage" Mr. Ferrara does *not* mean the rate of hire that employer and prospective employee non-coercively agree to, *regardless of whether the latter has no other opportunity for employment unless he relocates.* (For Mr. Ferrara, to have non such opportunity is tantamount to being coerced.) By a "just wage" he means one that *in justice the wage-earner must be paid*—and then he adds this odd proviso—*if the employer can afford to.*

We have, however, never heard of a requirement of justice, pertaining either to positive or negative rights, being subject to such a condition, e.g., "I will repay my debt to you . . . *if* I can afford to" or, "I will not mug you . . . *unless* I cannot afford *not* to." To offer wiggle-room is the prerogative of grace or mercy, not justice. What Mr. Ferrara fails to see is that if any employer is now paying what Mr. Ferrara deems a "just" or "living" wage, it is because he cannot afford *not* to if he wishes to stay in business.

To resume: according to Mr. Ferrara's claim, Wal-Mart, K-Mart, Nike, etc., *could* pay higher wages without putting at risk their operations—and the livelihoods of the impoverished people that depend on them. But he never spells this out and never justifies anything like such a claim. Above the level of barter, the zone of indeterminacy is vanishingly narrow, and the hire-price of labor tends to be set already at the high end, in which case the only way to go is down.[126]

Mr. Ferrara's sketchy history—excuse me, historical sketch distilled from his well-stocked library of material—is supported by equally sketchy references:

> The use of slaves or virtual slaves by Wal-Mart and other transnational corporations, acting through a complex web of subcontractors and sub-sub-contractors (thus permitting plausible deniability by upper management) has been documented beyond serious dispute. *See, e.g.,* "A Wal-Mart Christmas: Brought to You from a Sweatshop in China," National Labor Committee Report (2007).[127] (329 n. 30)

What is beyond serious dispute is that the NGO formerly known as the National Labor Committee in Support of Human and Worker Rights, now the Institute for Global Labour and Human Rights, is a propaganda arm of the international labor union movement, whose well-documented history of tender solicitude for the rights of human impediments to its goals does not merit Mr. Ferrara's concern.[128] When it comes to wage determination, the Institute is about as objective as is Greenpeace on climate change.

By announcing that TCATL will not treat economic theory (except to ridicule Austrian economics for an audience

---

[126] "It is curious that many writers move smoothly through rigorous price analysis until they come to wage rates, when suddenly they lay heavy stress on indeterminacy, the huge zones within which price makes no difference," allegedly, to the employment of a given factor of production. Murray N. Rothbard, *Man, Economy & State with Power & Market,* Chapter 10, "Monopoly and Competition," Section 4, B, 1. Freely available on mises.org.

[127] For a different view of Wal-Mart, see Art Carden, "Why Wal-Mart Matters," November 6, 2006 mises.org/daily/2377/Why-WalMart-Matters; and Paul Kirklin, "The Ultimate Pro-Walmart Article," June 28, 2006 mises.org/daily/2219

[128] Philip Taft and Philip Ross, "American Labor Violence: Its Causes, Character, and Outcome," *The History of Violence in America: A Report to the National Commission on the Causes and Prevention of Violence,* ed. Hugh Davis Graham and Ted Robert Gurr, New York, 1969. www.ditext.com/taft/vio-con.html

who, to enjoy the ridicule, must know even less about it than he does), Mr. Ferrara avoids committing himself to any theory of wage determination that we can examine. Such details are beneath his notice. He is content, apparently, to give the impression that wages are a function mostly of employer bad will and employee pressure. That is, if he believes that market forces have *anything* to do with wage determination, he doesn't say. It would be interesting to see where he lines up on the spectrum between pure market determination of wages as held by Austrians and pure exploitation theory as held by orthodox Marxists.

Every good, whether consisting of land, labor (human energy), or capital, has a rent or per-unit price. Since slavery is intrinsically inconsistent with free markets (because inconsistent with the "self-ownership" of laborers), labor cannot be bought on such markets, as is land or capital goods, but rather only *rented*. A wage is the rent or unit-price of labor. You may buy a plot of land from Smith, its owner, or rent its use from Smith. Smith himself, however, you may only hire; you may not buy Smith.

And no textile firm in El Salvador bought Rosa Martinez! She is the Salvadoran sewing machine operator exploited in Mr. Ferrara's second-hand propaganda, who works for thirty-three cents an hour (down, we're told, from fifty-seven cents). She is not a slave of any company operating in El Salvador, and it is offensive to the world's actual slaves to suggest that she is.[129] Mr. Ferrara copped his emotionally charged example—which comes from an ad in a textile industry journal—from John Médaille's *The Vocation of Business: Social Justice in the Marketplace* (Continuum, 2007), 252. Mr. Ferrara then reproduces his Foreword writer's analysis:

> [Rosa] lives in absolute poverty; her meager earnings provide little excess over subsistence to support the

---

[129] See the National Underground Freedom Center's site www.freedomcenter.org/slavery-today/

local economy, and the plant contributes nothing either to taxes or to import replacing abilities. (22)

Continuing his gloss on Mr. Médaille's putative textbook example of global corporatist slavery, Mr. Ferrara notes that at "one 'free-trade' zone' garment factory the daily output was valued at $30,000, while the labor cost came to $180. (22)

Ignoring Mr. Ferrara's tiresome, smarmy reference to "free trade" in scare-quotes, we ask for the meaning of his implicit comparison between output valuation and cost about which he writes with such confidence. Where does he get his data? And, more importantly, who is Rosa Martinez? What were her circumstances before that international textile company invested in her country? Did they not improve them? Does Mr. Ferrara even regard that as a relevant question?

Would it be better if the managed-trade agencies of various governments (e.g., USAID) were not involved, or even never existed? Yes, of course. But under these actual circumstances, which are beyond the control of either her employer or Sra. Martinez, did these two parties not make a deal that benefited both of them? Mr. Ferrara insinuates that wages could be, say, doubled to $360 with no perceptible degradation of the lifestyles of the alleged fat-cats who own the factory, whose greed is alleged to be the only impediment to that modicum of improvement in their workers' lives.

Such nice workerist propaganda. But where is the analysis? What *are* the margins that must be assiduously observed if there is to *be* a factory for Rosa Martinez to work in?

Silence. You're supposed to *feel* where Mr. Ferrara is coming from.

Ah, but we've been taken for a ride. Mr. Ferrara quotes Mr. Médaille, but what is *his* source? A case study from, say, the Harvard Business School or anything else equally authoritative? No. Courtesy of Mr. Médaille's own propaganda (*The Vocation of Business*), Mr. Ferrara's borrowed the material for his "historical sketch" from a 1995 video, *Zoned for Slavery: The Child behind the Label*. Who produced this agitprop?

Why, the National Labor Committee, now Institute, of whose propaganda output Mr. Ferrara already made us aware. It's right there in Mr. Médaille's 18th reference note on page 343.[130]

130 "Zoned for Slavery: The Child behind the Label."
www.youtube.com/watch?v=1XtYhfcEZ9A

Chapter 33

Corporations as "Psychopaths"

M ore rash language, propped up by biased sources, from Mr. Ferrara:

As it was in the 18th and 19th centuries, so it is today, even if the location has shifted: the wages that wage-slaves all over the world receive in transnational corporate gulags are hardly the result of "free" bargaining in a "free" market, but rather are dictated by employers to paupers who—*as Austrians themselves admit*—have no other means of survival. And there are still wage-slaves toiling in the garment factories of New York and Los Angeles, "back now, with a vengeance," and operating outside the law. (22. Emphasis in the original.)

Since the pre-Constantine Church "operated outside the law," it is hard to determine Mr. Ferrara's purpose in highlighting the legal status of the market transactions of which he disapproves. And since Mr. Ferrara never defines either "slavery" or "wages," we are left to guess what he means by "wage-slavery" and "wage-slaves." We have at least indicated in outline our own view of wage determination.

One looks in vain in TCATL for the names of Austrians who "admit" that a pauper has no other means of survival except to work in a "transnational corporate gulag" at wages "dictated" by employers. Whatever the objective reality intended by those words, that is certainly not a fair construction of the Austro-libertarian analysis of labor in countries in which capitalists from other countries have invested. What Austro-libertarians *acknowledge* is that everyone's range of choices is limited—a straightforward deduction from the undeniable truth that virtually all resources, including time, are scarce. In typical propagandistic fashion, however, Mr. Ferrara dips that recognition into the vat of his overheated, tendentious prose.

It may happen, of course, that one's range of choices is restricted because one has been the victim of aggression—that is, the initiation of physical force. Mr. Ferrara has not, however, even with the help of his unionist and social democratic literary sources, made out any such case. Let's look at one of them.

The reference note appended to the above-quoted sentences cites a book by Joel Bakan, a psychologist-*cum*-lawyer-*cum*-professor—a chilling combination of talents. Its title, as Mr. Ferrara cites it, is *The Corporation*. Now, he had just cited the subtitle along with the title of John Medaille's book, but for some reason he elected to omit the rather provocatively Ferrara-esque subtitle of Mr. Bakan's: *The Pathological Pursuit of Profit and Power*.

You see, Mr. Bakan believes he has found the secret of the corporation: criminal psychopathology (if not sociopathology). Blithely moving from the legal definition of "person" to a psychological one, he abuses his psychology training by treating the corporation as a collective psychological patient, and then diagnoses the latter as irresponsible, manipulative, grandiose, reckless, remorseless, and superficial. Just what Mr. Ferrara ordered for his assault on capitalism.

Mr. Bakan's imputation of criminal responsibility to the corporation is a case of the fallacy of misplaced concreteness: from the standpoint of the methodological individualism favored by Austro-libertarians, the collectivist notion of "corporate psychopathology" makes no more sense than does "corporate social responsibility," which phrase unfortunately enjoys wide currency in our culture.

But neither should it make any sense to any mind informed by Catholic anthropology. Limited liability ought to obtain on earth, as it obtains in heaven. It may be, according to Catholic doctrine, that every individual human being, excepting Mary, comes into the world deprived of sanctifying grace—that deprivation being the essence of what has traditionally been called "original sin"—but that is not to be understood as a form of "collective guilt."[131] Catholic theology teaches that Jews were and are no more "collectively guilty" of murdering Christ than Germans under Hitler were of Jews (Daniel Goldhagen to the contrary notwithstanding).

In the case of Mr. Bakan's oversized pamphlet, we seem to have a case of one propagandist finding polemical use for another's. It is certainly hard to find peer-reviewed commentary on this academic's work. Even Simon Fraser University Professor Gary Teeple, no fan of capitalism, has reservations about Bakan's brand of corporation-bashing propaganda.[132] Perhaps that's because *The Corporation*, along with the award-winning companion video of the same name, was intended for public consumption in the first place, a springboard for influencing "public policy."[133] According to Mr. Ferrara, Mr. Bakan documents on the pages cited (73-75)

---

[131] Some sources are cited collected in the article "Original Sin" for *The Catholic Encyclopedia*, on New Advent website. www.newadvent.org/cathen/11312a.htm

[132] Gary Teeple, "A Commentary on Joel Bakan's The Corporation, The Pathological Pursuit of Profit and Power," *Socialist Studies / Études socialistes*, Vol. 1, No. 2 (2005) www.socialiststudies.com/index.php/sss/article/view/49

[133] Joel Bakan, *The Corporation* (video). www.clickchoice.info/joel-bakan/the-corporation-video_8c77ab5b8.html

systematic violation of labor laws by sweatshop entrepreneurs paying one or two dollars an hour to tens of thousands of workers, "many of them illegal, and thus powerless, immigrants."[134] (330 n. 33)

Mr. Bakan has merely listed various liabilities that certain corporations have been threatened with or suffered—legal suits that have been brought against them in courts of law—due to noncompliance with "labor laws." The rhetorical force of his insinuated "indictment," however, depends logically on one's rational and ethical assessment of those edicts. For Mr. Bakan, if not also for Mr. Ferrara—those laws enjoy sacrosanct status, courtesy of democracy's mystique.

From our alternative perspective one must ascertain, on a case-by-case basis, whether any *aggression* (as defined above) occurred—not whether someone failed to reach a bureaucratically assigned numerical goal. As for instances of genuine aggression— the possibility of its occurrence no Austro-libertarian denies—the network of peaceful co-operators called the free market can solve the problem posed by violent non-cooperators not only at a lower cost, but also at a higher quality than what passes for "defense services" as provided by the state.[135]

Neither Mr. Bakan nor Mr. Ferrara distinguishes between the corporation as an expression of the free market and the anti-market political temptations to which particular corporation executives have succumbed, including seizing control of the state.[136] Corporations, Murray Rothbard writes:

---

[134] No scare-quote marks punctuate Mr. Ferrara's use of this loaded term. For an exorcism of this particular anti-market bogeyman, see Thomas J. DiLorenzo, "How 'Sweatshops' Help the Poor," *Mises Daily,* November 9, 2006. mises.org/daily/2384

[135] See, e.g., *The Myth of National Defense: Essays on the Theory and History of Security Production,* edited by Hans-Hermann Hoppe, Auburn, AL: Ludwig von Mises Institute, 2003. mises.org/etexts/defensemyth.pdf

[136] Mr. Bakan refers to the corporatist, virtually fascist "Swope Plan" (named after its author, General Electric's Gerard Swope) to overthrow the government of the United States in the early '30s of the last century (*The Corporation,* 19, 171 n. 34). Free market-oriented libertarians have been drawing upon this episode for their analysis of the state

. . . are free associations of individuals pooling their capital. On the purely free market, such men would simply announce to their creditors that their liability is *limited* to the capital specifically invested in the corporation, and that beyond this their personal funds are not liable for debts, as they would be under a partnership arrangement. It then rests with the sellers and lenders to this corporation to decide whether or not they will transact business with it. If they do, then they proceed at their own risk. Thus, the government does not *grant* corporations a privilege of limited liability; anything announced and freely contracted for in advance is a *right* of a free individual, not a special privilege. It is not necessary that governments grant charters to corporations.[137]

The state is, according to Austro-libertarians, the original natural outlaw. It has no resources it did not acquire by aggression. It is the ring of power that is too tempting for many of the wealthy to ignore. They must have it, wear it, and use it. Unfortunately, the *libido dominandi*, for which state power is a virtually irresistible near occasion of sin, deforms the ring-bearer. To ensure the redemption of the monopoly- and privilege-seeking corporation, therefore, the state and its false promises must be destroyed.

As one might surmise, however, Mr. Bakan is no anarchist. He regards the democratic state as *the* source of hope. *Its* wars, *its* lies, *its* psychopathic behavior get off Scott-free.

---

for decades. See our blog post, "Antony Sutton's Inconvenient Research: A Neglected Libertarian Resource." *AnthonyGFlood.com*, November 30, 2018.

[137] Murray Rothbard, *Power & Market*, Chapter 3, "Triangular Intervention," R. Policy toward Monopoly. Freely available on mises.org.

Chapter 34

Enclosing Debate

Mr. Ferrara's three-part, 10,400-word anti–Austrian broadside, filled to the brim with sarcasm and invective, entitled "The Austrian Version of the English Enclosures," is a critique without an object.[138] There is no such thing as *the* Austrian version of that or any other historical movement. There certainly was no such object in view when Mr. Ferrara wrote his few paragraphs on the subject in TCATL. As we have discussed, those thousands of acts of enclosure, which occurred legally and extra-legally over centuries in England, and which Mr. Ferrara conflated with Henry VIII's brutal seizure of Church lands, were convenient sticks with which to beat Austrians. Unfortunately for his propaganda, they are irrelevant to the Catholic assessment of Austro-Libertarianism.

---

[138] "The Austrian View of the English Enclosures," *The Distributist Review,* July 25, 2011, distributistreview.com/mag/2011/07/the-austrian-version-of-the-english-enclosures/; "The Austrian View of the English Enclosures, Part II," *The Distributist Review,* August 9, 2011,
distributistreview.com/mag/2011/08/the-austrian-version-of-the-english-enclosures-part-ii/; "The Austrian View of the English Enclosures, Part III," *The Distributist Review,* August 21, 2011, distributistreview.com/mag/2011/08/the-austrian-version-of-the-english-enclosures-iii/

We know of no Austro-libertarian who is a fan of the English Parliament *except* for the libertarian import of its resistance to absolute monarchy. In Mr. Ferrara's code, however, Austrians' support for free markets—*not* so-called "free" markets, but actual, non-coerced exchanges between traders *regardless of how their trading situations evolved*—implicates them criminally in the support of any aggression any capitalist ever waged on another person. As libertarian ethicists, that is, independently of their praxeological analysis of the distorting effects of political advantages upon markets, Austro-libertarians condemn them all.

It is good to recall, however, that Austro-libertarians did not, after all, influence the course of English history. If they could have, they no doubt would have ensured that the greater efficiencies that some have discerned in the consequences of enclosure would have been promoted without aggression, whether Henrican, parliamentary, or distributist in inspiration.

But such counterfactuals are the stuff of methodology, not history. And Mr. Ferrara chose not to treat praxeology or the non-aggression axiom in his book until his sketchy stories and their sordid impressions poisoned the well. We have already raised questions about what such analogously irresponsible approach to history would mean for the Catholic Church.

It bears repeating that in our lexicon the term "free market" refers to a real, interpersonal network of voluntary cooperation that naturally and persistently expresses itself through historical actors. The eminently ontologically real free market is the norm—the *ideal* norm, *not* the statistical norm—of human history for anyone guided by a eudaemonistic (good-life-seeking) ethics. (We would argue that a Catholic Christian ethics is a species of eudaemonism—with the good life sought being everlasting.) Ethics needs an anthropological framework, of course, but praxeology is not anthropology, and no Austrian ever said it was. But let's not get ahead of ourselves.

Therefore—or so goes the Austrian "version" of any historical episode—human action has an intelligibility or *logos* that any episode will illustrate. The facts of a given episode and their weight are for specialists to explore and argue about. What the Austrian distinctively claims is that no specialist will ever discover anything that contradicts the logic of human action (let alone "confirm" that there is no such logic). No contingency can determine the outcome of such a philosophical and methodological debate.

Now, while there's no such thing as "the Austrian version of the English enclosures," there is apparently a Ferraran version. It's based on reading a few century-old books that confirmed his anti-capitalist prejudices. He was momentarily flummoxed when Tom Woods, an historian, pointed out lacunae in Mr. Ferrara's reading, specifically highlighting a book by G. E. Mingay that questioned the received opinion that had been built on the Hammonds' research. Dr. Woods's point was not that Mingay was "the last word," so to speak, but that Mr. Ferrara wrote as though the Hammonds were. Even as late as the second part of his article—that is, before Mr. Ferrara was relieved to find scholars on his side of what he calls the "modern research game"— he revealed the true dimensions of his exigent mind:

> But why are the past fifty years of scholarship on the
> enclosures more reliable than the past two centuries
> of scholarship? Woods offers no demonstration.

Well, if reliability is to be decided after one determines whose ideological ox is being gored, then I suppose one does need a demonstration of the cumulative effect of collaborative scholarship! Mr. Ferrara forgot all about that, however, when he discovered that a more recent scholar, Jeanette Neeson, author of the award-winning *Commoners: Common Right, Enclosure and Social Change in England, 1700-1820*, allegedly swung the dialectical pendulum to the "pessimist" side of the enclosure controversy for the nonce.

Chapter 35

Rothbard Shaves Ferrara's Quasi-Marxist "Beard"

While it is possible to write a history of the Catholic Church (or of any institution and its key documents) that considers only the material interests of the participants in the recorded events, such a narrative would necessarily distort its object. That is because material interests—including the interest in acquiring authority over others, justly or unjustly, to steer the allocation of scarce resources in one's preferred way—are real, but do not exhaust the class of human interests.

Every human being's interest in enjoying material goods competes with equally real interests in truth, beauty, and goodness (to which last transcendental we refer justice as the virtue that orders the actions of persons toward the good of personal rights [*jures*]). We normally strive to coordinate the pursuit of these interests, so that one's honoring of those transcendentals does not obstruct one's pursuit of the good life (*eudaimonia*) and its constituent goods. The story of our lives is how we manage that competition. And so, while there might be an "economistic" analysis of the "secular" history of the Catholic Church, focusing on the venality of many of its representatives over the centuries, there can be none of the spread of the Gospel and its martyrs.

Just as crass material interests can assert themselves in the conduct of members of the Body of Christ, so non-material interest can find their head in movements of people who do not enjoy Her divine favor and protection. When we turn to sketchy story number 4, we find Mr. Ferrara once again venturing out into a field for specialists with no obvious connection to a "defense of the Catholic Church's teaching on man, economy, and state" (the subtitle of TCATL):

The protections for creditors and slave-owners built into the United States Constitution. (22)

For eighteen centuries, as we have seen, such protections were also built into the actual constitution of the Catholic Church, as evidenced by many documents, but that did not stop her from preaching the Gospel or dispensing the sacraments. In the fullness of time She adjusted Her constitution to achieve greater conformity with the *logos* of the Gospel. We will return to this.

Mr. Ferrara goes on to note what we Austro-libertarians have no difficulty noting, namely, that government confers advantages on its friends. Why he and others don't draw the anarchist inference from the intrinsic moral hazard that is government remains a mystery. We are sorry the Founding Fathers didn't.

> It was hardly the "free" market that favored the holders of worthless securities of the Continental Congress by redeeming them at par value, forbade the states to issue paper currency and required them to allow only specie (gold and silver coins) as payment for debts, forbade the states to impair contracts for private debt or commercial exchanges, preempted any state regulation of interstate and foreign commerce, required the return of escaped slaves, and guaranteed the continuation of the slave

trade for at least another twenty years. (22; the reference note cites several articles of the U.S. Constitution)

No, a free market didn't do any of those things. *People* do things *on* more or less free markets. Austro-libertarians do, of course, prefer legal tender laws that require payment in gold or silver rather than those that privilege paper currency that can be produced more promiscuously, and fraudulently, than gold and silver can be mined, refined, and minted. They'd rather, however, not have any legal tender laws at all. Let people use whatever they want as money. What's wrong with that?

Mr. Ferrara's criticism of particular interferences with markets is a tad disingenuous, for it is clear that he just prefers different modes of hampering. That is, he has no problem with hampering *per se*, for "true freedom" (as he defines it) may call for a dollop of it. The voluntary or involuntary aspect of a trade seems to be for him its least important aspect: liberty is, after all, the "god that failed."[139] He disguises that agenda when he professes that he is only exposing the hypocrisy of defenders of free markets. And as we saw earlier in this blog's history, the distinction between "spiritual freedom" and "political freedom" only makes for confusion.

Equally disingenuous is his implicit solicitude for slaves, for (as we saw earlier) the Vatican, the font of "Catholic Social Teaching" (CST), was still affirming the compatibility of slavery, and its attendant fugitive slave edicts, with "the natural and divine law"—not two decades after the ratification of the U.S. Constitution, but even a year after Appomattox. Why demonize the Founding Fathers but give the Vicars of Christ a pass on slavery? What's bad for the gander is bad for the goose.

---

[139] This is the title of his subsequent literary adventure, foretold at 330 n. 37. It was published in 2012 by Angelico Press.

And then, out of the blue, comes an endorsement of an old historical thesis:

Despite a fusillade of critical reviews of Charles A. Beard's famous "economic interpretation" of the Constitution, his basic thesis remains intact: the Constitution is an economic document crafted to serve business interests either possessed or represented by the fifty-five delegates to the Constitutional Convention. (23)

It is odd for a Catholic writer trying to dissuade Catholics from Austro-Libertarianism and promote the Catholic teaching feel compelled to dredge up and defend Beard's economistic thesis. When one first entertains it, "Catholic thought" is not the first description that comes to mind. No reason is given. We suppose he just felt like it.[140] We commend to our readers Murray Rothbard's thoughts on Beard.[141] The polished thoughts of a

---

[140] Mr. Ferrara's one cited source on Beard is Alan Gibson, "Whatever Happened to the Economic Interpretation: Beard's Thesis and the Legacy of Empirical Analysis."

citation.allacademic.com/meta/p_mla_apa_research_citation/0/8/2/9/1/pages82912/p82912-1.php

Professor Gibson, who teaches at California State University at Chico, delivered this paper at the Midwest Political Science Association meeting in April 2004. We would be happy to cite evidence of its publication in a peer reviewed journal if we had information to that effect.

[141] Murray N. Rothbard, "Marxism and Charles Beard," April 1954. Text taken from *Strictly Confidential: The Private Volker Fund Memos of Murray N. Rothbard*, edited by David Gordon. Ludwig von Mises Institute, 2010, 69-75. Freely available on mises.org. Historian Joseph Stromberg did not have access to this earlier, well-rounded assessment of Beard when he wrote "Charles Austin Beard: The Historian as American Nationalist," *Anti-War*.com, November 9, 1999, in which he wrote that Rothbard "always acknowledged a debt to Beard" (but without citing instances). antiwar.com/stromberg/?articleid=3336 Stromberg almost certainly, however, had at hand Rothbard's later, shorter, but complementary critique of the "Charles Beard-Carl Becker 'economic determinist' model of human motivation . . . so fruitful and penetrating when applied to statist actions of the American government, [but which] fails signally when applied to the great *anti*-statist events of the American Revolution." It appeared in Rothbard's *Conceived in Liberty, Volume III: Advance to Revolution, 1760-1775*, Arlington House, 1976, 354. Freely available on mises.org. Rothbard continues:

The Beard-Becker approach sought to apply an economic determinist framework to the American Revolution, and specifically a framework of inherent conflict between various major economic classes. The vital flaws in the Beard-Becker model were twofold. First, they did not understand the necessarily primary role of *ideas* in guiding any revolutionary or precocious 28-year-old provide the perfect prophylactic against our Catholic polymath's intellectual confusion. Rothbard's trenchant criticisms are worth publishing at the slightest provocation but in fact, for the reason offered in the first paragraph above, they can inform a just evaluation of the Catholic Church no less than of the American Revolution. It is ironic that Mr. Ferrara uncritically admires Beard's quasi-Marxist thesis which, on the relevant point, bears affinity to the thought of Founding Father James Madison.

---

opposition movement. Second, they did not understand that there are no inherent economic conflicts in the free market; without government intrusion, there is no reason for merchants, framers, landlords, et al. to be at loggerheads. Conflict is created only between those classes that rule the state and those that are exploited by the state. Not understanding this crucial point, the Beard-Becker historians framed their analysis in terms of the allegedly conflicting class interests of, in particular, merchants and farmers. Since the merchants clearly led the way in revolutionary agitation, the Beard-Becker approach was bound to conclude that the merchants, in agitating for revolution, were aggressively pushing their class interests at the expense of the deluded farmers.

But now the economic determinists were confronted by a basic problem: If indeed the Revolution was against the class interest of the mass of the farmers, why did the latter support the revolutionary movement? To this key question the determinists had two answers. One was the common, mistaken view . . . that the Revolution was supported only by a minority of the population. Their second answer was that the farmers were deluded into such support by the "propaganda" beamed at them by the upper classes. In effect, these historians transferred the analysis of the role of ideology as a rationalization of class interests from its proper use in explaining *state* action, to a fallacious use in trying to understand antistate mass movements. In this approach, they relied on the jejune theory of "propaganda," pervasive in the 1920s and 1930s under the influence of Harold Lasswell: namely, that no one sincerely holds any ideas or ideology, and therefore, that no ideological statements whatever can be taken at face value, but must be regarded only as insincere rhetoric for the purposes of "propaganda." Again, the Beard-Becker school was trapped by its failure to give any primary role to ideas in history (354-355).

Chapter 36

Shall We Prefer Government by Naked Coercion?

The last paragraph of Mr. Ferrara's fourth sketchy story contains three sentences, each of them a puzzle:

The U.S. Constitution, largely inspired by Lockean theories of "liberty," contained a clause that required the interstate rendition of escaped slaves to the owners of these human chattels, a clause that stood until the adoption of the Thirteenth Amendment in 1865, abolishing slavery in the United States. (23)

Does Mr. Ferrara accept the sturdiness of the word "liberty"? One wonders, since he almost never sends it outdoors without its scare-quote jacket. It is sheer obfuscation to insinuate that John Locke did not have a theory of that real object, liberty, whatever that theory's imperfections. We can comprehend each other's criticisms only if our words pick out the same things in our common experience.

And it was Congress, not the "free" market, that provided the Fugitive Slave Acton of 1793 and the Fugitive Slave Law of 1850, both of which mandated

the return of escaped slaves pursuant to the Constitution's unamended text, the latter statute requiring
federal marshals to effect the forcible repossession of
human chattels. (23)

It is hard to make out Mr. Ferrara's intended irony here.
Would it have been better if the free market, excuse me, the
"free" market had provided those laws? Was it morally inferior
to Congress for not having done so?

Without suggesting in any way that Lincoln was justified
in waging total war on the South at the costs of 600,000 lives, it
has to be said that the stated legal pretext for southern secession
was the federal government's *failure to assist* the "free" market by
compelling the states to honor the constitutionally and statutorily
mandated rendition of escaped slaves. (23)

In the reference note attached to this paragraph, Mr.
Ferrara quotes from several southern declarations of secession.
While we catch our breath, we ask again how they might bear
on a Catholic's assessment of Austro-Libertarianism. Is Mr.
Ferrara just indulging his interest in the legal dimension of
early American history at the expense of his reader's? Whatever
the answer, it is hard to see how he could satisfy the latter
interest without addressing centuries of Catholic apologetics
and involvement in, on the demand-side at the highest levels,
the slave trade.

The northern manufacturers did have a pact with southern
plantation owners against British rule, a pact that not only
acquiesced in but explicitly recognized in law the right of an
American, post-colonial rule, to own certain human beings. The
southerners who entered into this alliance were given to
understand that should their legal property wander away from
their territory, their northern confederates would help that
property find its way back.

A thoroughly shameful ingredient of human and American
history, all agreed. Now, what has this to do with the price of

Boston tea? Before America was founded as an independent country, there were Christians in its territory who were cordially opposed to slavery, and they left evidence of their activity as early as 1688. These abolitionists were Quakers, however, not Catholics. The latter distinguished themselves as *anti*-abolitionists.

Before that reference note (attached to the numeral 600,000), Mr. Ferrara attaches one wherein he enlarges upon his loathing of Lockean "consent" and with much hand-waving promotes a book whose arguments we cannot examine:

> As I argue in *Liberty: the God that Failed*, it was the height of absurdity for Lincoln to contend that the immediate descendants of the same Protestant revolutionaries who had overthrown King George on account of such grievances as a trifling tea tax of the local quartering of troops in riot-torn Boston, were somehow bound in perpetuity, under pain of death, to a central government in Washington, D.C.—a government, moreover, to which they had supposedly "consented" under Locke's nonsensical theory of sovereignty as "government by consent of the governed." But such are the absurdities unleashed by the revolutions Austro-libertarians hails as great triumphs for "liberty," even as they bemoan the rise of the "statism" those same revolutions made possible. (330 n. 37)

We are hardly obliged to analyze a string of gratuitous assertions, but let's take note of how Mr. Ferrara goes about his propagandistic business.

Surely Mr. Ferrara knows that those grievances were merely symptomatic of widespread colonist distaste for being ruled from abroad—that is, *for being colonists*—although making light of the disutility of imperial measures is uncalled for. It is not clear, however, that Mr. Ferrara even believes the colonists *ought* to have thrown off British rule in the first place, even failing any return of

England to the status of a Catholic confessional state. Between one group of Protestants and another, it seems, he has no preference.

Upon being parsed, that run-on sentence ironically confirms the anarchist suspicion that governments or states—or rather the people who run them, be they deistic presidents or Catholic kings—cannot be trusted to keep the promises they make to the governed or even to each other. Was it Mr. Ferrara's intention to confirm that suspicion? Probably not. It is not clear to this anarcho-Catholic that Lincoln's federalist-centralist presupposition was more "absurd," or at least less morally warranted, than George III's imperial one, but then Mr. Ferrara's sentence is not a model of clear expression.

The matter might be put this way: *if* good life-seeking (*eudaimonia*) is the standard of the good in human affairs, *then* moving from colonial to republican status was arguably a step in the right direction. Why? Because that direction was libertarian and good-life seeking requires liberty, i.e., the right or *jus* to use one's property as one sees fit, uncoerced by another (Matthew 20:15). That rules out using one's property to coerce others regarding the use of theirs.

Toward the end of exposing the futility of the goal of "self-limiting government," that move (from colonial subjects to independent nation) was probably pedagogically necessary. But Mr. Ferrara directed his theatrical laughter, not at the propensity of rulers to self-aggrandize—for that vice has not ensnared only deists and Protestants—but at the notion of "the consent of the governed," arguably the least morally objectionable aspect of an admittedly hopeless program.

Instead of throwing around hyperbolic language like "height of absurdity," "nonsensical theory," and "absurdities," he might have reviewed, or promised to review, an extended (1,616-page) study of the American Revolution by a leading Austro-libertarian. We refer, of course, to Murray N. Rothbard's four-volume *Conceived in Liberty*. Perhaps Mr. Ferrara is saving his analysis of them until the publication of his *Liberty*. (We're surprised he didn't put scare quotes in that title.)

It pertains to the dignity of a divine image-bearing creature above the age of reason to be asked his or her consent for the use of his or her labor or property. The notion is at the heart of covenant-making, e.g., marriage, and of covenant-breaking, e.g., sin. Now, one may not withdraw one's consent if, after giving it, another in good faith committed his person or property. This obtains in all contractual undertakings: one may not "withdraw one's consent" to pay one's bills! Apart from those circumstances, however, one may without prejudice withdraw any consent one may have given to any state of affairs involving himself or herself.

As for the phrase "the consent of the governed." Rulers may be blamed for *traducing* the principle they pretend to honor. They may justly be shamed for stretching the meaning of "consent" beyond reason so that a generation of the long-dead may be said to have "bound" the living, which bonds take the form of taxation, regulation, and conscription—and then for insisting to their hapless subjects that they are only taxing, regulating, and conscripting themselves (which, lamentably, so many of the "themselves" foolishly believe).

But not for *enunciating* the principle.

Chapter 37

Slavery for the Corporation?

Mr. Ferrara's fifth sketchy story concerns: "The rise of the limited liability, publicly held corporation." (23) The limited liability corporation (LLC) is the distinctive invention of liberal societies, according to prolific pro-market (but non-libertarian) Catholic scholar Michael Novak, whom Mr. Ferrara disparagingly calls a "hyper-capitalist." (23) (Is Mr. Ferrara a hyper-Catholic?) What is wrong with the idea of a legal person to which no personal liability attaches? (24)

> With the rise of the *publicly held* limited liability corporation, capitalists achieved the ability to amass capital without limitation, operate anywhere in the world, and undertake without personal liability ventures that would have been considered immorally reckless (*sic;* as opposed to morally reckless?) during all the centuries of Christendom (24. Emphasis in the original.)

Those were the centuries, we recall, when the slave trade blended into the soundtrack of Christendom. The Catholic monarchs who profited from that trade certainly enjoyed limited liability. State personnel always have and always will. If Mr.

Ferrara has a problem with that state of affairs, it would be good for him to say so. That inconvenient episode aside, he never makes a topic out of the *alternative* to the limited liability corporation, which occurs to any half-awake reader, namely, the *unlimited* liability corporation.

If those who pool their capital to undertake a large-scale enterprise can be personally sued for harm that might befall anyone due to its operations, they would stand to lose not only their investment, but also their shirt, so to speak. Under those circumstances, it is highly unlikely that the enterprise would be undertaken. That is, there would be very little "amassing of capital."

Now, we expect an anti-capitalist writer to favor policies that inhibit the pooling of capital, even if the inhibition keeps productivity and living standards lower than they would be without it. We do, however, also expect him to take responsibility for that preference. How far, for example, would Mr. Ferrara extend the law of conspiracy so that liabilities attach to the actions of corporate personnel as such? Instead of exploring such issues, Mr. Ferrara prefers to give currency, once again, to the thoughts of that paragon of impartiality, Joel Bakan: "by leveraging their freedom from the bonds of location . . . could *now* dictate the economic policies of government."[142]

"Now," Mr. Bakan writes, as though the powerful had resisted the temptation to dictate until the modern age. Let us hear him further. To remain in a location voluntarily, as opposed to being forced to stay, those responsible for investing the corporation's assets must find it attractive:

> To remain attractive, whether to keep investment within their jurisdictions or to lure new investment to them, governments would now have to compete among themselves to persuade corporations that they provided the most business-friendly policies. A

---

142 *The Corporation*, 22. Emphasis added.

resulting "battle to the bottom" would see them ratchet down regulatory regimes—particularly those that protect workers and the environment—reduce taxes, and roll back social programs, often with reckless disregard for the consequences.[143]

Maybe even immorally reckless disregard. The Bakans of this world support the imposition of taxes and social programs in violation of property rights with reckless disregard for consequences; the Austro-libertarian supports the end of both types of aggression because justice demands it, regardless of consequences. Note well that it is for Mr. Bakan's support for "bonds of location" that Mr. Ferrara cites him.

A few pages ago, however, Mr. Ferrara told us that one of the evils allegedly attending the Industrial Revolution was the state terror that "prevent[ed laborers] . . . from moving about in search of higher wages." Those are the words of Kevin Carson, another muse of Mr. Ferrara's. Why, if we may ask, may not the corporation enjoy the freedom from the "bonds of location," which freedom is held to be a personal right? Does he favor slavery for corporations? Out-of-the-blue Mr. Ferrara asks:

> How can the market be "free" when its fundamental business unit, created and advantaged by legislative and judicial fiat, shields its human officers, directors and investors from the normal consequences of misdeeds and bad judgments?" (24)

Didn't he really mean to ask "How can the market be free . . ." (without scare quotes)?

No truly free market, *which would be one on which no legislative or judicial fiat either creates corporations or advantages one over another,* would shield a corporation's officers, directors, and investors from the consequences of any aggression they may commit under the color of limited liability. There would be no

---

[143] Ibid., 22

government as we know it, and therefore no "friends in government," to grant subsidies.[144] The term "bad judgment" is ambiguous, however, and should not be confused with a bad will. The parties that pool their capital for the purpose of corporate investment put that capital at risk, which may very well amount to being at the mercy of bad judgment. There is no shield from market consequences for bad judgment, nor in the law for aggression.

From there Mr. Ferrara leaps to the financial meltdown of 2008 as confirmatory of the theory of the corporation that he selectively borrows from others.

> . . . the very governments that purport to regulate them grant them regulatory exemptions and other market-skewing privileges not available to small businesses. The mere threat that a corporate hegemon will pack up and leave, or go bankrupt, is often sufficient to extract what it wishes from government at all levels. (24)

Have we caught Mr. Ferrara implicitly affirming the reality the free market? After all, if the latter is an illusion, no privilege can skew it. In any case, his value judgments are merely implicit: he has not argued for them. The reader is apparently expected to go with the flow, occasionally nodding his head in agreement. And so, for instance, speaking of "hegemons," is it better for a government to be so powerful as to *prevent* a corporation from packing up and leaving, to "bind" it to a "location" like the English government once did those hapless laborers?

---

144 That libertarians have long recognized, and *condemned*, corporate lobbying and subsidy-seeking is another inconvenient fact that Mr. Ferrara ignores (when he's not repeating Mr. Carson's mocking "diagnosis" of "vulgar" libertarians as absent- or double-minded, which says more about Mr. Ferrara than it does about the targets of his perjoratives). See the literature cited in Walter Block and J. H. Huebert, "Defending Corporations," *Cumberland Law Review*, 39:2, 377, n. 75. See also agriculture economist Richard W. Wilcke's anti-lobbying study, "An Appropriate Ethical Model for Business and a Critique of Milton Friedman's Thesis," *The Independent Review*, IX:2, Fall 2004, 187–209.

The method of the propagandist, however, is not to enter into the thought of others and wrestle with it before assessing it, but to take the parts he likes, cafeteria-style, and discard the rest. (During the Cold War, Soviet propagandists would ransack the news for quotes from many people in the news who said something that could be construed as support for this or that Soviet position, thereby creating an impression of a chorus of support.) Mr. Ferrara does not pay attention to the diverse non-Catholic worldviews underlying the works he ransacks. And so, for example, he elects Kevin Carson the left-libertarian as *"the man"* for one purpose, Joel Bakan the democratic socialist for another, and quasi-Marxist Charles Beard for yet another. When it comes to the corporation, the man of the hour is "legal commentator" Daniel J. H. Greenwood, whom he quotes to support his leftoid demonizing of the corporation.[145]

Professor Greenwood does not, note well, share Mr. Ferrara's presuppositions about God, man and state, but is a democratic socialist theoretician—*Dissent* is one of his literary venues—whose argument is presuppositionally democratic. That is, democracy is the unquestioned assumption underlying his academic brief against the corporation. Since it is not Mr. Ferrara's, however, why does he quote Professor Greenwood? How does that help Catholics form an opinion about Austro-Libertarianism? That is, in the light of Mr. Ferrara's Catholic and anti-democratic worldview, why should a Catholic care what non-Catholic and pro-democratic Professor Greenwood has written on the corporation?

> There are two most important differences [Professor Greenwood writes] between a democracy and the other forms of government. First, democracies take their citizens to be the ends of the law: the good of the citizen is the good of the state. In a democracy,

---

[145] "Markets and Democracy: the Illegitimacy of Corporate Law," *University of Missouri Kansas City Law Review*, vol. 74, 2005, 102.

the citizens are never only tools to some goal greater than themselves, means simply to be exploited, or strangers to be treated entirely at arms [*sic*] length. Second, democracies allow the citizens to debate and decide their own good; it is not imposed on them by government or some supra-governmental movement. Democracies do not have established churches, in the broadest sense.

Well, "in the broadest sense" Professor Greenwood is excluding as incompatible with democracy not only a state-established church, or "confessional state" to borrow Mr. Ferrara's preferred terminology, but also any undefined "imposition" by "some supra-governmental movement" on citizens. That is, the words of Mr. Ferrara's academic expert are not reassuring to a Catholic, and so perhaps we were being generous in characterizing its author as merely non-Catholic. For should there arise a "democratic consensus" to the effect that the preaching of the Gospel tends to undermine the efficacy of that consensus, citizens would be within their democratic rights, according to Professor Greenwood, to resist such "imposition."

The note Professor Greenwood attaches to this description of democracy takes us to another article of his, one that "begin[s] to explain the theory of democracy as partnership."[146] There we find this personal credo, remarkable for a peer reviewed academic journal (or maybe not so remarkable):

> ... I place myself firmly in the pluralistic tradition of the United States Constitution: our different decision-making systems serve irreducibly different values, and that is the way it should be. (863)

Should? Where did that come from? On the sacred subject of democracy, Professor Greenwood is neither a pluralist nor

---

146 "Beyond the Counter-Majoritarian Difficulty: Judicial Decision-Making in a Polynomic World," *Rutgers Law Review*, 2001, Vol. 53, 781-864.

relativist, but quite the monist and absolutist. We are not inclined to cut him any slack.[147] But why on Earth does Mr. Ferrara—a chief columnist for *The Remnant* newspaper, whose writers regularly denounce pluralism as symptomatic of the Americanist heresy—recommend the opinion of this pluralist to his Catholic readers? Is it because his worldview is internally incoherent?

Maybe. But there's a simpler hypothesis. In the war Mr. Ferrara has decided to wage on Austro-Libertarianism, such apparent incoherence doesn't matter. What matters is that one has a stick with which to beat them. What Mr. Ferrara thinks he can get away with, he will try.

---

[147] Mr. Ferrara is a qualified admirer of Austro-libertarian Hans-Hermann Hoppe's *Democracy: The God that Failed.* He believes Dr. Hoppe made a compelling case for the moral inferiority of democracy to monarchy with respect to the exhaustion of state resources. The charitably disposed reader might reasonably expect Mr. Ferrara to qualify his citation of Professor Greenwood, if only to clarify the difference between the latter's democratic worldview from his own. But a propagandist is concerned only with the intended immediate effect of the cited work, not with the burden of living up to such a reader's expectation.

Chapter 38

The Corporation as "Sociopath"

Given Mr. Ferrara's stated purpose, namely, to demonstrate the incompatibility of Catholic teaching and Austro-Libertarianism, it is hard to regard the material in Part 1 as anything other than one, long Emily Litella-like *ignoratio elenchi*. Besides misrepresenting everything Austro-libertarian, his only counterpoint so far is a farrago of non-Catholic opinion. In a particularly egregious appeal to emotion riddled with reification and false juxtaposition, Mr. Ferrara judges it to be "morally bizarre" that

> corporations, the exclusive vehicle of worldwide "free" market activity today, are immortal "legal persons" under the meaning of the law with all the rights of human beings, yet are not subject to incarceration for their crimes, whereas millions of unborn children put to death all over the world by machines and drugs sold to abortionists on the "free" market—by corporations—do not even have the right to life. (25)

How cautiously he proceeds. The implicit syllogism is: abortion is murder; corporations trade in abortifacients; *ergo*, corporations are accessories to murder—a propagandistic gem worthy of Goebbels and Ehrenburg, and unworthy of critical reply. When he writes like that, which is almost always, Mr. Ferrara reminds us of no one more than the so-called New Atheists.[148]

Mr. Ferrara shows no interest in understanding the networks of trade that human persons spontaneously generate in the peaceful pursuit of their ends. This lack of interest in what his adversaries actually defend in controversy effectively concedes the case to the latter, who are keen to remove impediments to markets that fallen human beings have erected. Mr. Ferrara is fixated on the *hampered* market, which hampering Austro-libertarians have always condemned. And so:

> The demise of Enron and the Meltdown have made it clear to the world that these gigantic entities are not operating in a "free" market but rather in a vast supranational fiefdom, built upon government privileges, whose collapse could wreck entire nations. (25)

Exactly, they're operating on hampered markets, but the darkness does not overcome the light. The hampering is not absolute. The economies of the world are, as they say, "mixed," so the analysis of how the various factors—voluntary trade and politically inspired trade-hampering privilege—is complicated. To say so does not reflect double-mindedness or forgetfulness about what one is saying "from one moment to the next" as Mr. Ferrara impudently insinuates (inspired by Kevin Carson).

---

[148] "The books by [Richard] Dawkins, [Sam] Harris, and [Christopher] Hitchens are not mild treatises like those that trickle tentatively, and often unreadably, from departments of philosophy. They are works of passion, and I suspect that most philosophers would be embarrassed by their intemperate style of presentation. So, I do not expect that philosophers will recommend these writings to their own students either, although the books might usefully serve as case studies for classes in critical thinking." John F. Haught, *God and the New Atheism: a Critical Response to Dawkins, Harris, and Hitchens,* Westminster John Knox Press, 2008, 25.

And it was not government alone that caused the Meltdown, but also "free" market actors, hiding behind the corporate veil, who created and sold on an immense international scale a web of interlocked "toxic assets," traded with the lacunae of securities regulations. (See Chapter 13) (25) But Austro-libertarians never said it was "government alone." They have rather argued that it was government *in the first place*, that is, governmental policy as the indispensable prime mover and *sine qua non* without which the other historical factors that crowd the pages of Mr. Ferrara's yellow journalism could not have even arisen, let alone conspired, to cause the Meltdown. His acknowledgement that the "very existence" of multinational corporations "would be impossible without government support" (25-26) provokes the anarcho-Catholic to ask: What governmentally provided goods compensate for that evil? And: So why do you rationalize and tolerate the existence of that intrinsic moral hazard?

Without the Act of Congress that authorized the creation of the Federal Reserve System, bankers could have *hoped* that their cartelizing desires would be satisfied one day in a central bank. There would, however, have been no legal protection for that racket from market forces, which inexorably erode such collusions of convenience. (The most efficient producer in any cartel is usually the first cartel member to have second thoughts about the arrangement, and on free markets that firm is free to break ranks.) On this point Mr. Ferrara's next sketchy story will outline much of what every Austro-libertarian has known for most of the last century.

No, not government alone, for in themselves, no governmental personnel can produce the cartel's economic effects, that is, lower quality at higher prices. Only the cartel itself, and the market players who are at its mercy, can do that. Facilitated by legal tender laws, the Federal Reserve functions as a central planner and therefore as a market signal-distorter. As fallen human beings, market players are indeed motivated by greed, but greed is necessarily balanced by fear of loss—*unless a market-hampering agency enters the scene to take fear out of the equation,* to cite again Peter Schiff's memorable aphorism.[149]

No sooner does Mr. Ferrara acknowledge that the "very existence" of multinational corporations "would be impossible without government support" (25-26)—thereby inspiring an anarchistic thought or two—than he reveals his grasp of economics by declaring that corporations do not passively abide by "market forces." Rather, they direct them with State assistance. (26)

It is hard to know what to make of this admission. He is saying either that there *are* market forces that corporations can and do direct as, say, a cop directs traffic; or that corporations direct only *so-called* "market forces," which strips the assertion of content and interest. But which does he mean? *Of course,* market forces—shorthand for "the totality of trades being made right now, followed by the totality of trades to be made immediately thereafter, etc."—are beyond the ken of human beings to direct, whether organized as governments or corporations.

Perhaps he meant to write that market players are not above trying to *influence* market events in the short term (often foolishly unmindful of the consequences). That is, they seek advantages over the rivals in the market that have nothing to do with improving the intrinsic appeal of their products or services, whether by way of higher quality or lower price. They may, for example, seek to restrict supply or entry into a market "with State assistance." (Sort of the way the Church can influence, and historically sometimes has influenced, the religious choices of its citizens "with State assistance." The Catholic confessional state of Mr. Ferrara's longing can't actually *direct* such behavior, but it can influence it.) But Mr. Ferrara didn't say the corporations with State assistance *seek to influence* markets. He said they *direct* them.

---

[149] Peter Schiff, "Don't Blame Capitalism," *The Washington Post*, October 16, 2008.

Not being a man to let his ignorance on any subject hold him back, Mr. Ferrara then decides to attack "corporate advertising" with a zeal that would have made John Kenneth Galbraith blush.

> . . . shielded from censorship by the courts, . . . [corporate advertising] has created an entire mass culture of "happiness" through the satisfaction of an ever-expanding catalogue of stimulated desires. Here the Austrians argue that the advertising on which corporations spend billions has no influence on human will but merely provides "information," and that consumers besieged by commercial messages from infancy "freely" choose every single thing they buy, including goods and services that waste vast amounts of their time, addict them, ruin their health, corrupt their morals, and kill both body and soul. (26)

If Mr. Ferrara does not favor "censorship [of advertising] by the courts," he should not have mentioned it, thereby putting that unhappy thought in the reader's head. If he does favor such censorship, however, he should have said so plainly. But then, that's only one of ten ideas he decided to throw into that one sentence. That's what propagandists do.

No Austrian ever said that advertising has *no* influence on human will and, of course, Mr. Ferrara, our arbiter of taste, morals, health, and happiness, doesn't cite any. All information conveyed in advertising, whether relevant or irrelevant to making a sound judgment about the product or service, influences the recipient. What a person does with that information will depend on his or her moral development, background knowledge, etc. We choose as we please, but rarely (if ever) please as we please, for as we form habits, seeking or resisting God's grace, the effective range of choice for each of us narrows. But however constricted that range may be, it is never zero. That is, behaviorism is not true, and no Christian should give credence to that ideology, as Mr. Ferrara's anti-advertising tirade implicitly does.

Having already planted the word "kill," Mr. Ferrara now moves in for it with histrionics worthy of pulp fiction. Dear reader, take a deep breath:

> In sum, the corporate "personality" unleashed upon the world by the laws and courts of secular post-Christian nations exhibits all the features of a human psychopath, as [Joel] Bakan has noted: singularly self-interested (because by law the first duty of corporate management is to protect shareholder profits), lacking in empathy, irresponsible, manipulative, grandiose, unable to feel remorse or to accept responsibility for its actions, superficial in relations with others, and afflicted by a tendency to asocial behavior. But, unlike a mere flesh and blood psychopath, the mega-corporation of the capitalist world economic order, linked everywhere to government and to the bureaucracies it captures (such as the World Trade Organization), has the power to affect entire nations and even the whole human race with its self-interested decisions. (26)

In short, the modern limited liability corporation (LLC) is a criminal conspiracy, one little better than, for example, the Brooklyn Combination, A.K.A. "Murder, Inc."

Apparently, such an irresponsible introduction of the concept of corporation to his readers does not embarrass Mr. Ferrara, a lawyer who deals professionally with that form of business organization. We are embarrassed for him.

Every corporation is a conspiracy, a literal "breathing together," a voluntary union of independent natural persons who recognize their interdependence in achieving a common aim. Jesus' disciples formed a conspiracy whenever two or three of them were gathered in Jesus' name. Roman law regarded the Catholic Church as a criminal conspiracy until Constantine decriminalized Her. Catholics hold that when a person is baptized, he or she is *incorporated* into the Body of Christ (*Corpus Christi*). And so, while some conspiracies are criminal (Psalm 2:1-2), some are not (Isaiah 8:12).

The idea of treating a collective entity as a legal (fictitious, artificial) person is therefore not to be held up for ridicule, at least not responsibly. There is ancient precedent for that idea, which has noble as well as ignoble, Christian as well as pagan motivations. The Roman State that once outlawed the Church regarded itself, as least implicitly, as an international, perpetual, property-holding, and business-transacting non-natural person. As though to illustrate God's sense of irony, however, the Church's self-consciousness as an international, perpetual, property-holding, and business-transacting non-natural person was formed during the senescence of that Christian-immolating State. The Body of Christ is also the Bride of Christ (if Christ is the Bridegroom of Matthew 9:15), and we presume Mr. Ferrara's interpretation of reference to that non-natural Person is realistic, not nominalistic.

Rome eventually collapsed, but not before unwittingly providing Her with an imperfect but serviceable real-world model of legal organization. And so, the language and structure of Eastern Roman Emperor Justinian's *Corpus Juris Civilis* (539-534) is reflected in the Church's *Corpus Juris Canonici* a millennium later, coinciding with Her explicit self-recognition as a corporation.

By a further cunning of history, the secular world later imbibed the theory and practice the corporation from the Church. As soon as they were powerful enough to do so, states as rent-seeking criminal enterprises arrogated to themselves the right to grant licenses to private corporations and charge for the privilege. The salient point, however, is that *the corporation developed in the West when states were weak*. They in turn emulated the organizational entrepreneurship of the corporation that was the Church. As Austro-Reformed economist and historian Gary

North succinctly puts it: "The historical model for the limited-liability corporation was the Church."

> Over time, civil law in the West formally recognized the existence of an implicit agreement with respect to the legal immunity of church members. The state does not create this legal immunity. On the contrary, the state has recognized a previously existing legal immunity. To argue that the state should no longer recognize this immunity in the name of a universal principle of full liability without any exceptions is to grant enormous power to the state to undermine both custom and contract.[150]

Dr. North does not explore this gradual "recognition of immunity," which was a function of relative State weakness, not necessarily of respect for the rights of the Church. For when the nascent modern state picked up where the moribund Roman State left off, it seized the opportunity to interfere with voluntary contract and declare incorporation a privilege rather than a personal right of property. For that dimension of our story, we must turn to Duke University Professor Timur Kuran.

As a prelude to for explaining why Islamic law got around to recognizing the corporation as an artificial person only a little more than a century ago, Professor Kuran sheds light on a critical chapter in the Church-world dialectic:

> Following the split of Christianity in 1054, and during the struggle to emancipate religion from the control of emperors, kings, and feudal lords (1075-1122), the Roman Catholic Church began calling itself a corporation. This struggle, considered to have culminated in the Papal Revolution, gave rise to the new canon law (*jus novum*) of the Catholic Church. Canon law, which dealt with a wide range of

---

[150] "Rothbard's Defense of Contractual Limited Liability," *LewRockwell.com*, September 28, 2005, www.lewrockwell.com/north/north408.html

issues, including jurisdiction, property, and contracts, built on innumerable concepts, enactments, and rules belonging to the inherited secular and ecclesiastical legal systems. Unlike its forerunners, however, it emerged as a systematized body of law. Articulated in texts, it was supported by theories pertaining to the sources of law.[151]

By contrast, Mr. Ferrara's Bakanalian "psychoanalysis," while perhaps entertaining, is wholly unenlightening. It potentially subjects all non-natural persons to its morbid diagnosis. Language appropriate for describing the behavior of deranged natural persons cannot without grave fallacy be used to describe, let alone indict, the corporate person whose constituents they are.[152] In the hands of an anti-Catholic propagandist, Mr. Ferrara's method will almost certainly portray Holy Mother Church as Mommy Dearest.

Mr. Ferrara never mentions the elements of limited liability, namely, that it protects (a) shareholder assets from personal claims made against any member and (b) personal assets of members from claims made against the corporation. Business corporations are about resource-pooling, asset-shielding, and owner-shielding. Their virtues are durability, perpetuity, transferability. And since corporation law also protects non-business corporations like the Catholic Church, She finds it in her interest to incorporate according to such laws in the territories in which She operates. There was a time, of course, when mere public announcement of

---

[151] Timur Kuran, "The Absence of the Corporation in Islamic Law: Origins and Persistence," *The American Journal of Comparative Law*, Vol. 53, No. 4 (Fall, 2005), 791, http://www.helsinki.fi/iehc2006/papers3/Kuran.pdf

[152] To infer the character of the whole from the character of its parts is to commit the fallacy of composition. This is a fallacy even in the case where the validly drawn conclusion is true. (For examples, a floor whose every tile is all-green is necessarily all-green.) A given LLC may indeed be a criminal conspiracy, and we may rightly suspect it to be one if it is exhaustively comprised of criminals who incorporated just to further their several criminal interests. That is no warrant, however, for imputing criminality to the LLC as such or insinuating that the LLC is intrinsically a ruse for evading accountability.

incorporation sufficed. As Rothbard explains in *Power and Market*, which Dr. North cites:

> . . . corporations are not at all monopolistic privileges; they are free associations of individuals pooling their capital. On the purely free market, such men would simply announce to their creditors that their liability is limited to the capital specifically invested in the corporation, and that beyond this their personal funds are not liable for debts, as they would be under a partnership arrangement. It then rests with the sellers and lenders to this corporation to decide whether or not they will transact business with it. If they do, then they proceed at their own risk. Thus, the government does not grant corporations a privilege of limited liability; anything announced and freely contracted for in advance is a right of a free individual, not a special privilege. It is not necessary that governments grant charters to corporations.[153]

But there are earthly as well as heavenly reasons for embracing the corporate form. Unincorporated partnerships being risky to the capital they pool, economic advance tends to follow that embrace, stagnation its repudiation.[154] The LLC is not a sufficient condition of such advance, but it seems to be a necessary one. Dr. North again: ". . . the most rapid period of economic growth in mankind's history," if one condescends to consider such crass things, "took place from about 1875 to 1914—the era of the modern limited-liability corporation." It took place because the state, at long last, extended the same right of contract to businessmen that churches had enjoyed from the beginning. Rothbard wrote in *Man, Economy, and State* (1962): "The great advantage of the joint-stock company is that

---

153 Murray Rothbard, *Power & Market*, Chapter 3, "Triangular Intervention," R. Policy toward Monopoly. Freely available on mises.org.

154 See Kuran, op. cit. No law of corporations passed the Ottoman Parliament until 1908.

it provides a more ready channel for new investments of saved capital." (Ibid.)[155]

In his tribute to Han-Hermann Hoppe, Sean Gabb devotes a few pages that address the politically tainted contemporary reality of the LLC. One section of that paper is actually entitled, "Limited Liability: The Worm in the Free-Market Bud," which unfortunately (in our opinion) is not followed by a question mark. In that section and in the pages that follow (10-14) Dr. Gabb addresses, calmly and urbanely, libertarian concerns that can in the hands of others become grist for a quasi-Marxist propaganda mill. Consider Dr. Gabb's treatment of the issue (and contrast it with Mr. Ferrara's).[156]

To show he is not the first libertarian to express a sensibility that some might deem "leftist" (and in fact was first expressed by the Old Right), Dr. Gabb quotes Murray Rothbard (the last of the Old Rightists). Here is that germane (if long) passage (which we have extended slightly on both ends and broken up into sentences for greater ease of reading):

> Indeed, the New Deal was not a revolution in any sense; its entire collectivist program was anticipated: proximately by Herbert Hoover during the depression, and, beyond that, by the war-collectivism and central planning that governed America during the First World War.
>
> Every element in the New Deal program: central planning, creation of a network of compulsory cartels

---

155 North, "Rothbard's Defense of Contractual Limited Liability," op. cit. North also observes: ". . . long before the limited-liability corporation, there was a limited-liability church. I want to go to join a church without worrying about what the U.S. Supreme Court determines regarding my liability as a member. A 5-to-4 decision by this most monopolistic of all American institutions does not in fact constitute the really supreme court."

156 Sean Gabb, "Hans-Hermann Hoppe and the Political Equivalent of Nuclear Fusion," in *Property, Freedom, and Society: Essays in Honor of Hans-Hermann Hoppe*, Jörg Guido Hülsmann and Stephan Kinsella eds., Auburn, AL: Ludwig von Mises Institute, 2009, 7-20. Freely available on mises.org.

for industry and agriculture, inflation and credit expansion, artificial raising of wage rates and promotion of unions within the overall monopoly structure, government regulation and ownership, all this had been anticipated and adumbrated during the previous two decades.

And this program, with its privileging of various big business interests at the top of the collectivist heap, was in no sense reminiscent of socialism or leftism; there was nothing smacking of the egalitarian or the proletarian here.

No, the kinship of this burgeoning collectivism was not at all with Socialism-Communism but with Fascism, or Socialism-of-the-Right, a kinship which many big businessmen of the 'twenties expressed openly in their yearning for abandonment of a quasi-laissez-faire system for a collectivism which they could control.

And, surely, William Howard Taft, Woodrow Wilson, and Herbert Clark Hoover make far more recognizable figures as proto-Fascists than they do as crypto-Communists.[157]

Toward the end of his fifth sketchy story, Mr. Ferrara declares rather arbitrarily that

Whatever good corporations have done in the relentless pursuit of their own ends is not the result of the corporate form as such, which invites and protects a thousand abuses. (26)

---

[157] Rothbard, *Beyond Left and Right: Prospects for Liberty*, Auburn, AL: Ludwig von Mises Institute, 2002, 13. Freely available on mises.org. See also Rothbard, *The Betrayal of the American Right*, edited and with an introduction by Thomas E. Woods, Jr. Auburn, AL: Ludwig von Mises Institute, 2007. Freely available on mises.org.

One would think that the corporate pooling of capital bears some causal relationship to the good of higher living standards, itself an effect of the greater productivity that the pooling makes possible. Not a word about that, of course.

The *unlimited* liability corporation—the sole logical alternative to the LLC Mr. Ferrara reviles—would be formed only rarely, if ever, for few investors would care to put not only their own well-being but also that of their families at risk just because they went into business with others. Since Mr. Ferrara brought up the topic of abuse, however, we remind him that the Catholic Church seeks that corporate form of protection so that liability for millstone-meriting abuse committed by some of its officers is confined to corporation assets and does not ensnare every Catholic who ever donated money to Her.

If what bothers Mr. Ferrara is an organizational form that "invites and protects a thousand abuses," then he should direct his animus against the state as such, whose income stream is predicated on a squishy reading of the Eighth Commandment. The *state* is a moral hazard, if there ever was one. If one does not like the partnership between the taxing state, which is intrinsically rights-violating, and limited liability corporation, which is only accidentally so, it is not rational to abolish the latter in favor of the former. Certainly Mr. Ferrara provides no argument for that preference.

Mr. Ferrara should consider that if there were no attractive helm of state for them to influence or seize, *all* LLCs would be utterly exposed to the rigors of the free market with no "Sugar Daddy" Federal Reserve System to bail them out should they fail. There would, for example, be no non-market regulatory burdens and taxes at all, let alone of a magnitude that only the biggest market players can afford to pay. But if those barriers to market entry were lifted, "expiration dates" on the dominance of those larger firms would materialize on their backsides.

Anarcho-Catholics join Mr. Ferrara in supporting the separation of corporation and state. We part company, however, over the probability of success as long while the state exists. There was never a time when the economically wealthy and the politically powerful did not form a symbiotic relationship, with members of each group morphing into members of the other, perverting both into social parasites. People who, like Mr. Ferrara, claim to favor genuinely free markets, as distinct from today's hampered markets, should join our effort to "hamper the hamperer" and, frankly, phase it out. For as small as it was a century ago (in comparison to today), the Federal Government was not then so small as to be overlooked by the financiers who conspired to form the Federal Reserve System, a story that Mr. Ferrara will tell in his tenth sketch—and then, like the drunk who, sick after ten consecutive cocktails, swears, *"That's it! No more ice for me!,"* fails to draw the anti-statist moral therefrom. If certain large LLCs that benefit from the State are the mainstay of the State, then they will never keep their mitts off it. And they will resist with all their might the formation of any State they do not control. The only remedy, as we see it, is cold turkey: *"No more State for you guys . . . ever!"*

We must also remember that the State is effectively an LLC—"on steroids," so to speak: it is a Hellmouth that recognizes no limits to its appetites. In the end, however, it is but a configuration of imperfect men, one which other imperfect men can disband if they would only set their mind to it.

Mr. Ferrara closes this section with an hypothesis about the moral breakdown in society, one that cannot wait for the appropriate time and place for hypothetical expression:

> The publicly held corporation thus involves the same morally deadly disjunction between "public" and "private" morality exhibited by the secular State of political modernity—the disjunction that underlies

the Austro-libertarian "ethics of liberty" and post-Enlightenment.

The corporation and the "free" market, as the Austrians call it, are perfect together. In one sense the "free" market of corporate activity, which has never been without its coercive partner, the secular State, is indeed free: free from all moral constraint, as any viewing of television for a few hours will demonstrate with sickening impact. (26-27)

Still in his arbitrary mode, Mr. Ferrara asserts that that disjunction is "morally deadly" without specifying the fatal ingredient. Perhaps he expects his readers to just nod their heads in unison when he writes this way, and perhaps most of them do as expected. But such throw-away lines come under the microscope here.

Now, there is a sense in which Austro-libertarians deny that disjunction: the moral quality of an action does not depend on whether state personnel engage in it. If A may not steal, then B may not steal, not even if B claims he's ordained by God to steal. Not even if A and C, and D, and . . . n endorse B's claim to have the right to pick their pockets. But that is probably not Mr. Ferrara's point.

He says he looks to the LLC for the source of televised moral degeneracy (among other species). If only agents of the "public"—preferably Catholics—would subject the "private" to moral constraint! But would Catholics get to do the subjecting? (Should they even *want* to, in the light of Matthew 20:25?) And since that has been tried before, one hopes that Mr. Ferrara would tell us why things would be different the next time. (We charitably assume he does not think the last time left nothing to be desired.)

The *non*-secular State of yore, after all, the one whose personnel often professed Christ with their lips and betrayed Him with their deeds—no shortage of that discrepancy today!—

has at least an ambiguous record on this score. The professedly Christian monarchs and princes of those confessional states may have been restrained in their behavior, but we suspect that their comparative restraint was mostly a function of technological limitations.

Mr. Ferrara does not, at least here, essay an account of the role of philosophical ideas in moral decline, but it is hardly obvious that there is a simple answer to the question of why his late, lamented Christendom fell apart, with the help of both friend and foe. The Protestant revolt? Against what was it in revolt? The scientific revolution? What role did the Church's favoring of mechanism over Aristotelianism and hermeticism play in that episode? Mr. Ferrara will not go there. He's content to blame the LLC. Or the Enlightenment. Or greed. And this is supposed to pass for Catholic social analysis.

Chapter 39

Railroading the Free Market

M r. Ferrara's brief eighth historical "sketch"
8. The government-subsidized transportation
network (27)

is surreal in its virtual repetition of Murray Rothbard's
case against government subsidies to corporations without
"connecting to the dots" for the reader who fail to see how this
expose undermines the Austro-libertarian defense of the free
market. One would think it tends to exonerate Austro-
libertarians of the Carsonian charge of vulgarity.

When given the opportunity, no Austro-libertarian fails to
condemn such subsidies on the explicitly Rothbardian grounds
Mr. Ferrara adduces. He then delivers this revelation:

Without government-subsidized transportation systems,
the modern "free" market could never have developed
as it did nor continue to function as it does. (27)

And Rothbardians, those "vulgar libertarians" who have
created almost a cottage-industry of historical revisionism
regarding the career of Lincoln the Corporate Railroad Lawyer,
join Mr. Ferrara in condemning anything that interferes with
free markets.

What we wait in vain for Mr. Ferrara to acknowledge, however, is the significance of the reality of persons who generally seek mutually agreeable terms of trade even if they also irrationally pursue opportunities to cheat and plunder each other. We acknowledge both sets of facts, while affirming the eminent reality of free markets, a reality that asserts itself through the major and minor distortions, betrayals, and perversions committed by every kind of market player, rich and not-so-rich.[158] The freedom is exercised in spite of the subsidies.

Mr. Ferrara doesn't need more than these three paragraphs, however, to display once again his already well-documented penchant for misdirection:

> Even Rothbard notes that the railroad companies "received vast subsidies of land from the government: not only rights-of-way for their roads, but fifteen-mile tracts on either side of the line." Through federal, state and local government land grants and outright land seizures by eminent domain as authorized by the "takings clause" of the Fifth Amendment, tort law exemptions that insulated railroads from damages liability, the issuance of government railway bonds, the use of tax dollars to construct and maintain interstate highways, and numerous other government favors, it is the State— not the "free" market—that has "built an artificial ecosystem to which large-scale, mass-production industry was best 'adapted'" while small local firms were fatally disadvantaged by new, government-subsidized economies of scale.

> This was only part of the process by which "the growth of big government continued to parallel that

---

[158] We acknowledge both sets, but do not equate them ontologically: distortions, perversions, and betrayals are dependent, even parasitic, upon what they distort, pervert, and betray. Wealth, to be looted, must first be produced.

of big business, introducing newer and larger-scale forms of political intervention . . . to insulate the giant corporation from the market forces that would otherwise have destroyed it."

To his credit, Mr. Ferrara quotes approvingly and accurately from Murray Rothbard's *Power and Market*—perhaps the most hardcore anarchocapitalist economics textbook ever written— but then unfortunately creates the impression that his next two quotes are from the same source.[159] In fact they are from *The Homebrew Industrial Revolution* by Carson the Accuser, a fact discovered only in the reference notes.[160] Rothbard's position on large-scale or small-scale industry is not quoted. We cannot recall where he has ever written on it. That aside, why would Mr. Ferrara not make it clear that the "Pope" of the Vulgar Libertarian Church and Carson are on the same page when it comes to the free market and anti-market government subsidies? Would such forthrightness undermine his propagandistic purpose?

---

[159] Murray Rothbard, *Power & Market*, Chapter 3, "Triangular Intervention," M. Conservation Laws. Freely available on mises.org.

[160] Mr. Ferrara's ellipsis obscures Mr. Carson's phrase, "to address the corporate economy's increasing tendencies toward destabilization," which omission makes one wonder whether Mr. Ferrara is uncertain about whether there is such a thing as a "corporate economy." There is certainly such a thing as an economy progressively destabilized by governmental interference. Kevin Carson, *The Homebrew Industrial Revolution: A Low-Overhead Manifesto*. Booksurge, 2010, 23. dl.dropboxusercontent.com/u/4116166/NewHomeBrew.pdf

Chapter 40

(Fan)Fanning the Embers of Fascism

T he next sketch continues Mr. Ferrara's recitation of historical examples of some capitalists seeking and winning governmentally granted privileges, subsidies, and other non-market advantages over their market rivals—as though such stories bore on the Catholic reception of Austro-Libertarianism:

> 7. The use of State power to impose the legal and social uniformity required for "efficient" large-scale commerce (27)

to which our by-now equally boring response is that such episodes only reinforce our case for ethically regarding the State—no matter how "constitutionally limited," no matter how "small" by today's measure—as an unacceptable moral hazard.[161] Here's the latest laundry list:

---

[161] Catholics wary of drawing an anti-state, i.e., anarchistic, conclusion should remember that man's fallen nature and the nature of the state as the territorial monopolist of the means of violence form a fateful combination. It is just *because* "men are not angels" that they should not be trusted to exercise that monopoly. Anarcho-Catholics are happy to have a discussion about how social order is to be maintained in the absence of such a

Capitalists were instrumental in achieving State-imposed uniform legal codes and weights and measures, the abolition of the guilds and other intermediary social bodies, the repeal of the Sunday closing laws and legal religious holidays, the repeal of laws against usury, and a host of other State-imposed "reforms" that cleared away all the underbrush in the once Christian socioeconomic landscape that had interfered with the business of buying cheap and selling dear over as large a territory as possible. Capitalism thus achieved, through the exercise of State power, "still greater advantages from being able to expand over the wide territories of a State in which the feudal sub-structures were demolished one by one." (27-28)

Our first reaction to this was: *"So, for crying out loud, work to abolish the State instead of trying to influence it!"* Taking these items on a case-by-case basis, we notice problems that the market solves when it is free to (e.g., standards), and others that are not problems at all ("usury"). Mr. Ferrara's generalization "were instrumental in achieving" is a template of conceptual laziness that dilutes any content poured into it. If he laments the passing of "feudal substructures" (along with their intertwining royal and papal intrigues) or prefers buying dear and selling cheap to the alternative arrangement, he should step up to the microphone and remove any doubt.

---

monopoly. We only ask that those who see it as indispensable to such maintenance entertain our skepticism for an evening. We remind them the State does not "abuse" its power the way a bad parent abuses his or her parental authority or a bishop his ecclesiastical. As a network of interpersonal relations, the state is constituted and sustained by aggression, the initiation of violence against persons and their property. It is intrinsically, not accidentally, a rights-violating agency. The monopoly it enjoys in the provision of defense, police, and judicial services only underscores the state's constitutional instability and the incoherence attaching to "the state" as a summary term for such diverse activities as taxation, defense, and ensuring the delivery of mail.

Our second reaction was based on what we found in the reference note appended to the concluding quote, whose author is not identified in the main text. We were surprised, at least initially, to his seemingly nonchalant reference to Amintori Fanfani's *Catholicism, Protestantism, and Capitalism*, an erudite anti-capitalist tome that should give its readers, especially Catholics among them, a whiff of the ideological hothouse within which early 20th-century anti-capitalism grew.[162]

Mr. Ferrara's note gives the impression that *Catholicism, Protestantism, and Capitalism* is a new book, as it bears a publication date of 2005 and the imprint of IHS Press, a pro-"Catholic Social Thought" outfit after Mr. Ferrara's own heart. (In the next sketchy story, he obscures more than identifies Fanfani, but let's not get ahead of ourselves.) In fact, it was first published 70 years earlier. At the Cattolica del Sacro Cuore, from which Fanfani graduated in 1932, Fanfani wrote a thesis that was published three years later as *Cattolicismo e Protestantismo nella formazione storica del capitalismo*, also published in the United States by Sheed & Ward as *Catholicism, Protestantism, and Capitalism*.

The Thirties were a busy time for Signore Fanfani. In the late 1930s, a few years after this Italian Fascist Party member's book was published (while Mussolini's troops were mustard-gassing Haile Selassie's), he found regular outlet for his literary production in a magazine with the charming title *La Difesa della Raza* (*The Defense of the Race*), whose first issue appeared in August 1938.[163] Furthering the goals of its movers and shakers was a "Manifesto della razza," which many public figures and

---

[162] Coincidentally, Murray Rothbard prepared a brief report bearing that title for the Volker Fund. In 2004 the text was published online under the title, "Catholicism, Protestantism, and Capitalism," following a prefatory note by historian Joseph Stromberg. Memo to Richard C. Corneulle, August 8, 1957.
www.lewrockwell.com/rothbard/rothbard56.html

[163] One ordinarily shouldn't judge a periodical by its covers, but an internet search for this one's will yield pictures worth thousands of words.

academics, including our devout Catholic social scientist, signed.[164] The Manifesto quickly metamorphosed into a law in July 1938 that deprived Italian Jews of their citizenship, thereby provoking the displeasure of Pope Pius XII with equal alacrity. In short, to say that Amintore Fanfani was a Fascist is not to engage in name-calling. According to the July 14, 1958 issue of *Time* magazine, Fanfani "once wrote" that

> the European continent will be organized into a vast supranational area guided by Italy and Germany. Those areas will take authoritarian governments and synchronize their constitutions with Fascist principles.[165]

"Once" was probably fifteen to twenty years before that article was written. Certainly, no Italian dreamt such dreams after July 25, 1943, the day King Victor Emmanuel III had Mussolini arrested, a month and a half before Italy's surrender to the Allies. Signore Fanfani was probably not even in town at the time: having been drafted into the service of the lost cause of that grand synchronization, he fled to Switzerland to teach Italian expatriates and conceptually alchemize his fascisto-Catholic or "corporatist" ideology as "Christian Democracy." This former Fascist cheerleader, who continued to expound Fascist principles as late as 1942, when his anthology *Il Significato del corporativismo* appeared, reinvented himself as Catholic Prime Minister of post-war Italy five times (not to mention numerous other governmental posts).

Mr. Ferrara didn't think any of this was worth bringing to his readers' attention.

Some scholars entertain the possibility of a less than enthu-siastically Fascist Fanfani. According to MIT Political Science Professor Richard J. Samuels, for example: "Some historians do not

---

[164] See http://en.wikipedia.org/wiki/Manifesto_of_Race.

[165] "Italy: Moving to the Left," *Time*, July 14, 1958.
www.time.com/time/magazine/article/0,9171,868573,00.html

believe that Fanfani was ever a committed fascist, e.g., Pombeni 1997, 173. See also Bocci, 1999."[166]

Not having those sources at hand, of course, we cannot yet evaluate their "beliefs" about someone else's "commitment." We would, of course, be interested to see how their considerations could reverse, or even bevel the sharp edges of, the unflattering verdict to which the facts seem to lead. Certainly, in that Fascist Party member's own mind, the public evidence of his commitment, which included signing the Manifesto della Razza in 1938, was enough to induce Fanfani to flee Italy five years later, that is, once the military tide had turned irreversibly against Il Duce. Until we do see how, Mr. Ferrara's promotion of Fanfani's chameleon-like adaptation to various forms of the demonic state remains grist for the anarcho-Catholic mill.

Fanfani makes another appearance in TCATL in Mr. Ferrara's eighth historical sketch, this time by name. We will get to him presently.

8. Corporate cost externalization: the "nanny state."

Here he exposes the alleged hypocrisy (or perhaps merely the inability to remember "from one moment to the next") of Austro-libertarians who rail against the welfare-warfare state "while failing to mention the role of corporations in its emergence and persistence." (28) By now you probably know how this goes: first, the overgeneralization dressed in scare quotes followed by a *mélange* of extraneous matters, each of which needing a reply:

> Under the corporate status quo of our "free" market society, which institutionally rejects the Catholic concept of the just or living wage (*see* Chapter 12),

---

[166] Richard J. Samuels, *Machiavelli's Children: Leaders and Their Legacies in Italy and Japan* (Cornell University Press), 2003, 395 n 165. Professor Samuels cites Paolo Pombeni, "I partiti e la politica dal 1948 al 1963." *La Repubblica*, Vol. 5 of *Storia d'Italia*, ed. G. Sabbatucci and V. Vidotto (Bari: Laterza, 1997), 127-251; and Maria Bocci, *Oltre Lo Stato Liberale: Ipotesi Su Politica E Societa Nel Dibattito Cattolico Tra Fascismo E Democrazia* (Roma: Bulzoni, 1999).

corporations are able to "exter-nalize" onto govern-ment (i.e., the taxpayer) not only transportation costs, as discussed above, but also the costs of supporting wage-dependent employees, including health and retirement benefits. (28)

The salient "failure to mention" here is Mr. Ferrara's, whose yellow journalism overlooks Murray Rothbard, for his exposure of this very externalization (why the scare quotes?) was a major theme of his scholarly career. Here is a sample of his thought on this matter:

> Under cover of the Civil War, then, the Lincoln Administration pushed through the following radical economic changes: a high protective tariff on imports; high federal excise taxes on liquor and tobacco (which they regarded as "sin taxes"); massive subsidies to newly established transcontinental railroads, in money per mile of construction and in enormous grants of land all this fueled by a system of naked corruption; federal income tax; the abolition of the gold standard and the issue of irredeemable fiat money ("greenbacks") to pay for the war effort; and a quasi-nationalization of the previous relatively free banking system, in the form of the National Banking System established in acts of 1863 and 1864.
>
> In this way, the system of minimal government, free trade, no excise taxes, a gold standard, and more or less free banking of the 1840s and 1850s was replaced by its opposite. And these changes were largely permanent. The tariffs and excise taxes remained; the orgy of subsidies to uneconomic and overbuilt transcontinental railroads was ended only with their collapse in the Panic of 1873, but the effects lingered on in the secular decline of the railroads during the 20th century. . . .

The chief architect of this system was Jay Cooke, long-time financial patron of the corrupt career of Republican Ohio politician Salmon P. Chase. When Chase became Secretary of the Treasury under Lincoln, he promptly appointed his patron Cooke monopoly underwriter of all government bonds issued during the war. Cook, who became a multi-millionaire investment banker from this monopoly grant and became dubbed "the Tycoon," added greatly to his boodle by lobbying for the National Banking Act, which provided a built-in market for his bonds, since the national banks could inflate credit by multiple amounts on top of the bonds.[167]

The article concludes:

The northeastern Republican Establishment is still cartelizing, controlling, regulating, handing out contracts to business favorites, and bailing out beloved crooks and losers. It is still playing the old "partnership" game—and still, of course, at our expense.[168]

Rothbard's remedy, of course, was the opposite of Mr. Ferrara's "freedom through moral restraint" program. It was rather *to free markets from the State by reducing and ultimately abolishing the latter.*

---

[167] Murray N. Rothbard, "Government-Business 'Partnerships,'" appears in Rothbard, *Making Economic Sense*, Second Edition, 2006, Ludwig von Mises Institute, 190-192. Freely available on mises.org.

[168] Ibid., 192. ". . . what does one do with the legion of pro-New Deal, -Fair Deal, -Great Society big businessmen: the Paul Hoffmans, the Averell Harrimans, the Rockefeller brothers? Neither the liberal explanation that these were unusually 'enlightened' or 'intelligent' sports, nor the conservative psycho-smear that they were brainwashed into feeling guilty about their wealth by liberal prep-school teachers, was particularly compelling. Especially when everyone knew that such government intervention as tariffs or import quotas on steel, for instance, were lobbied for, neither by altruists nor by the brainwashed guilt-ridden, but by steel manufacturers anxious to secure their profits from more efficient foreign competition." Rothbard, "The Business-Government Alliance," *Inquiry*, January 1983. http://www.lewrockwell.com/rothbard/rothbard99.html

As it becomes clearer with each page that Mr. Ferrara offers only fallacy-infected, anti-capitalist litanies, we will take the occasion they provide to push the antithesis between his viewpoint and ours. His authorities are clues to the affinities that his Distributism bears to one form or another socialism, be it corporatism, guildism, democratic industrial organization, or, we now see in the case of Amintore Fanfani, Fascism. We are aware of Mr. Ferrara's formal denial of socialism, if no other reason than that Pope Pius XI declared in *Quadrogesimo Anno* that "No one can be at the same time a sincere Catholic and a true socialist." Mr. Ferrara is nothing if not a sincere Catholic. Since, however, his criticisms display the same economic ignorance that distinguishes franker socialists, draped in the same historical romance, then his denial rings hollow. Now, back to Fanfani.

> The renowned Italian economist Amintore Fanfani, who served as Prime Minister of Italy and President of the United Nations General Assembly, summarized, this truth about capitalism thus: "The State, by carrying out public works in a capitalist-liberal régime, lessens the risks of producers, and almost plays the part of an insurance system." (28)

Readers had to wait until Mr. Ferrara quoted Fanfani a second time to get an insight into the meaning of this appeal to authority. Just why did Mr. Ferrara cite him? Because he was a scholar, a specialist in economic history, who taught at the Universities or Milan and Venice? Mr. Ferrara never mentions those facts. Mr. Ferrara doesn't even tell us that Fanfani was a *Catholic*, arguably relevant to Mr. Ferrara's purposes. Does he believe that "Amintore Fanfani" is a household name, like, for example, "Abraham Lincoln," in which case further denotation would insult the reader? We learn a bit of Fanfani's post-war career but not why we should pay heed to the utterances of Italian Prime Ministers or Presidents of the U.N. General Assembly.

Most remarkably, he doesn't mention Fanfani's career as a fascisto-Catholic theoretician (before he reinvented himself as a center-left Christian Democrat).[169] Remarkably, we say, for in the 21st century one does not responsibly quote such a figure without also distancing himself from that political commitment. One so distances himself especially if one is a Catholic—unless, of course, one is attracted to aspects of Italian fascism. We're anarcho-Catholics. If you're a fascisto-Catholic, you should't hope no one will notice that you're quoting an earlier fascisto-Catholic. If you're not, however, then you should take pains to ensure that no one draws that fateful inference from your words.

---

[169] In *Machiavelli's Children,* Richard J. Samuels reveals facts about Mr. Ferrara's expert that in turn raise questions that are neither anticipated nor answered.

> The Christian doctrine of "voluntarism" was his [Fanfani's] connection to fascism. On this view, the economy is subordinate to politics, and politics is subordinate to Christian morality. . . . Corporatism was a fundamentally reactionary "third way" between capitalism and communism that suited Catholics and fascists alike. 250

> Although his central concern was social justice, he was not beyond nationalist sentiment. Fanfani celebrated Italian imperialism in Ethiopia, for bringing "Roman virtue combined with Christian consecration" to Ethiopia. He praised Mussolini, whom he called "the conqueror of all in the struggle for civilization," for inculcating a new patriotism among youth and for raising Italy's stature abroad. . . . In 1937 he wrote that he did not consider fascism a form of tyranny because it limited "only the noxious and dysfunctional liberties." Totalitarianism, he argued, was acceptable because it organized the inequalities among citizens for desirable collective ends and subordinated rights to duties." 250

> Fanfani continued to write of its [Fascism's] virtues as late as 1942, arguing that it had succeeded traditional corporatism with its powerful ideas for "organic reconstruction of society and cross-class cooperation." At this point Fanfani was convinced that fascist corporatism echoed the moral teachings of the Catholic Church, a "coincidence [that] should not serve to diminish the originality and merit of fascist corporatism, but [that] should demonstrate the profound sense of justice that animates the new [fascist] doctrine." 251.

> Fanfani had been attracted to fascism in part because fascist corporatism was consistent with Catholic social doctrine and in part because fascism was politically dominant. He reinvented himself as a center-left Christian Democrat at a time when democracy had become the only means to realize his social doctrine or to achieve political power. Samuels, *op. cit.,* 252.

This evidence certainly helps position TCATL within a longer tradition!

As Fanfani was a scholar, a note on his contribution to the current state of economics education is germane. For light on the roots of one of Fanfani's ideas, we once again turn to Murray Rothbard, this time his magisterial *Austrian History of Economic Thought*. He traced several symptoms of the economic ignorance on display in TCATL to the 14th-century theologian and mathematician Heinrich von Langenstein the Elder. [170] This gentleman was rescued from obscurity by scholars who were unfortunately impressed, not by his expertise in divinity or math, but rather by his economic notions.

In his entertaining way, Rothbard exposed the ageless rationale for the intervention known as price-fixing—the desirability of maintaining one's station in life, draped in moralizing solicitude for the poor. Elements of 20th-century corporatism and guildism are discernible. Rothbard shows the power of ideas, especially bad ones, to influence scientific inquiry for centuries:

> Von Langenstein was scarcely important in his own or at a later day; his great importance is solely that he was plucked out of well-deserved obscurity by late-19th-century socialist and state-corporatist historians, who used his station-in-life fatuity to conjure up a totally distorted vision of the Catholic Middle Ages. That era, so the myth ran, was solely governed by the view that each man can only charge the just price to maintain him in his presumably divinely appointed station in life. In that way, these historians glorified a nonexistent society of status in which each person and group found himself in a harmonious hierarchical structure, undisturbed by market relations or capitalist greed. This nonsensical view of the Middle Ages and of scholastic doctrine was first propounded by German socialist and state

---

[170] Henry of Langenstein, *[The Original] Catholic Encyclopedia*, 1907-1912, Volume VII, 236-237. oce.catholic.com/oce/browse-page-scans.php?id=5cd13aec0f88587e04855574fb39821f

corporatist historians Wilhelm Roscher and Werner Sombart in the late 19th century, and *it was then seized upon by such influential writers as the Anglican Socialist Richard Henry Tawney and the Catholic corporatist scholar and politician Amintore Fanfani.* Finally, this view, based only on the doctrines of one obscure and heterodox scholastic, was enshrined in conventional histories of economic thought, where it was seconded by the free market but fanatically anti-Catholic economist Frank Knight and his followers in the now highly influential Chicago School.[171]

How irenic of Rothbard to describe Fanfani so politely and how interesting that Mr. Fanfani's partner in this intellectual escapade was the Anglican Socialist Tawney, whom Mr. Ferrara has drawn upon.

---

[171] Murray N. Rothbard, "The Doctrines of One Obscure and Heterodox Scholastic," *Mises Daily*, January 8, 2010. mises.org/daily/3923; excerpted from Rothbard, *An Austrian Perspective on the History of Economic Thought, Vol. 1: Economic Thought before Adam Smith*, 78. Freely available on mises.org.

Chapter 41

Scrooge on Externalization

Continuing his eighth sketchy story, Mr. Ferrara rails against state-facilitated externalization or socialization of the cost of doing business. In his attempt to make this a case against the free market, however, Mr. Ferrara has, as we have seen, summoned to the witness stand an unrepentant Catholic Fascist. Remarkably, he then reinforces his argument by quoting the words Charles Dickens put into the mouth of Ebenezer Scrooge in *A Christmas Carol.* You know, where he suggests that the poor repair to the prisons and workhouses of Victorian England, etc:

> Well, I'll be tougher than the toughies, and sharper
> than the sharpies—and I'll make my money square!

All right, that was Scrooge McDuck.[172] That cartoon character's lines may be more irrelevant to the matter at hand than Ebenezer's, but not much. For the matter at hand is Mr. Ferrara's accusation that

---

[172] Brother to Viennese polymath Ludwig von Drake. I owe my awareness of this genealogy to Dave Rogers.

. . . it is precisely Scrooge's reliance on the State to do what he should do in justice that Austrians defend. (28)

Yet Mr. Ferrara does not—because he could not—quote any Austro-libertarian to the effect that employers either (a) morally owe their employees certain welfare benefits or (b) should evade that "obligation" by persuading their employees to join the welfare rolls. The Austrian condemnation of the welfare state in all its incarnations does not allow for that inference. Let's overlook that typical shortcoming, however, and instead make sure we understand the apparent slander: Austrians allegedly defend the fictional Scrooge's reliance on the State (which they want to dismantle) to do what that fictional miser was allegedly morally obliged to do.

Mr. Ferrara's implicit slander that any given capitalist is presumptively a meanie—a Scrooge—informs the tenor of this section. And he is not finished: here he is merely foreshadowing the chapter (15) that he will devote to Michael Levin's contrarian, pro-market interpretation of Dickens' classic. Mr. Ferrara's slander is not based on evidence we can examine, but rather trades on the negative emotional charge attaching to "Ebenezer Scrooge" enhanced by (as we shall see) a poorly documented anecdote. As there's no real defendant here, no defense is required.[173] We wonder why Mr. Ferrara didn't omit this appeal to the fictional and instead move directly from Fanfani to one of his favorite whipping boys, Wal-Mart:

> A perfect example of how the "free" market uses government to "externalize" its operating costs so that it can scrimp on employee compensation is the declaration by Wal-Mart's CEO that Wal-Mart employees without medical coverage should consider public assistance. (28)

---

[173] Mr. Ferrara once before treated us to his sophomoric use of the novelist when he referred to Albert Jay Nock's unfortunate reliance on Dickens' *Hard Times* to express disapproval of the enclosure of the English commons.

What does this have to do with Austro-Libertarianism? Markets, whether "free" or free, don't use government. Individuals use government to seek power over other individuals, and historically the State has served as the convenient facilitator of such exploitation. We Austro-libertarians don't think that moral hazard should exist.

Mr. Ferrara insinuates that the interest of big business in getting others to pay their costs of doing business was the prime mover of the rise of the welfare state *in America*, which would not, of course, explain its earlier rise in Europe. We agree that the effort to externalize costs was *one* factor, but hardly the only one. It is certainly not the kind of explanation that should satisfy a Catholic intellectual. Unless one is committed to Marxist—or Beardsian, quasi-Marxist—interpretation of history, one will look for ideological drivers.[174] The silent, unsupported premise of Mr. Ferrara's indictment of Wal-Mart is that "medical coverage" is somehow a morally necessary part of an employee's compensation. Mr. Ferrara has not even attempted to show that it is any more such a part than is a Social Security "insurance premium."

Compensation—money paid to "compensate" employees for the leisure they forego when they produce goods or services their employer prefers to that money—is determined by market forces, including the supply of and the demand for their particular skill sets. It is also, as we have argued, a function of the capital investment that increases the productivity of labor, which in turn increases the wages or "compensation" that labor can command.

Market forces—not ethical desire or the imperatives of justice—also determine the production of the goods and services for which wage earners exchange the money they receive in wages, including health care insurance. Markets cannot—

---

174 Murray Rothbard has shown how much ideology Mr. Ferrara's economic determinism omits in "Origins of the Welfare State in America," *Journal of Libertarian Studies*, 12:2, Fall 1996, 193-232. This is the text of a paper delivered at the Mises Institute's "Evils of the Welfare State" conference, Lake Bluff, Illinois, April 30—May 2, 1993. Freely available on mises.org.

logically cannot—be blamed for political interference with markets, which distorts pricing. One form that such interference takes is the mandatory pooling of people who incur greater risks to their health through their lifestyle choices with those who incur lesser. That is, the same coverage is offered both to those who don't eat well and exercise and to those who do.[175] But to the degree that health is subject to one's control, to that degree the acquisition of an adverse health condition is not a risk that can be pooled as is, say, the occurrence of a catastrophic accident. Yet insurance underwriters get raked over the coals every time they insist on following the logic of pooled risk rather than that of welfare benefits.

Such interference has made health care insurance coverage virtually unaffordable for most people.[176] Many of them conclude, unfortunately, more emotionally than rationally, that such coverage is not something they must either (a) pay for themselves or (b) receive as charity from others. It is rather something that is theirs as a matter of justice, as Mr. Ferrara suggests. This moral imperative does not, however, immunize companies from the central bank-spawned alternation of boom and bust, and during the bust, when many of them are forced to cut costs, including those associated with their compensation packages, healthcare insurance coverage is vulnerable. But Mr. Ferrara has not demonstrated that there is any presumptive right to such coverage: as far as we can tell, that's just his dogma, and therefore it is but another form that compensation has taken historically and can one day cease to take.

---

[175] As Hans-Hermann Hoppe tersely put it: "Subsidies for the ill and diseased breed illness and disease, and promote carelessness, indigence, and dependency. If we eliminate them, we would strengthen the will to live healthy lives and to work for a living." "A Four-Step Health-Care Solution," *The Free Market*, Vol. 11, No. 4, April 1993. mises.org/freemarket_detail.aspx?control=279

[176] See the resources cited in Thomas E. Woods, Jr., "Find It Hard to Defend Free-Market Medicine?," TomWoods.com, October 27, 2011. www.tomwoods.com/blog/find-it-hard-to-defend-free-market-medicine/

If, in fairness to former Wal-Mart CEO Lee Scott whom Mr. Ferrara seems to quote, you would like to read for yourself what he said, even what else he may have said immediately before or after his alleged comparative judgment

> In some of our states, the public program may actually be a better value with relatively high income limits to qualify and low premiums (28-29)

do not look to Mr. Ferrara. He fulfills his obligation as a propagandist once he has held up his target for mockery, sourcing only the latter's adversary: his reference note cites something called wakeupwalmart.com/facts, but that link does not take one to the transcript of Mr. Scott's speech mentioned in Mr. Ferrara's note. (331 n. 51) Rather, it redirects to the site of the United Food and Commercial Workers International Union.

If fact, do not bother to look anywhere for the origin of those words, which seem to reproduce themselves, meme-like, across the Internet. On the Wiki article on criticism of Wal-Mart one can find a contemporary source for this alleged speech-fragment, but its linked reference, Susan Bucher's impartially titled study, "Walmart: the $288 billion welfare queen," *Tallahassee Democrat,* April 19, 2005, also redirects to that union site. In short, Mr. Ferrara's "perfect example" is an anecdote, from which nothing may be reliably inferred.

For the sake of argument, however, let's assume that Mr. Scott said what he is quoted as saying and that it fairly represents his attitude toward the "public program," that is, the welfare rolls. Let's also assume the veracity of the facts Mr. Ferrara appended to Mr. Scott's words:

> And this from a company whose CEO earns more than $25 million annually and whose founding family is worth more than $80 billion collectively thank to the labor of the "sales associates" Wal-Mart declines to provide with medical coverage .... (29)

The undefended implicit premise here seems to be: "And employers who are worth that much and pay their officers that much ought to pay larger compensation packages than those mutually agreed upon." But that "ought" begs the question.

> While corporations are externalizing these operating costs [Mr. Ferrara writes], wage earners are paying for them almost entirely. In fiscal year 2008, for example, federal personal income taxes and payroll taxes combined represented 81% of federal tax revenues, while the corporate tax represented only 12%. (29)

Tax avoidance is everyone's game, however, and we should not be surprised that those with more money and power will be better at protecting their money from the taxman than those with less. So, in the interest of equity as well as justice, why not abolish all such systems by which the few loot the many and find a more intelligent way to pay for socially necessary goods and services? Let's try free markets. On this very point, we are pleased to note *partial* agreement between Mr. Ferrara and ourselves. After imputing another silly "panic button" to us (*"So, you want to soak the corporations?"*), he "replies":

> . . . this is not an argument for increased corporate taxation. Rather, it is an argument for *abolition* of the personal income tax *and* the federal corporate income tax . . . (29)

Actually, we haven't seen much of an *argument* at all, but if Mr. Ferrara wishes to number himself among the tax abolitionists, however, we will take him at his word. But then he drops the other shoe. (Same sentence; take a deep breath.)

> . . . followed by payment of just wages and benefits to employees in the Catholic spirit of commerce, along with privatized retirement plans and public provision only for those truly in need, and then only at the local level. (29)

Hmmm. How will that be paid for? He will attempt an argument for this opinion later, but here it is a gratuitous, question-begging assertion, meriting only gratuitous denial.

* * *

The rest of Mr. Ferrara's sketch concerns the role of big business in the creation of the welfare state and its infamous socialistic "programs," an involvement we lament and deplore, but to the origin of which there was much more by way of ideological inspiration than he shows any awareness of or interest in.[177] We do, however, question what this indictment of "the Keynesian model of the managed economy," as he refers to it, has to do with the defense of free markets, hampered as they are by the implementation of that model. He tops off his narrative with this flourish:

> . . . every single Western nation today . . . combines a "free" market of privileged corporations with government assistance programs by which corporate costs for employees are externalized. "We're all Keynesians now," as Milton Friedman has famously observed. (29)

---

[177] Rothbard writes:

J. Douglas Brown was head of Princeton's IRC-created Industrial Relations Department, and was the point man for the CES [FDR's Rockefeller-dominated Committee on Economic Security.—A.F.] in designing the old-age pension plan for Social Security. Brown, along with the big-business members of the Advisory Council, was particularly adamant that no employers escape the taxes for the old-age pension scheme. Brown was frankly concerned that small business not escape the cost-raising consequences of these social security tax obligation. In this way, *big businesses, who were already voluntarily providing costly old-age pensions to their employees, could use the federal government to force their small-business competitors into paying for similar, costly, programs.* Thus, Brown explained, in his testimony before the Senate Finance Committee in 1935, that the great boon of the employer "contribution" to old age pensions is that it makes uniform throughout industry a minimum cost of providing old-age security and protects the more liberal employer now providing pensions from the competition of the employer who otherwise fires the old person without a pension when superannuated. It levels up cost of old-age protection on both the progressive employer and the unprogressive employer.

"Origins of the Welfare State in American." Our emphasis.

But he has not shown that they are necessarily "corporate costs" at all. They are simply various goods and services (e.g., "social security" financed by a Ponzi scheme) that people demand through the political system, which large corporations effectively control. The latter warrants the aim of abolishing, not the corporate form of organization, but rather the State.

As for his use of Friedman, Mr. Ferrara's source for his words is not the December 31, 1965 issue of *Time* magazine, which is where they first appeared, but rather (once again) a book by John Médaille (331 n. 53). The latter author, however, merely reproduced the fragment of Friedman's words that President Nixon echoed when he closed the U.S. "gold window" in 1971. Words "as quoted" by Médaille, however, is apparently good enough for Mr. Ferrara. We have seen how unreliable that can be. Let's explore that defect in this instance.

Mr. Médaille wrote: "The conservative economist Milton Friedman somewhat impishly suggested 'We're all Keynesians now!'"[178] If the following qualified remark by the late dean of the Chicago School of Economics sounds like an impish suggestion to our readers' literary ears, then perhaps something is wrong with ours:

> In one sense we are all Keynesians now; in another, no one is a Keynesian any longer. We all use the Keynesian language and apparatus; none of us any longer accepts the initial Keynesian conclusions.

As for Mr. Médaille's political characterization of Friedman, Jacob Sullum writes:

> In 1994 Milton Friedman wrote a letter to *Policy Review* to complain that the magazine, then published by the Heritage Foundation, had inaccurately described his mentor and friend F.A. Hayek as a conservative. Noting that Hayek had included a postscript in his

---

[178] Médaille, *The Vocation of Business*, 79.

classic work of political philosophy, *The Constitution of Liberty*, explaining "Why I Am Not a Conservative," Friedman said, "Hayek, to the best of my belief, like myself, always considered himself a 'Whig'—a 19th century liberal, never a conservative." *Policy Review's* editor, Adam Meyerson, was unfazed. Not only was Hayek a conservative, he told Friedman, but "you are a conservative, too. Sorry."[179]

We never said Mr. Ferrara is the first practitioner of the art of persistent misquotation and mischaracterization.

---

179 Jacob Sullum, "Milton Friedman, Archliberal: Why the great free market economist was not a conservative," *TownHall.com*, November 22, 2006. Emphasis ours.

Chapter 42

Ferrara's Reserve of False Notes

M r. Ferrara's ninth sketchy story is entitled "Fractional reserve banking" (29). He joins Austro-libertarians in regarding it as a Ponzi scheme, that is, a fraud perpetuated by bankers against their customers, but does not wish to emphasize that agreement. He prefers to create the arguably slanderous impression that Austrians indict only the government's legitimizing of capitalists who engage in it.

> One of the oldest State-supported capitalist scams is the system of "fractional reserve banking," a legalized Ponzi scheme that allows banks to treat depositors' funds as the bank's own reserve against which it can "lend" out a multiple of the reserve amount, thus literally creating wealth out of nothing. This practice, a foundation of the modern capitalist social order, attained formal legal approval by the State in the English common law via judicial decisions (obtained by bank lawyers) to the effect that a bank deposit is not a bailment—an entrustment of one's property to

another for safekeeping—but rather an "investment" in the bank. (29-30)

Not bad. Of course, a bank really does lend what it creates—and expects the borrower to repay it—so it's less clear than usual what skepticism his scare quote marks are intended to express. And by increasing the quantity of money at a much lower cost than that associated with mining and refining precious metals, the bank does not so much "literally create wealth" as create money substitutes—even if they are only entries on a computerized ledger—that facilitate the transfer of wealth away from their producers to the scammer (often via the inevitable inflation). In other words, the fraction implicit in "fractional reserve banking" (FRB) is the numerical relationship of a bank's deposits to lendable assets. The bank has X, but lends more than X, e.g., X+Y. The fraction is therefore $X/X+Y$. The bank thereby effectively creates out of thin air more of its chief, if not only, productive asset.

And so, the bank risks, not its own money, but rather that of its depositor-customers. The rarely questioned premise of the whole business is that the bank may lend to B the deposited funds of A, regardless of A's understanding of his property's exposure to risk. Depositors might, for example, think that they are simply placing valuables in a warehouse for safekeeping, for which bailment the bank reasonably charges them a fee.

What one archives, stores, or warehouses, however, one may retrieve upon demand. That is not so in the case of an investment and, regardless of what they may believe, depositors are indirect co-investors in the borrowers' enterprises, sound and risky alike. At least that's what the courts will tell them, should they be naïve enough these days to take their bank to court. For that's what plaintiffs were told in 19th century courts.[180]

---

[180] We both acknowledge and deplore the role played by material beneficiaries of that "judicial finding" in determining court personnel. We suggest, however, that the answer

These days, every child knows that his "deposit" is not only warehouse inventory but also someone else's investment capital. And few children care, for Big Daddy Government says their "deposits" are "insured"—according to the fairy tale in which insurable risk attaches to a conspiracy to commit systematic fraud. And the children believe.

Since some or all of the new loans may not "perform"—especially likely during the "bust" following a central bank-generated "boom"—there might not be enough money to satisfy the demand of the (self-)deluded "depositors," whereupon the inherent bankruptcy of the banking operation is immediately exposed. It must collapse unless it is bailed out by the cartel of which the insolvent bank is a member.

Exacerbating the exposure of deposits to the risks of investment (sustained by the lullaby of FDIC "insurance") is the fact that the relationship of deposits to lendable assets is not 1/1, but rather 1/2 or 1/6 or (as in Mr. Ferrara's text) 1/9. If one makes money charging interest on a loan, one's ability to profit from lending is limited by how much of other people's money is on "deposit."

If, however, one can create money analogously to the way God created light—*Fiat lux*, as Saint Jerome rendered the Hebrew of Genesis 1:3—then one can break free of that restriction. Fiat currency supplied by the central bank sustains the moral hazard, which virtually no bank resists. Inevitably, they all feel compelled to do more "business," to decrease the value of the fraction's "quotient" further and further until the unsustainable character of the scam becomes obvious even to the bank's most gullible customers. This cannot be done with gold or any other durable, portable, divisible commodity whose utility as a medium of exchange was discovered, not by bankers, but rather by those actually involved in the exchange of goods and services on the

---

does not lie in the quixotic search for incorruptible personnel as in the demand for a free market in judicial services, which process would tend to weed out corrupt competitors.

free market. But it can be done by applying ink to paper and substituting the result for money. And it will almost certainly be done in any society that has repudiated its biblical patrimony, which includes the precept, "Ye shall have honest weights and measures" (Leviticus 19:35-36). What reigns in the land is rather: *"I will use any standard that I can fool anyone else into accepting and, if I can, get the authority of the State to ratify and reinforce by the threat of violence my designs on the wealth of others."*

Bernard Madoff's Ponzi scheme was private, and so when the U.S. economy melted down, not only did he no longer have new "investors," i.e., dupes, parading into his office, but also he also could not meet the demand of the old dupes standing in another line demanding the return of the money they entrusted to him. As he was not a dues-paying member of the banking cartel, however, there was no one to bail him out. Although one notes that financial regulators, whose powers many want to expand these days, either couldn't or wouldn't catch Madoff in the act.

And now for the snottily expressed slander:

Even a scholar of the Mises Institute recognizes that this capitalist scheme is a fraud involving a deliberate effort to create confusion in consumers' minds between strict money titles to deposited funds and mere bank IOUs. In typical Austrian fashion, however, the same scholar blames "government" as "one of the most important driving forces for the establishment of fractional-reserve banking," even as he also admits that the fractional-reserve fraud "is *not necessarily* the result of government activity" and that in some instances in the long history of this abuse "bankers themselves *took control of the government or even set up their own,*" and that "this tendency seems to be very strong in the United States." To say the least. (30; needless to say, emphasis *not* in the original.)

The scholar is Jörg Guido Hülsmann.[181] Imagine that: "even" Professor Hülsmann, the author of *The Ethics of Money Production,* would recognize fraud when he sees it! This "recognition" is hardly undermined by his claim, patently supported by scholarship, that government was "one of the most important driving forces for the establishment of fractional-reserve banking." The *establishment* of the fraud, that is, its institutionalization, requires more than greed. It requires the threat of violence against anyone who would dare compete with the fraudulent operation and thereby potentially put it out of business.[182]

The occurrence of sin must precede its institutionalization. And so there will be Bernie Madoffs until Doomsday. The question is whether FRB—a Ponzi scheme that makes Mr. Madoff's look like cookie-jar pilfering by comparison—could be institutionalized without State coercion. As Professor Hülsmann wrote in *The Ethics of Production,* the State, although not the source of the fraud or "falsification" (which is the wicked heart of fallen man), but it certainly is its great facilitator and multiplier:

> ... the legalization of false money certificates, though harmful, is virtually insignificant from a quantitative point of view, at least in comparison to the inflationary impact of legal monopolies and legal tender laws. Nevertheless this privilege is fundamental because it is the foundation of all other monetary privileges. It would seem impossible, for example, to establish legal tender laws in favor of some debased coin, or of some fractional-reserve banknote, if the latter are *per se* illegal. And thus it follows that the moral case for

---

[181] See note 46.

[182] Try using gold to pay debts in accord with Article I, Section 10 of the U.S. Constitution, in contempt of "federal reserve notes" and in defiance of legal tender laws and see what happens when your experiment comes to the attention of the Treasury Department.

invigorated the government, extending its size and scope of activities beyond what they would have been without fraudulent banking. In city-states and other communities with plebiscitarian or democratic forms of government, which facilitate political takeovers, the bankers themselves took control of the government or even set up their own. Whether the bankers reinforced cooperation with government, took it over, or set up their own, the same basic scheme of political cover-up was used: the initial violation of property rights (fraudulent banking) was covered up with increased political involvement and cooperation.

That is, while fraudulent banking is not *necessarily* the result of government activity, sometimes is an instance of the spontaneous emergence or reinforcement of government.[185] The State may not be the originator but is certainly the great facilitator and aggravator of the moral hazard, ultimately enabling its own further engorgement at the expense of its subject. This causal story, borne out by the facts, provokes the perfectly legitimate question, and not only for anarcho-capitalists, as to whether such an institution does, on balance, more harm than good.

And what about that reference to bankers taking over governments, especially American governments? It's nice that Mr. Ferrara concurs with Professor Hülsmann, but why did he suppress the Austrian scholar's other, non-American, historical example?

> This tendency [of capitalists to dominate govern-ments] seems to be very strong in the United States. Another example is republican Florence, which the Medici family came to dominate in the fifteenth and sixteenth centuries. The house of Medici had purely commercial origins in the Medici merchant company,

---

[185] Hülsmann, "Has Fractional Reserve Banking Really Passed the Market Test?," 418.

which "after the manner of these organisations from the time of their origin represented a combination of trade and banking."[186]

Ah, yes, the Medicis. Those pious Florentines certainly didn't resist the ring of power, did they! They gifted not only Europe with bankers, but also the Church with four popes, some of whom ran Rome as they did Florence. And all this during the height of Christendom of Distributist romance. But that's all right. At least they didn't enclose the commons or build factories. They just subsidized Renaissance porn![187]

* * *

Mr. Ferrara's tenth sketchy story is entitled "The Federal Reserve System" (30). We have shown that his interpretation of the Austrian case against fractional reserve banking as exonerating its capitalist prime movers is without merit. As he pursues this bootless gambit into an area in which Austrian scholars long ago distinguished themselves, he invites the suspicion that the indispensability of the State in the establishment of the relevant moral hazard is not a topic he wishes to pursue. He does this by reprising the worn-out tune that corner-cutting by some market players somehow negates the deeper social ontology of trade, the font of the eminently real free market that ever presses against the confines of statist distortion.

Mr. Ferrara's insolent tone is undiminished. Whereas before it was "even a scholar of the Mises Institute recognizes that this [fractional reserve banking] capitalist scheme is a fraud. . . .," now it's: "Even Rothbard describes it [the Fed] as a "cozy government-big bank partnership, the government-enforced banking cartel, that big bankers had long envisioned."

---

[186] *Ibid.,* n. 12. Hülsmann cites Ferdinand Schevill, *The Medici.* New York: Harper, 1949, 58.

[187] See Lynn Hunt, *The Invention of Pornography: 1500-1800,* MIT Press, 83, 86, 91, 95, 203. See also the Wiki article on that ribald recipient of Medici largesse, Pietro Aretino: en.wikipedia.org/wiki/Pietro_Aretino

(32; emphasis not in the original, as the reader by now has grown to expect.) Yes, big bankers long envisioned it, but they could not effect it without the State. The State is the *sine qua non* of this vast criminal enterprise. Mr. Ferrara obscures the key causal connection: the bankers could not have achieved their goal of expedient expansion of the money supply without first achieving the intermediary institutional goal of an enforceable cartel. The State is the enforcer.

Private cartels are not self-enforcing and therefore vulnerable to "runs," that is, demand that cannot be satisfied. That's why bankers "envisioned" their instrumental relationship to government: it backs their vision with the threat of violence. Yes, the bankers made government its partner, if not also its tool. But they always will endeavor to do that. Again, what it the great compensating advantage of this territorial monopoly of violence called the State such that we should maintain this moral hazard in business?

Rothbard had been writing about the malevolent anti-market forces behind the creation of the Fed, *many of whom started out as market players,* throughout his scholarly life. In a passage from his 1963 *America's Great Depression* we see an example of his judicious balancing of factors:

> Instead of preventing inflation by prohibiting fractional-reserve banking as fraudulent, governments have uniformly moved in the opposite direction, and have step-by-step removed these free-market checks to bank credit expansion, at the same time putting themselves in a position to direct the inflation. In various ways, they have artificially bolstered public confidence in the banks, encouraged public use of paper and deposits instead of gold (finally outlawing gold), and shepherded all the banks under one roof so that they can all expand together. *The main device for accomplishing these aims*

has been Central Banking, an institution which America
finally acquired as the Federal Reserve System in 1913.
Central Banking permitted the centralization and
absorption of gold into government vaults, greatly
enlarging the national base for credit expansion: it
also insured uniform action by the banks through
basing their reserves on deposit accounts at the
Central Bank instead of on gold.[188]

Government vaults.

The government assured Federal Reserve control over the
banks by (1) granting to the Federal Reserve System (FRS) a
monopoly over note issue; (2) *compelling all the existing "national*
banks" to join the Federal Reserve System, and to keep all their legal
reserves as deposits at the Federal Reserve; and (3) fixing the
minimum reserve ratio of deposits at the Reserve to bank
deposits (money owned by the public).[189]

Rothbard *never* sought to exonerate the banksters. (And, if
any other Austro-libertarian ever did, we would like to know his
or her name.) On the contrary, for forty years he named their
names.[190] But Mr. Ferrara's studied failure to address the
intrinsic evil of their "main device" is consistent with a desire to
exonerate the State. He certainly does not betray awareness of
the possibility that government personnel have interests distinct
from those of the financial movers and shakers who put them in
office, that the fallen human interest in "lording it over others"
(Matthew 20:25; 1 Peter 5:3) is not reducible to an interest in
money, but rather the root of which the latter is a flower.

---

[188] Rothbard, *America's Great Depression,* Fifth Edition, Auburn, Al: Ludwig von Mises
Institute, 2000, 25. Emphasis added. mises.org/rothbard/agd.pdf

[189] Rothbard, *America's Great Depression,* 26. Emphasis added.

[190] *The Case against the Fed,* Auburn, AL: Ludwig von Mises Institute, 1994. Freely available
on mises.org. See also his earlier *Wall Street, Banks, and American Foreign Policy,* Auburn, AL:
Ludwig von Mises Institute, 1984. Freely available on mises.org.

Mr. Ferrara does cite Rothbard's *The Case against the Fed*, but only for the description of the Fed as a cozy partnership, not for any of the historical facts he adduced in a sketch of the Jekyll Island conspiracy, all of which are developed and sourced in that book. (Whom *does* Mr. Ferrara cite for those facts? Nobody.)

As for the operational and structural facts about the Fed that puff up this section, including factoids about the Open Market Committee and another rehearsal of fractional reserve banking covered in the last sketch, these materials bear no obvious relationship to his polemical aim. Only the last paragraph seems to do that, but there is nothing new there:

With the entire money supply and the availability of money and credit in the U.S. economy under the control of a private banking cartel that has made government its partner, and which illegally buys up failing mega-firms to save their principals and shareholders from ruin, the term "free" market is little more than a place-holder for what Austrians wish existed. (32)

May we presume that Mr. Ferrara also wishes to see a totally unhampered market? If he does, then it seems there is only one road to travel, a road he will not take. For if one disapproves of the cozy bizgov partnership, and if the wealthy inevitably seek to control the State (and usually succeed), without which they cannot enforce their cartel and its attendant frauds, then the only logical alternative to abolishing the wealthy is abolishing the State.

Appendices

Appendices

Appendix
A

Murray Rothbard on Abortion: My Late Friend's Lamentable Error

Originally published on AnthonyGFlood.com, January 7, 2019

"I was sure I was going to predecease him."

That's how my friend Father James A. Sadowsky (1923-2012) confirmed the news of the passing of Murray Newton Rothbard (1926–1995) two dozen years ago today.

It was after Sunday Mass at St. Agnes. Finishing breakfast with friends in a 42nd Street a coffee shop, I excused myself to call (using a pay phone) my wife who, enduring a cold, couldn't join me in Manhattan that wintry day.

"Father Sadowsky called," she said. *"Murray Rothbard died yesterday."*

It's now been almost 36 years since the first chat that began my friendship with Murray, which continued through his last dozen years. His writings, illuminated by conversations, formed a major part of my education in economics, history, and politics. His personal influence makes it difficult to make a selection among the many memories.

Reading *Man, Economy & State*, a project I began on March 22, 1983, inspired me to call him one evening. Barely two months into it, I looked up his number (in a 20th-century phone book) and made bold to use it on May 18 (my diary says): "I got six new [libertarian] leads from him, including a Fordham [University] history professor who lives in Jackson Heights [John McCarthy] . . . . Rothbard is so easy to talk to and make laugh. . . . Look forward to meeting him in the Fall [at the Libertarian Party National Convention]."

Finishing that stout tome on June 19th marked the end of my political wilderness-wandering to which I had sentenced myself after breaking with Marxism six years earlier. By the time my "Jürgen Habermas's Critique of Marxism" was published in the Winter 1977/1978 issue *Science & Society*, a Stalinoid academic journal, I was in the free market camp.[191] But I didn't find *National Review* conservatism sufficiently inspiring.

Less than a year later I was invited to participate in Murray's 1984 seminar on the history of economic thought:

> Last Rothbard class was a damning critique of Adam Smith. Smith has almost no libertarian credentials. Marx can have him. . . . [T]here's an essay in the latest *Libertarian Vanguard* that Rothbard wants me to read, and Mark [Brady] is going to copy for me . . . . Murray Rothbard was very friendly again with me after class. He's busy packing for his move to Stanford CA, so, he says, he's sorry he couldn't have invited Gloria and me to dinner. Discussed my

---

[191] Its text with corrections and editorial notes is available here: http://www.anthonyflood.com/habermasmarxism.htm

Christian libertarian idea with him on the bus. I'm flattered." (May 4, 1984; unless otherwise marked, dates refer to diary entries.)

I met him for first time at the 1983 Libertarian National Convention at the Sheraton Hotel in New York. "He remembered my name," I recorded, "and when I discussed [Bernard] Lonergan's economics briefly, he said Lonergan struck him as an 'institutionalist.'" (September 4, 1983)

After one session of that seminar there was a small celebration for his 58th birthday:

> Very fortunate to have spent Murray Rothbard's birthday with him at the souvlaki restaurant at 102 MacDougal St. [H]e sat at my table before any one else [from the group] got there. . . . It was a real pleasure to talk about my political past, his intellectual development . . . . There's nothing I can't broach with him. He gave me another perspective on Nathaniel Branden. The class on medieval economics was excellent as was the discussion afterwards on philosophy. (March 2, 1984)[192]

I will continue to treasure his writings and share them with anyone who'll listen. But as I settle accounts with my erstwhile political conscience, I have to point out where, in my opinion, he was wrong.

For starters: his appropriation of the natural rights tradition was idiosyncratic. His reasons for uncoupling it from the natural law metaphysics that informed its classical exponents were never clear to me. (I'll take my share of the blame for any failure of insight.) But that metaphysics (and anthropology) is not so easily set aside.

---

[192] "The Great Women's Liberation Issue: Setting It Straight," *The Individualist*, May 1970. Reprinted as Chapter 8 of Rothbard, *Egalitarianism as a Revolt against Nature*, Auburn, AL: The Ludwig von Mises Institute, 157.) Freely available on mises.org.

A modernist cannot solve the problems of modernity, which are legion. It's one thing to demonstrate a proposition without explicitly referring to God. It's another to be satisfied with a theoretical life that, at its base and superstructure, is agnostic about God and evicts "God-talk" (however benignly and tolerantly) from scientific discourse.

Rothbard was so satisfied, and that marked him as thoroughly modern.

In my opinion, Murray's agnosticism about God's existence and revelation produced a defective anthropology; and one's view of man cannot help but affect every branch of one's theory.

Agnosticism (really, a function of one's suppression of one's innate knowledge of God) encouraged our culture's trade-in of the *imago Dei* for the pseudo-autonomous "self," as in the alleged "axiom" of "self-ownership."

If one does not locate the absolute in God, then one must locate it in something other, and less, than God. For Murray, the "self-owning" person is at once the accidental product of nature's flux *and* the absolute legislator thereof who someone stands over and above it.

One terrible consequence of this is to regard the human fetus as the mother's property which, merely upon change of location (from *in utero* to *ex utero*) *becomes* a potential bearer of absolute rights.

According to Murray, a pregnant mother, her offspring's natural *protector*, no more has duties toward what she carries in her womb than she does toward her limbs or organs.

On the contrary, she has, according Murray's reasoning, the right to procure an abortion. That is, the absolute right to have the human being, whose genetically distinct body naturally came to be inside hers, killed. His anthropology made the individual, rather than the family, the starting point for social theorizing.

One's man's logical deduction is another's *reductio ad absurdum.*

I regret I couldn't persuade Murray to recoil from this fatal consequence of his fateful premise of "self-ownership" as he articulated it in *The Ethics of Liberty*. There he arbitrarily asserted, with italicized emphasis, that "birth *is* indeed the proper line of demarcation" separating allegedly subpersonal fetal tissue from the allegedly "future" rights-bearer.

His discussion of abortion with my friend James Sadowsky is germane.[193] Murray's rhetorical question, "Does birth really confer no rights?" is not an argument.

Murray N. Rothbard and James A. Sadowsky, S.J.,
at the Scottish Games, Stamford, Connecticut, July 4, 1987

Scanned from a snapshot given to Tony Flood
by the late JoAnn Rothbard in 1998

Note the *slightly* sarcastic words that precede it: "[the] act of birth, which I had always naively assumed to be an event of considerable important in everyone's life, now takes on hardly more stature than the onset of adolescence or of one's 'mid-life crisis.'"

Murray rejected the idea that a human person comes to be the instant his or her body comes to be. The embryo is an immature, but complete human being. It needs nothing more than to be allowed to gestate.

Murray's suggestion that the mother's state of mind might equate the legal status of her "unwanted" fetus with that of a

---

193 James A. Sadowsky, "Abortion and the Rights of the Child," *The Libertarian Forum*, July-August 1978, 2-3. Murray Rothbard's reply follows. It may be searched for on mises.org's complete *Libertarian Forum* archive (1969-1984) on https://mises.org/library/complete-libertarian-forum-1969-1984 or, more perhaps more conveniently, the text of this exchange may be read on my old site: http://www.anthonyflood.com/sadowskyabortion.htm

parasite shows how far the acids of modernity had eroded his common sense (of course, not his alone).

His assertion that "no human has the right to reside unwanted within the body of another" is gratuitous and deserves only gratuitous denial. It is best understood as the conclusion toward which he landscaped a garden path of argument.

The man who began an article with: "It is high time, and past due, that someone blew the whistle on 'Women's Liberation'" and proceeded to lampoon feminist economic ignorance, conceded to that movement the validity of their sacrament.[194]

Paul, the Apostle to the nations, listed 21 signs of the "concluding" ἔσχατος (*eschatos*) days of the present dispensation. One of them is "without natural affection" (2 Timothy 3:3 KJV). The Greek is ἄστοργος (*ástorgos*), which the RSV renders "inhuman."

These last days coincide with "the fag-end of the Enlightenment," to borrow the late Fr. Francis Canavan's charming phrase, so we shouldn't be shocked when brilliant thinkers like Murray

---

[194] Further diary entries may interest some readers:

> After [Rothbard's class] . . . I walked him to the 8th St. Playhouse where he was meeting his wife to see *To Be or Not to Be*. This gave me a chance to discuss strategy and get his side of the Voluntaryist issue. What a pleasure it was . . . . he thinks Voluntaryism blurs the line between the aggressor and the victim. If voting is immoral, then voting is part of the crime. If paying taxes is immoral, then the taxpayer is an enemy. Rothbard sees Voluntaryism as a dangerous misdirection of energy. The L[ibertarian]P[arty] is the best base of operations for a libertarian. (March 9, 1984)

> Dog-tired, but enjoyed Murray Rothbard's discussion of the Reformation. Before the class, he gave [me] two issues of his *Libertarian Forum* and the address of the *Journal of Historical Review*, a revisionist historical journal. . . . Rothbard wanted to go for a drink, but Gloria was suffering [from a cold] at home (as it is I got home late), so at least we talked on the way to the 6th Ave. bus, on the bus to 42nd St., and while waiting for his crosstown bus. We discussed privatized roads and, more importantly, strategy. He made a cogent case for LP electoral politics as long as one fights for the pure anarchist line and never compromises it. (March 16, 1984)

> Enjoyed Rothbard's class tonight, and am enjoying the friendship he extends to me. . . . He liked my idea of paraphrasing Man, Economy and State, and is encouraging me to do so. Too bad in five weeks he'll be gone for almost a year, first California and then University of Nevada at Las Vegas. (April 6, 1984)

Rothbard blunder.[195] (Although as Wittgenstein remarked in another context, "For a blunder, that's too big.")

A thinker who would meet the issues of our times will reject modernity's anthropological errors on pain of joining the other flickering embers in history's ashtray. Classical liberals and libertarians are not exempt from this imperative (and fate).[196]

Recently Lew Rockwell summed up Murray Rothbard's vision: a world of free markets, with no exceptions for any class of services (e.g., defense, police, and courts). He emphasized Murray's lifelong theoretical *consistency.*

> [Some people, Lew wrote] even among those who knew and admired Murray, fail to realize this because they view him through a political lens. They point to shifts in his political alliances, seeing him as shifting from Old Right to Left and finally to Paleolibertarian. They miss the essential point. Of course, Murray wanted to put his vision into practice. But for him the vision was primary. If you concentrate on

---

[195] Many have attributed this term to Father Canavan, but Charles Rice has cited its source: Francis Canavan, "Commentary," *Catholic Eye* (New York), Dec. 10, 1987, at 2. See Charles E. Rice, Rights and the Need for Objective Moral Limits, 3 Ave Maria L. Rev. 259 (2005), 266 n. 42. My 1994 correspondence with Father Canavan can be read here: http://www.anthonyflood.com/replytocanavan.htm.

[196] Timothy Gordon explores the devolution from (what he calls) "Catholic Natural Law" to the Protestant and Enlightenment deformations that informed the founding of the American republic in *Catholic Republic: Why America Will Perish without Rome.* Dangerous Books, 2018. Despite the signal contributions of Catholic theologians to the articulation of the natural law (centuries after Aristotle gave it classical expression), I see no reason to follow Gordon in his modification of "Natural Law" by "Catholic." Outside of the Biblical worldview, enunciating first truths (which we see to be true as soon as we understand them) and systematically relating them makes no sense. All historical circumstances illustrate those truths, and so the latter "transcend" the former; the modifier "Roman Catholic" obscures that transcendental character. Gordon does, however, make intelligible the sorry modernist perversion of natural law philosophy by showing it to be a reaction to the common ecclesiastical rival of Protestant and Enlightenment thinkers, viz. the Roman Catholic Church. My only other comment on Gordon (for now) is that natural law philosophy may be a necessary condition of republic-making (if that's what we're interested in doing), but the Catholic Church's political history demonstrates that it not a sufficient one.

Murray's political tactics you will miss the real Murray.[197]

But we who have been drawn to the life and writings of Murray Rothbard want to know how to get out from under the modern state, not (contrary to the impression Lew's column gave me) how to evaluate his theoretical legacy (as important as that may be). Theoretical consistency and fidelity to one's vision may be necessary conditions of success, but they are hardly sufficient. Lew didn't say they were sufficient, but neither did he say what is.

And if one's "consistent vision" includes the deduction of the "right" to commit infanticide, then we could do without that hobgoblin. (Romans 1:22)

In the House of Representatives Ron Paul courageously championed Rothbardian economics and anti-interventionism. "If you want to know what Rothbard's vision applied to contemporary America would be like in practice," Lew wrote, "you should look to Ron Paul. Dr. Paul's career in Congress, marked by his opposition to war and the Fed, is the best example of the anti-elitist free market values that Murray supported."

Murray's vision *applied* to America? What it *would be like in practice?* With all due respect to Rockwell and the great educational work of the Mises Institute, political success is not merely about getting the words right or even about disseminating the right words. (I know Lew knows this.)

Despite his articulation of Rothbard's vision, the American electorate rejected Paul's bid for the White House, twice. They didn't give him (or anyone else) a chance to enshrine Rothbardian principles in the White House.

"Where there is no vision, the people perish" (Proverbs 29:18).

---

[197] Lew Rockwell, "Rothbard Was Right," *LewRockwell.com*, December 18, 2018. https://www.lewrockwell.com/2018/12/lew-rockwell/rothbard-was-right/

And if they don't know how to *realize* their vision, they can also perish *with* it.

America's perishing. Murray's America was on its way out when he died. Now it's virtually gone. So's the time for implementing his vision.

I'll spend what time remains "standing aside under shelter of a wall in a storm and blast of dust" (*The Republic*, Book VI, 496d). Murray's books will comprise a share of my comfort reading for the storm's duration. But I will pray, "Thy Kingdom come, thy will be done on earth, as it is in heaven" from the only Book that, in the end, matters.

We may delight in studying history and the passing scene. We may even be addicted to doing so. But I've come to the conclusion that there is no sound pre-Kingdom politics.

A Profound Philosophical Commonality

This review of Thomas E. Woods, Jr., The Church and the Market: A Catholic Defense of the Free Economy, *was originally published on LewRockwell.com, April 23, 2005. In this review, numbers in parentheses refer to pages of* The Church and the Market.

The writings of Thomas E. Woods, Jr., remind one that truth has a chance of being heard if at least one courageous soul is expressing it. One truth he wants people to hear is that Catholics are not only at liberty to embrace the free market but, given their ethical concerns, ought to give it a bear hug.

A Traditionalist Catholic resister to Vatican II's "regime of novelty," Woods is the author of several books. (With the popular ascription of not only "conservative" but also "traditionalist" to the late Pontiff and to many of the Cardinals he created, a term is needed to distinguish Catholics like Woods from the usurpers. I suggest "restorationist.") Besides the book under review, he has in the past three years given us *The Politically Incorrect Guide to American History*, Regnery, 2004; *The Church Confronts Modernity: Catholic Intellectuals and the Progressive Era*, Columbia University Press, 2004; and, with Christopher A. Ferrara, *The Great Facade: Vatican II and the Regime of Novelty in the Roman Catholic Church*, Remnant Press, 2002. In 2005, Regnery published his *How the Catholic Church Built Western Civilization*.

Woods fights a two-front war against both the modernist menace within the Catholic Church and an obscurantist tendency among traditionalists. Against the latter streak Woods has now given the free market its first book-length Catholic defense. Given the suspicion that many Catholic intellectuals have harbored against capitalism over the past century, such a book has long been overdue. (By "intellectuals" I do not mean the frankly Marxist "liberation" theologians (diabologians?) whose literary droppings have soiled so much paper, but rather giants of traditional Catholicism like Belloc and Chesterton and learned exponents of mainstream Catholic Social Teaching [CST] like Monsignor John A. Ryan.)

And the appearance of *The Church and the Market* is as surprising as it is welcome, for I remember how Woods once curtly dismissed classical liberalism during a brief conversation I had with him after Mass one Sunday in the late '90s. Sometime afterwards, however, I began to notice the writings of a startlingly different Tom Woods on the Rockwell, Mises, and Acton web sites. An "if-you-can't-beat-'em-join-'em" convert, Woods not only imparts with a veteran's ease ideas he has only relatively recently mastered, but also shares a delight with their beauty. His coverage of a vast terrain (economics, history, theology, philosophy, and politics) is concise, but not breezy. As Brand Blanshard noted in his talk *On Philosophical Style*, good style is "so transparent a medium that one looks straight through it at the object, forgetting that it is there." The best writing draws attention to itself only after it has been read. If the reader reflects on the human source of his literary delight, he may feel a debt of gratitude such as I felt after reading each of Woods' chapters. Woods' firm literary hand assures the reader that he is not in over his head and delivers a work that, for all its learning, goes down smoothly.

Much as a professor of logic might dissect a newspaper editorial, Woods parades his opponents' sentences before the reader in order to expose their fallacies with the help of Mises, Rothbard, Hayek, Hoppe, Reisman, and other seminal Austrian minds. There is no rancor; if any emotional response is due, Woods lets the reader supply it. After each lesson, however, the reader will likely wonder, as I did, "How could anyone have thought otherwise?," or "Isn't that policy obviously tantamount to fraud?," or "How could any Catholic with the slightest knowledge of the historical record, not to mention the least sense of Original Sin, exonerate that behavior by these scoundrels?"

Aside from serving as polemic against defenders of certain aspects of CST, *The Church and the Market* offers one of the best introductions to Austrian economic theory available anywhere. It is especially good to see the relatively neglected writings of James A. Sadowsky figuring so prominently among the references. (One may read every essay of Sadowsky's that Woods cites on anthonyflood.com.) This is not an explicitly libertarian or anarchocapitalist book, although it is implicitly so. For instance, Woods notes that unlike "any alternative, the market order does not require the use of coercion—the initiation of physical force—but amounts instead to a system of peaceful social cooperation." (205) Since he does not make an exception for the means whereby social cooperators restrain, deter, and punish violent, anti-social, non-cooperators, he invites an inference to anarchism, but he does not draw it. Earlier, he claims that if "the rights of private property were respected across the board, without exception, we would have reason to expect a substantial improvement in the cultural and moral health of the American people." (198; emphasis added—A.F.) Again, "without exception" does not mean "except in order to provide police, armies, or courts," but I will not go further than he has in characterizing his thought.

The Church and the Market has seven chapters, each on a different matter of controversy, including the last, which is an irenic, Augustinian plea for charity in the conduct of controversy. Woods' primary aim, however, is to discredit the imputation of theological dissent to the Catholic defender of Austrian economics. Economics is simply not a matter of possible theological assent or dissent. It makes no sense, he argues, "to speak of 'dissent' from teaching one believes to be based on factual error on a matter on which the Church has been promised no divine protection from error."

We are not dealing here with the pertinacious denial of a solemn dogma believed by the Church for two thousand years, which the conscience is absolutely bound to accept, but rather with a good-faith effort on the part of loyal Catholics to amend certain economic positions and prudential judgments which, though advanced in the name of helping the poor or rectifying alleged injustice, must have the opposite effect. (214; emphasis added)

Catholics have the right to engage in "selective appropriation of the best of secular thought whenever it contain[s] an insight that might be of benefit to the Church." (7) In conscience, Woods argues, I cannot be obliged to support (say) trade unions if I believe their overall effect is to impoverish workers. Such technical matters, which govern the adjustment of means to ends, are "very far from Church competence." Principles set only ends, not means; economics concerns only aspects of the means by which men attempt to realize their plans; and there is a lawful diversity of opinion with respect to means. Even popes recognized that they could overstep the boundaries of their office if they suggested otherwise. But if, as Pius XI recognized, economics has "an internal coherence of its own," how is a Catholic to receive papal statements that suggest that Catholic doctrine overrides that coherence?

(In popular Catholic apologetics, one often meets the charming conjecture, followed by the predictable refutation, of the Pope who would give odds on the Super Bowl or the World Series. The apologist assures his audience that papal infallibility does not extend to that. Nevertheless, I fear what a CST defender would say were seven consecutive Popes to ignore his Office's limitations in this way. I can also imagine a world in which seven consecutive Popes unburdened themselves of their opinions of, say, the kind of architecture or music that promotes the common good and which, therefore, every Catholic must take to heart. Such a world would need its Tom Woods.)

"Over and against our critics," Woods confesses, "I am convinced that a profound philosophical commonality exists between Catholicism and the brilliant edifice of truth to be found within the Austrian school of economics." (216) Indeed, what "is especially interesting," however, is that "some of the Church's own theologians" "anticipated the best of modern economics." (7) For a Catholic, Woods argues, the world is intelligible because it is the product of infinite intelligence. From this it follows that we have a duty to unearth and explore that intelligibility. Following St. Thomas Aquinas, Woods affirms a category of knowledge "attainable by reason alone," and into it he firmly places economics and its laws. (34)

The Austrian school classifies economics as a division of praxeology, the logic of human choice and action. We may derive its structure by reflecting on the concept of purposive behavior by agents who are certain they are going to die but uncertain as to when. For them, therefore, time is a scarce resource. The logic of human action provides the same backbone to social theory as sentential logic does to reasoned inquiry in general. The first rule of any good theorizing might therefore be: commit no fallacy. The absence of fallacy is no proof against errors of fact, but its presence will impair one's grasp of fact.

Woods critically examines an alternative, popular misconception of economics as a tool of the politically willful. That view, unfortunately, has informed the thinking of many educated and influential people, some of them Catholics, a few of them popes. CST's defenders, Woods argues, reveal "profound confusion regarding the very nature of economics, not to mention the nature and scope of the Church's Magisterium." (214) They are misinformed about the relevant facts (which popes as such have no special competency to establish). The thought that economic reality sets limits to their will is offensive to them, as it is to many other sorts of people. Although no Catholic in his right mind would say, "You can erect any edifice your heart desires, no matter how high, or what shape, or out of whatever material, so long as you are motivated by charity," the resistance of many Catholics to the logic of markets is no less foolish. Unfortunately, they do not keep that foolishness to themselves, but rather seek to impose it on others. No Catholic can be indifferent to the charge that many CST-inspired policies must harm their intended beneficiaries (e.g., the poor, the laborer, and the family provider), but that is the charge Woods levels against CST's advocates.

Woods isolates the scientific task, uncoupling it from the appreciation of those ends which science may help one achieve, and then shows why this view of science is consonant with Catholicism. Economic law cannot contradict moral law: "The moral law tells us what we ought to do. Economic law, on the other hand, is purely descriptive and necessarily amoral, having nothing to do with morality one way or the other." (29–30) He quotes Sadowsky: "Economics indicates the probable effects of certain policies, while ethics determines what one should do." (38 n. 6) (This is Woods' translation from the Spanish-language interview of Sadowsky, conducted in English by Lucia Santa

Cruz; published in the Chilean newspaper *El Mercurio*, November 22, 1987; later reprinted in *Cristianismo, Sociedad Libre y Opción Por Los Pobres*, Eliodoro Matte Larrain, ed., Santiago, Chile: Centro de Estudios Publicos, 1988. My deficient grasp of Spanish did not impede my stubborn, and ill-fated, attempt to render into English the whole valuable conversation. I have waited decades in vain to find someone fluently bilingual who would execute what, no doubt, would be for him or her an easy task.) Economics is as *wertfrei* or value-free as metaphysics, and in that very freedom lies its utility for moral reasoning, which does explicitly advert to ends.

Woods accurately summarizes Austrian methodology and, in my opinion, successfully defends its compatibility with Catholic dogma. His treatment of their interface, however, reminded me of some outstanding philosophical issues whose exploration was not to Woods' immediate purpose and so falls outside of the scope of any fair review of his book.

Woods then shows us what economics teaches about prices, and therefore about wages as the price of labor. State-enforced efforts to raise real wages (i.e., to increase their purchasing power) directly through legislation or indirectly through sanctioning coercive unionism are ill-fated. They are doomed because a price is a rate of exchange between goods, and what determines that rate is the supply and demand for that good. Period. A change in either its supply or demand will therefore affect the rate of exchange. With each additional unit of that good, the demand for it falls. This is not a psychological observation that happens to hold most of the time, but an unfalsifiable implication of human action. The actor will use the first unit to satisfy his or her most urgent wants, and the second unit the next most urgent, and so on. There are no precautions one can take to prevent a good's marginal utility, so described, from decreasing.

Woods reminds the reader that supply and demand determine price even when what is demanded and supplied is labor. The price of any kind of labor is the value of its contribution to the production process, discounted by the going rate of interest. Laborers are paid in advance of the sale of the fruits of that process with money that would have earned a rate of interest had its owners deployed it otherwise. Wages are therefore discounted by that percentage. (Employers might never use such a formula, but if their own estimates vary from what that formula yields, they soon learn, the hard way, whether they have discounted too much or too little.)

"The question," Woods insists, "is not whether some employer for some limited time might possess the means to exercise charity" by raising wages. "The question is whether wages as a whole can be permanently increased through mere good will, voluntary or otherwise, rather than through increases in productivity made possible by increased capital investment." (68) That is, through an increase in the value of what labor offers in exchange for wages. This is virtually a point of logic. Encyclicals cannot effect that increase. Moral exhortation cannot. A collective decision by employers to raise nominal wages cannot. Only capital investment can. (See also Woods' talk, "Catholic Social Teaching and Economic Law: An Unresolved Tension," *Proceedings of the Austrian Scholars Conference 8*, "Liberty, Tradition, and Faith" panel, chaired by Woods, March 15–16, 2002.) Therefore, Woods argues:

> . . . the attempt to elevate such principles as the "just wage" to the level of binding doctrine [for Catholics] is . . . fraught with error. To maintain that private property is just . . . requires nothing more than simple reflection on the teaching of Christ, the Fathers, and natural law itself. The same cannot be said for exhortations to employers that they pay a "just wage," for embedded within such counsel is a

set of unproven assumptions about how economic relationships work, and the belief that all that stands between the world today and the great society of tomorrow is wise legislation, rather than the capital investment which is alone capable of increasing the overall stock of wealth." (79–80)

Woods turns his attention to the nature of money and banking. Mises once quipped that the governmentally protected banking cartel takes a perfectly good commodity and ruins it by engraving pictures and numbers on it. The serious point behind the joke is that, unlike gold or silver, central bank notes have no utility apart from their use as money. Money arose on free markets when one commodity began to facilitate the exchange of otherwise incommensurable commodities, thereby permitting progress beyond the stage of barter. The commodities that best served that function had attributes like durability, divisibility, and portability. Precious metals like gold and silver had all of them.

While an increase in the production of other commodities may engender a social benefit, none accrues to an increase in the supply of money. Any supply of it suffices as a means of exchange. Therefore an increase in its supply will only tend to decrease the purchasing power of each unit of money. There is, however, "money to be made" in the legally sanctioned counterfeiting of central bank notes. When depositors originally paid banks a fee to warehouse their money, they had a moral right to receive any or all of it back on demand. Citing Rothbard's discussion, Woods points out that this warehousing service was bailment. That is, the depositor was not understood to have "lent" money to the bank, but rather to have paid the bank to store it. When it dawned on bankers that they could lend at interest fictitious multiples of deposits, they set up that fraudulent operation (known as "fractional reserve banking") as soon as they could provide legal protection for this racket.

Aiding and abetting this fraud was the word merchant who redefined bailment as debt. As Woods notes, the effect of this verbal engineering has been to ethically upgrade the banker who cannot redeem your note from the thief that he is to merely an "insolvent." He didn't really steal your money, you see. Rather, you lent money to him and, unfortunately, he cannot repay. Since the Great Gold Robbery of 1933, Federal Reserve Notes are redeemable, not for gold, but for the banking cartel's diktat that they are "legal tender for all debts public and private." We live in a world of "fiat" currencies that, as Woods puts it, have been created "out of thin air," i.e., *ex nihilo*, if you will. (The allusion to Genesis 1 suggests the apotheosis of the State. "Let there be money!" And there was money.) Inflation follows fiat currency as the night the day. What encyclical condemns this racket?

The great bugbear of CST, once upon a time at least, was "usury," the charging of interest on a loan. Now since the borrower clearly values the money he receives at present more than he does future money (with which he presumably intends to repay the loan), what obligates the lender to equate those two amounts? That is, just how does being a lender make one's greater valuation of an amount of money an example of exploitation? Woods shows that a sainted theologian who condemned "usury" (because it allegedly amounts to "charging twice for the same good") also approved of profit-sharing by investors in business ventures. Economic analysis, however, reveals no essential difference between these two acts of risking money in the expectation of future reward.

If a great saint's apparent contradictions can addle a Catholic's pate, how much more can magisterial backtracking? To put it bluntly: did the magisterium err when it first condemned usury? On this point, Woods cites Patrick O'Neal:

> When better theory became available (along with the lessons of practical experience), the Church could change its position because the fundamental form of

her judgment was: If W is the economic function involved in the charging of interest, then the charging of interest is immoral, because economic activities must adhere to rule X (or rules X, Y, & Z). Changes under these circumstances do not threaten the claims of the magisterium of the Church in any way. The discovery that the charging of interest does not (necessarily) involve exploitation, but represents instead legitimate payment for the time-value of the money and for the risk factors endured by the lender, denies the antecedent of the hypothetical. (121–122)

This kind of reasoning gives apologetics a bad name. After all, for an orthodox Catholic, nothing may count as "threatening the claims of the magisterium." Unfortunately, O'Neal's proposed "solution" only raises a thornier question: Was the Church protected from error in her moral denunciation of usury, but not in her identification of the behavior that counts as usury? Are we to conclude that, yes, usury is a sin, but there are no instances of it; or at least, one of the behaviors we had traditionally regarded as an instance of it, wasn't? Moral competency, however, includes the ability to identify relevant particulars. I'm sure there's some distinction I'm failing to make.

Economic fallacies and follies in the international arena are Woods' next target.

[The] specific application of Catholic social principles, which is a debatable matter of rational judgment based on circumstances and contingent factors rather than a matter of strict Catholic doctrine, can never bind the Catholic conscience – especially . . . when a trained economist knows very well what their outcome will be. (137)

One such economist was Lord Peter Bauer. His specialty was the economics of development, and his ground-breaking studies were available to Paul VI when that Pontiff was calling for massive increases in "foreign aid." The latter is the racket by which wealth is mulcted from the taxpayers of one state for the benefit of the apparatchiks of another, any alleviation of the plight of the poor being purely coincidental. What is not coincidental is the adverse impact of such "aid" on the accumulation of capital that alone could benefit the recipient country's poor. Bauer's studies might have dampened Paul VI's enthusiasm for the racket, but only if he had read them. As Woods notes, Leo XIII wrote of a "realm of fact" wherein secular matters were to be decided. Bauer offered a scholarly tour of that realm, but Paul VI declined to take it, just as he ignored certain strictures on the exercise of his authority.

As in the case of the welfare state, virtue is assumed to lie, not in the result, but in the good intentions and process. Are you transferring billions of dollars with the intention of alleviating the misery of the poor? Then you have merited the praise appropriately bestowed on one who has actually alleviated it, even if you worsened their condition and left them less able to improve it. Forty years and $2 trillion worth of "aid" later, things are pretty much the same, for after the tribal syndicates that pass for Africa's post-colonial "governments" have financed their drunken orgies, very little remains to quell a baby's hunger pangs. Again, where is the Catholic outcry?

Woods then traces the etiology of various economic diseases that ravage civil society and its fundamental unit, the family. The Catholic Church is second to none not only in its defense of the family, but also in the defense of what has eroded familial and intergenerational bonds: the welfare state. The free market, which is Pareto-optimal for all, making the rich richer while making the poor richer, too, has always been and always will be the "preferential option for the poor." The willful blindness of many Catholic intellectuals to this reality and the anti-family consequences of "progressive" economic policies is a mystery as well as a tragedy. It deserved a more ruthless diagnosis than Woods was apparently willing to make, at least in this book.

I invite the reader to guess who wrote the following:

[I]t is a necessary inference that there will be under capitalism a conscious, direct, and planned exploitation of the majority (the free citizens who do not own) by the minority who are owners . . . . If you left men completely free under a capitalist system, there would be so heavy a mortality from starvation as would dry up the sources of labor in a very short time. . . . The main body of citizens, the Proletariat, are not sufficiently clothed, housed and fed, and even their insufficient supply is unstable. They live in perpetual anxiety. (165–66)

The author of this astoundingly ignorant passage is none other than Hilaire Belloc, who was, among other things, a prolific writer on historical subjects. Since it has been firmly established that capitalist-owned factories in the towns saved the peasants from starvation, why do Catholics still repeat socialist propaganda? We know where the specter of mass starvation roams, and it is not the lands that are "completely free under a capitalist system." (205) (Woods observes that anti-market critics shift ground when cornered: once you've shown them that capitalism lifts up rather than grinds down the poor, they retort with "there's more to life than material things," the very material things of which the capitalists allegedly deprive them. Anti-market types simply move on and concede nothing.) One may choose the hell of North Korean–like autarky for oneself, Woods argues, but not impose it on others. He urges this in a chapter, alone worth the price of the book, in which he buries Belloc's "distributism."

Distributism is a morally licit option, Woods grants, but only for people who don't mind a lower standard of living. The distributist's way of honoring private property is a bad joke: A should have property, even if that means forcibly expropriating some of B's. Woods notes that while there may be a political function called "distribution" (or "redistribution"), there is no economic one: unowned factors of production do not lie about awaiting distribution. On free markets, such factors are either produced or exchanged. Distributism is a riot of statism, anti-savings propaganda, and disregard for consumer preferences. Its attacks on the division of labor, which have a peculiarly Marxist odor, are wholly unoriginal. Distributists favor a society dominated by "guilds" (think of the AMA, ABA, SAG, etc.) which restrict entry into certain labor markets, thereby driving up the price of whatever depends on certain kinds of labor for its production. They act, therefore, in the interest of members at the expense of non-members. They get away with it only because they have the backing of legally sanctioned force.

As Sadowsky noted: "there is no revealed solution to the problem of poverty any more than there is a revealed cure for cancer. Just as there is no revealed medicine, so there is no revealed economics." (39 n. 63) (See James A. Sadowsky, S.J., *A Christian Response to Poverty* (London: The Social Affairs Unit, 1985.) Woods' anti-Austrian Catholic challengers, however, imply that the economic opinions of seven consecutive Popes virtually are revealed economics. Woods, however, does not ask his fellow Catholics for more than a respectful hearing and thoughtful reflection for his own viewpoint:

> Those of us within the Church who advocate the Austrian approach to economics are not demanding that the popes preach Austrian economics from the Chair of Peter. . . . What we stand for . . . is the legitimate liberty of opinion that is supposed to be permitted in matters that do not touch upon Catholic dogma. (215; my emphasis.—A.F.)

Not all of his fellow Catholics will allow this liberty. This reminds me of how my own narrowness once led to embarrassment.

In 1983, new to the libertarian movement and seeking out fellow Christian libertarians, I assumed that all I had to do was find a pro-lifer. I was soon put in touch with Doris Gordon of Libertarians for Life. Within the first minute of talking with her, however, I discovered that she was, and is, an atheist. (There are also non-libertarian atheistic pro-lifers: Catholics should exploit these "anomalous" facts, especially when exposing Catholic public figures who are more afraid of "imposing their religion" than of undermining the rationalization of murder.)

We may be confident that Gordon arrived at her pro-life position without the help of the magisterium. One may, of course, derive a true conclusion validly from false premises, but is that what Gordon did? She may have drawn it from premises whose truth ultimately depends upon a metaphysics she rejects, but that is a different kind of criticism. Even so, Gordon is not "wrong on abortion" because she does not affirm theism. At worst her philosophy might ultimately underserve her moral convictions. (Some Calvinist apologists I have known would have argued that Gordon had no epistemic warrant for the premises from which she derived her conclusion about unborn human life. One was Greg L. Bahnsen [1948–1995]; another is John H. Robbins [1948-2008]. Respectively, they were protégés of Calvinist philosophers and theologians Cornelius Van Til [1895–1987] and Gordon H. Clark [1902–1985].)

I adduce the (for some) irritating fact of pro-life atheists because it goes to the heart of the Catholic view of reason, which Tom Woods champions. If we are to conclude that Mises and Rothbard are wrong about economics, more evidence is required than that their views do not square with that of seven consecutive popes.

My repeated references in this review to "seven consecutive popes" reflect a recent conversation with a Catholic critic of Austrianism. He used that phrase several times as if to underscore its centrality to his case against Catholic free-market defenders like Woods. As I mentioned, we are not going to find popes handicapping sporting events. And when it comes to faith and morals, it would not take seven but only one pope speaking *ex cathedra* to bind a Catholic's conscience. If it does not pertain to those matters, if it is instead about, say, music, architecture, or economics, then not even the considered opinions of 265 consecutive popes, in themselves, would suffice to bind it. Especially ironic about this critic's line of argument was its sharp contrast with his powerful defense, delivered in a lecture just before he and I chatted, of Archbishop Marcel Lefebvre's 1988 consecration of bishops without the Pope's explicit permission (and arguably against his wishes). According to this critic, therefore, a faithful Catholic may withstand Paul VI to his face on *Novus Ordo Missae*, but not on the living wage, or John Paul II on episcopal consecration, but not on "consumerism."

Nonbelievers can (surprise!) arrive at knowledge of the world despite their unbelief, and believers can learn from them. When that knowledge bears on the application of faith to practice, they have a duty to learn from them. *The Church and the Market* will help them discharge that duty.

Lord Acton: Libertarian Hero

This was first published on LewRockwell.com, April 4, 2006

"**Y**ou would spare these criminals, for some mysterious reason. I would hang them higher than Haman, for reasons of quite obvious justice; still more, still higher, for the sake of historical science."[198]

Thus ends a long passage of a letter from John Emerich Edward Dalberg Acton, First Lord Acton (1834–1902) in which appears his famous aphorism regarding power's tendency to corrupt its possessor. In a few words to a fellow historian, who regarded his critic as the "most learned Englishman now alive," his vast historical knowledge, passion for justice, and love for his Church are fused and brought to a fine point.[199]

What revolted Acton, what he devoted his life to exposing, was the rationalization of crime when the criminals are authorities,

---

[198] *Selected Writings of Lord Acton*, J. Rufus Fears ed., Indianapolis, Liberty Classics, 1985, Volume II, 383–384. Hereafter, this indispensable collection will be cited as "SWLA," followed by volume and page numbers.

[199] Roland Hill, *Lord Acton*, New Haven, Yale University Press, 2000, 297. Hereafter, this definitive biography will be cited as "Hill."

whether civil or ecclesiastic. For Acton, the historian's calling was that of a "hanging judge," holding the strong and the weak to the same moral standard. As Acton's counsel was to "suspect power more than vice" when studying history, his moralism may have been intense, but it was never that of the petty vice-cop.[200]

When some years ago I first read Murray Rothbard's description of Lord Acton as "the great Catholic libertarian historian," I suspected overstatement, in spite of the opinion's source.[201] The abuse of "liberal" by twentieth-century statists cannot justify an anachronism, and (so it once seemed to me) attaching libertarian to a Victorian aristocrat, who once urged Marx's *Capital* on Great Britain's Prime Minister, just might be anachronistic.[202]

The more I learned from and about Acton, however, the more Rothbard's categorization rang true. I would go Rothbard one better and say that Acton was a libertarian hero. His championing of liberty against power was the central theme of his intellectual life. It was wide-ranging and without compromise, even when it cost him.

Acton described himself as "a man who started in life believing himself a sincere Catholic and a sincere Liberal; who therefore renounced everything in Catholicism which was not compatible with Liberty, and everything in Politics which was not compatible with Catholicity." (SWLA III 657) As Acton scholar J. Rufus Fears put it, in "liberty, Acton found more than the key to

---

[200] For criticism of Acton's moralism, see Herbert Butterfield, *The Whig Interpretation of History,* Chapter 6. In the opinion of Butterfield, a subsequent occupant of the Regius chair at Cambridge, "Creighton could not know enough to exonerate. Neither . . . did Acton in reality know enough to condemn [Pope Alexander VI] himself." *History and Human Relations* [London 1951], 119, cited in Hill 302.

[201] Murray N. Rothbard, *The Ethics of Liberty,* New York University Press, 1998, 18.

[202] "[That] remarkable book . . . the Koran of the new socialists." Hill 411. According to Herbert Butterfield, no man influenced that prime minister, William Ewart Gladstone, more than did Acton, who was raised to the peerage at his recommendation. It is therefore odd that biographer A.N. Wilson could not spare a line for Acton in his *The Victorians* [New York & London, W. W. Norton & Co., 2003], which devotes so much space to Gladstone.

the unity of history. He found the key to the unity of his life as a Catholic, as a Liberal, and as a historian." (SWLA II xxi)

We murder to dissect, Wordsworth warned, so we cannot understand any one of those life-vectors apart from its relationship to the other two without risk of distortion. Within the severe limits of a short article we shall try to minimize that risk.

Between his birth in Naples a few years before Victoria's accession to the British throne and his death in Bavaria a year after hers, John Acton led the fullest life possible to a Catholic intellectual of means in Protestant England. Related to many of Europe's nobility (and even royalty) and fluent in its chief languages, he traveled widely as a young man not only throughout Europe, but also to America and Russia (on the occasion of Czar Alexander II's coronation). He corresponded voluminously with many notables including his friend, the aforementioned Prime Minister Gladstone, and General Robert E. Lee.

Religiously disqualified from attending Cambridge University in 1850, Acton was apprenticed for seven years to Father Ignatz von Döllinger of Munich, Europe's most learned theologian and historian. Under his tutelage Acton unearthed archives to examine the primary sources of history. The result was that he gained an education that made him the peer of those who enjoyed the academic pedigree denied him as a Catholic. In 1895, however, Cambridge honored him with an appointment to one of its most prestigious chairs, the Regius Professorship of Modern History, the first Catholic to be so honored in three centuries. From it he planned (but never produced) a history of liberty, living only long enough to organize the Cambridge Modern History.

If the "one supreme object of all my thoughts is the good of the Church" (SWLA III 659), then Lord Acton was a Catholic before (in his hierarchy of goods as well as chronologically) he was anything else. Both his intellectual activity and even his libertarianism were forged within the hull of Peter's barque. He improved the reputation of English Catholic intellectuals with his editing of and impressive contributions to two scholarly journals, *The Rambler* and *Home and Foreign Review,* closing the latter in advance of almost certain papal censure. His determination, to the point of nervous collapse, was that of a man in love with the Church. "I would rather die than having [*sic*] to live without the sacraments and to leave the Church" (Hill 472 n. 55)

The reign of Pope Pius IX was the most unfortunate feature of Acton's world, and not just because the specter of absolutism that increasingly haunted his Church diverted his energies from the writing of books. This pontiff had once been the hope of liberals, Catholic and non-Catholic, until Europe's ascendant nationalist movements boxed the Vatican in, psychologically and, eventually, territorially and an illiberal, bunker mentality set in. As the de facto leader of the Church's ultimately victorious "ultramontanist" party, Pius not only dashed any hope that he would reconcile himself with liberalism, but also went so far as to identify his very person with Tradition. (Hill 500 n. 56)

Two issues surfaced for reflective Catholics: freedom for the Church and freedom within the Church. For Acton they were not incompatible goals. He doubted, not that the Church has implacable enemies, but that authoritarian governance helps Her fight them. If anything, he feared, it throws dry wood on the flames of anti-Catholic prejudice. Liberal self-governance will fortify the Church, not weaken Her, as She conducts Her spiritual battles. For Her "own everlasting foundation," he wrote, is

> the words of Christ, not . . . the gifts of Constantine. More than once since then . . . she has been stripped of that terrestrial splendor which had proved such a fatal possession; but she has stood her ground in the wreck of those political institutions on which she no longer relied, and alone has saved society. The old position of things has been reversed; and it has been

found that it is the State which stands in need of the Church, and that the strength of the Church is her independence.[203]

Acton made this fight his own, going so far as to wage journalistic guerrilla warfare in Rome against the foreordained course of the First Vatican Council. While the Council sat, he would meet with every delegate he could by day and write up his notes in his rented apartment on the Via Della Croce by night, the next day availing himself of a diplomatic pouch to dispatch his reports to Father Döllinger in Munich. From these reports Acton's scholarly colleague would, under the pseudonym "Quirinus," cobble together an article for the *Allgemeine Zeitung*. That paper's Roman subscribers would eagerly consume it within days—to the sound of pounding fists from inside the papal apartments. For the Pope's aim in convening the Council was to satisfy his burning desire to define papal infallibility as a dogma to be believed by all Christians on pain of damnation. But he didn't need the definition to feel, and assert, infallibility.[204]

Unlike John Henry Cardinal Newman, the Catholic convert from the Church of England with whom Acton is sometimes too casually linked, Acton opposed this proposal, because he thought doing so was not so much inexpedient as wrong. Infallibility meant that a solemn papal pronouncement on faith or morals was to be received by Catholics as true because it enjoyed (in the words of the Council) "the same infallibility with which the Divine Redeemer thought fit to endow his Church" and "not in consequence of the consent of the Church."[205]

---

[203] Acton, *Essays on Church and State*, Douglas Woodruff ed. [London, Hollis & Carter] 1952, 472.

[204] Gertrude Himmelfarb's description of the Council's all-too-human dimension makes for lively reading. See her *Lord Acton: A Study in Conscience and Politics*. The University of Chicago Press, 1952, 95–128. Hereafter, this pioneering study will be cited as "Himmelfarb, Lord Acton."

[205] For a perspective favorable to Newman and critical of Acton, who regarded the former with "deep aversion" as a "sophist" and "manipulator of the truth" (SWLA III xviii), see

Acton's conscience, extraordinarily well formed as it was historically and theologically, did not allow him to ratify that affirmation; and just because he was a Catholic, he could not ignore that conscience's directives. His opposition was not a symptom of doubt regarding any doctrine that had "always been believed, everywhere, by everyone." Rather, he feared that the ascription to a sinner of a divine attribute, however circumscribed, would tend to discredit the Faith and fortify harmful absolutist tendencies within the Church.

He also feared that were he to reveal his opposition to infallibility he would be excommunicated. With the zeal of a convert, Henry Edward Cardinal Manning had worked to contrive such a predicament. The prelate pressed his interrogation in a letter, asking the historian point blank whether he ought not to say that he submitted to the decrees of the Council.

In his reply of 18 November 1874—a model either of adroit evasion or of legal self-extrication worthy of a Saint Thomas More—Acton stated that a "misconception" was driving the Cardinal's inquisition:

> I can only say that I have no private gloss or favourite interpretation for the Vatican Decrees. The acts of the Council alone constitute the law which I recognize. I have not felt it my duty as a layman to pursue the comments of divines, still less to attempt to supersede them by private judgments of my own." (Hill 265) (". . . I cannot accept his [Manning's] tests and canons of dogmatic development and interpretation and must decline to give him the only answer that will content him, as it would, in my lips, be a lie. (Acton to John Cardinal Newman, 4 December 1874. Hill 268.)

Richard John Neuhaus, "Lord Acton, Cardinal Newman, and How To Be Ahead of Your Time," *First Things*, 105, Aug–Sep 2000.

In another reply (16 December 1874), this time to his diocesan bishop, who had the authority to quiet the whole matter, Acton protested "that I have given you no foundation for your doubt. . . . I have yielded obedience to the Apostolic Commission which embodied those decrees, and I have not transgressed ... obligations imposed under the supreme sanction of the Church." That satisfied Acton's ordinary, and that was that.

The self-imposed pressures of his journalistic, scholarly, and political activity, which often involved foreign travel, put some but not undue strain on his family life. All his considerable good fortune did not, however, spare him the sorrow of burying two of his children at very young ages. Given Cambridge's previously mentioned denial to him of the opportunity to study there in 1850, it is a pleasant irony that his most professionally rewarding, even happiest, years of his life were the last seven, dating from his acceptance of the Regius Professorship. He was a popular lecturer who spoke to standing-room-only crowds, who were sometimes charged admission. He left behind a library of nearly seventy thousand volumes, many of them annotated in his hand. They are now preserved at Cambridge, having been saved from certain dispersal and disintegration by a check from Andrew Carnegie.

Acton's understanding of the Church's mission was organically related to his libertarian philosophy of history. The Gospel that transformed individuals could not help but go on to transform their societies:

> The Church which our Lord came to establish had a two-fold mission to fulfill. Her system of doctrine, on the one hand, had to be defined and perpetually maintained. But it was also necessary that it should prove itself more than a mere matter of theory – that it should pass into practice, and command the will as well as the intellect of men. It was necessary not only

to restore the image of God in man, but to establish the divine order in the world. (SWLA III 22)

In summarizing the contribution of the Stoics to the Christian, i.e., Acton's, idea of liberty, he wrote:

They made it known that there is a will superior to the collective will of man, and a law that overrules those of Solon and Lycurgus. . . . That which we must obey, that to which we are bound to reduce all civil authorities, and to sacrifice every earthly interest, is that immutable law which is perfect and eternal as God Himself, which proceeds from His nature, and reigns over heaven and earth and over all the nations. . . . The liberties of the ancient nations were crushed beneath a hopeless and inevitable despotism, and their vitality was spent, when the new power came forth from Galilee, giving what was wanting to the efficacy of human knowledge, to redeem societies as well as men. (SWLA I 23–24, 26)

What did Acton mean by "liberty"? In one place he said it was "the assurance that every man shall be protected in doing what he believes his duty, against the influence of authority and majorities, custom and opinion." (SWLA I 7.[206] In another he grounded his concept of liberty in Catholicism and contrasted it with modernity's:

There is a wide divergence, an irreconcilable disagreement, between the political notions of the modern world and that which is essentially the system of the Catholic Church. It manifests itself particularly in their contradictory views of liberty, and of the functions of the civil power. The Catholic notion, defining liberty not as the power of doing what we like, but the right of being able to do what we ought, denies

---

[206] For a selection of quotations of Acton on liberty, see Gary Galles, "Lord Acton on Liberty and Government," *Mises.org*, posted November 5, 2002.

that general interests can supersede individual rights. (SWLA III 613)

For Acton, the principle of liberty always faces the counter-principle of power, and he linked this tension to the primary moral effort of the individual to suppress his own *libido dominandi*, which is secondarily expressed in institutions. That libido is the urge to "push people around" with impunity (as Rothbard would render the Latin). It is, as Acton put it, the insidious "enemy within." The greater that urge's potential range of expression, the greater the danger, be its subject mitered or crowned: "The passion for power over others can never cease to threaten mankind and is always sure of finding new and unforeseen allies in continuing its martyrology."[207]

That passion varies in intensity from person to person, as does the desire to cool it. As there can be no permanent moral victories against it, we cannot reasonably hope to establish a utopia in which liberty is enjoyed as a permanent victory, a settled attitude, immune to back-sliding. ("Liberty: Power over oneself. Opposite: Power over others." Undated note. SWLA III 490.)

Power tends not only to corrupt, but also to "expand indefinitely, and will transcend all barriers, abroad and at home, until met by superior forces." This "law of the modern world . . . produces the rhythmic movement of History."

> The threatened interests were compelled to unite for
> the self-government of nations, the toleration of
> religions, and the rights of man. . . . it is by the
> combined efforts of the weak, made under compulsion,
> to resist the reign of force and constant wrong, that,
> in the rapid change but slow progress of four

---

[207] Acton, "Beginnings of the Modern State," *Essays in the Liberal Interpretation of History,* ed. William H. McNeill, The University of Chicago Press, 1967, 401. Hereafter, "Beginnings." As Professor McNeill put it, Acton saw history as a "tortuous yet persistent advance toward liberty." xii.

hundred years, liberty has been preserved, and
secured, and extended, and finally understood.
("Beginnings," 419)

Man is therefore not only a liberty-seeker, but also a
power-grabber; his political maturity will arrive when he
becomes a consistent power-checker. In describing church-state
rivalry in pre-modern Europe, Acton reiterates the theme of
countervailing power as the key to liberty's progress, referring
again to that critical period of four centuries:

> The only influence capable of resisting the feudal
> hierarchy was the ecclesiastical hierarchy; and they
> came into collision, when the process of feudalism
> threatened the independence of the Church by
> subjecting the prelates severally to that form of
> personal dependence on kings which was peculiar to
> the Teutonic state. To that conflict of four hundred
> years we owe the rise of civil liberty. If the Church
> had continued to buttress the thrones of the king
> whom it anointed, or if the struggle had terminated
> speedily in an undivided victory, all Europe would
> have sunk down under a Byzantine or Muscovite
> despotism. For the aim of both contending parties
> was absolute authority. But although liberty was not
> the end for which they strove, it was the means by
> which the temporal and the spiritual power called the
> nations to their aid. (SWLA I 32–33.)

As Leonard Liggio confirmed Acton's point:

> [R]eligious institutions were totally separate from,
> and often in conflict with, political institutions only
> in the Christian West. This created the space in
> which free institutions could emerge. The idea of
> independent religious institutions is absent even in
> Eastern Christianity; their religious institutions are
> part of the bureaucracy of the state. In Western

Europe, though, the religious institutions were autonomous among themselves, and totally independent from and often in opposition to state power. The result was the creation of a polycentric system. And whenever this system was threatened by claims of total empire by the political rulers, Christian philosophy was utilized as part of its defense. ("Christianity, Classical Liberalism Are Liberty's Foundations," Interview with Leonard Liggio, *Religion & Liberty*, Sep–Oct 1996. My emphasis.—AF)

Acton again:

Real liberty depends not on the separate but on the distinct and appropriate, but continuous, action and reaction of Church and State. The defined and regulated influence of the Church in the State protects a special sphere and germ of political freedom, and supplies a separate and powerful sanction for law. On the other hand, the restricted and defined action of the State in ecclesiastical affairs gives security to canon law, and prevents wanton innovation and the arbitrary confiscation of rights. (Woodruff 467)

Acton once wrote that property was the "basis of liberty" (SWLA III 572), but he was no Lockean theorist of self-ownership; that is, he did not—regrettably in my opinion—define liberty in terms of property rights. It is therefore not surprising that he deems the "state . . . competent to assign duties and draw the line between good and evil only in its own immediate sphere. Beyond the limit of things necessary for its well-being, it can only give indirect help to fight the battle of life, by promoting the influences which avail against temptation, – Religion, Education, and the distribution of Wealth." (SWLA I 7) Acton limited, but did not eliminate, the State. But more on that problem presently.

The context of the famous "power dictum" is a letter, dated 5 April 1887, to Anglican Archbishop Mandell Creighton, whose five-volume history of the medieval papacy Acton had savaged (in a publication that Creighton edited!) for the double standard that he allegedly applied to crimes, depending on the social rank of their perpetrators. The recipient of the letter quoted at the beginning of this essay, Creighton was a Fellow of Merton College and Dixie Professor of Ecclesiastical History at Cambridge. He had sought out Acton as a reviewer because he "wanted to be told my shortcomings by the one Englishman whom I consider capable of doing so." As he later hoped Acton would succeed him when he left Cambridge to take up his see at Peterborough, he was most enthusiastic in support of Acton's appointment to that University's Regius Chair. (Hill, 296, 297, 368.) Yes, Creighton thought him incomparably learned, but "he never writes anything," referring to his notorious underproduction of publications. As an historian Acton was, nevertheless, according to Gertrude Himmelfarb, "perhaps the most learned and intellectually ambitious of his generation."[208]

The power under review was ecclesiastic. Let us view his epigram in its surroundings:

> I really don't know whether you [Creighton] exempt them [from criticism] because of their rank, or of their success and power, or of their date. It does not allow of our saying that such a man did not know right from wrong, unless we are able to say that he lived before Columbus, before Copernicus, and could not know right from wrong. It can scarcely apply to the centre of Christendom, 1500 [years] after the birth of our Lord. That would imply that Christianity is a mere system of metaphysics, which borrowed some ethics from elsewhere. . . .

Acton continues to turn the polemical heat up . . .

---

[208] "Lord Acton: In Pursuit of First Principles," *The New Criterion*, 18:10, June 2000.

I cannot accept your canon that we are to judge Pope and King unlike other men, with a favourable presumption that they did no wrong. If there is any presumption it is the other way against holders of power, increasing as the power increases. Historic responsibility has to make up for the want of legal responsibility.

Power tends to corrupt and absolute power corrupts absolutely. Great men are almost always bad men, even when they exercise influence and not authority: still more when you superadd the tendency or the certainty of corruption by authority. There is no worse heresy than that the office sanctifies the holder of it. That is the point at which the negation of Catholicism and the negation of Liberalism meet and keep high festival, and the end learns to justify the means.

. . . and then boils things down:

You would hang a man of no position, like [François] Ravaillac [assassin of Henry IV of France]; but if what one hears it true, then Elizabeth asked the gaoler to murder Mary, and William III ordered his Scots minister to extirpate a clan. Here are the greater names coupled with great crimes. (SWLA II 383–384)

Then follow the words with which this essay began.

Rothbard stressed the deeply anti-conservative nature of Acton's thought. "While natural-law theory has often been used erroneously in defense of the political status quo, its radical and 'revolutionary' implications were brilliantly understood by" Acton:

Acton saw clearly that the deep flaw in the ancient Greek— and their later followers'—conception of natural law political philosophy was to identify politics and morals, and then to place the supreme social moral agent in the State. From Plato and

Aristotle, the State's proclaimed supremacy was founded in their view that [as Acton wrote] "morality was distinguished from religion and politics from morals; and in religion, morality, and politics there was only one legislator and one authority."

Acton added that the Stoics developed the correct, non-State principles of natural law political philosophy, which were then revived in the modern period by [Hugo] Grotius and his followers. "From that time" [Acton wrote] "it became possible to make politics a matter of principle and of conscience." The reaction of the State to this theoretical development was horror.[209]

Rothbard then quotes Acton:

When [theologian Richard] Cumberland and [jurist Samuel von] Pufendorf unfolded the true significance of [Grotius's] doctrine, every settled authority, every triumphant interest recoiled aghast. . . . It was manifest that all persons who had learned that political science is an affair of conscience rather than of might and expediency, must regard their adversaries as men without principle. (SWLA I 42)

Here's what Acton wrote just before those words:

In a passage almost literally taken from St. Thomas, he [the philosopher Pierre Charron] describes our subordination under the law of nature, to which all legislation must conform; and he ascertains it not by the light of revealed religion, but by the voice of universal reason, through which God enlightens the consciences of men. Upon this foundation Grotius drew the lines of real political science. In gathering the materials of international law, he had to go beyond national treaties and denominational interests, for a

---

[209] Rothbard cites Acton, *Essays on Freedom and Power,* Glencoe, IL: Free Press, 1948, 45; and Himmelfarb, *Lord Acton,* 135.

principle embracing all mankind. The principles of law must stand, he said, even if we suppose that there is no God. By these inaccurate terms he meant that they must be found independently of Revelation. From that time it became possible to make politics a matter of principle and of conscience, so that men and nations differing in all other things could live in peace together, under the sanctions of a common law. (My emphasis. —A.F.)

If one reads Acton superficially, it seems as if the State is ever under suspicion, but never under indictment. That is, he does not seem to regard the State as such as the enemy of society. But we must take care not to equivocate. When 19th-century writers referred to "the State," they did not necessarily mean what anarchocapitalists mean. They may have meant something more fundamental, such as the principles according to which people implicitly regulate their mutual affairs, which principles they more or less accurately express in a legal code.

Therefore, if it is true of any possible society that its members' interactions are arranged intelligibly, that intelligible arrangement may be said to be its "state." It refers to the whole of society, not just that portion of the population arrayed against the rest by its monopoly of police. It is in the interest of those monopolists to identify their particular interests (those of "the State" in the Rothbardian sense) with the general interest (that of "the state" of the whole society). They have largely been successful in getting their victims to accept that identification.

So when a writer like Acton refers to "the divine origin and nature of authority," the last thing he means is that heaven smiles upon, or at least winks at, the anti-social gang that taxes, inflates, conscripts, rewards, punishes within its own turf and occasionally lays waste to the territories of rival gangs. Rather, Acton is referring to a dimension of human living that is no more dispensable than its biological dimension. For example, he once wrote that the State has

> the same divine origin and the same ends as in the Church, which holds that it belongs as much to the primitive essence of a nation as its language, and that it unites men together by a moral, not, like family and society, by a natural and sensible, bond. (Woodruff 424)

A society could, therefore, no more be without a State in that sense than it could be without families. Given that stipulation, "libertarian state" would not be an oxymoron, but rather name a society whose members are fundamentally libertarian in their settled convictions. To avoid the sin of equivocation we need only announce in advance which sense of "State" we intend. For Acton "a State in which the law is powerless to punish a thief ("anarchy"), or in which a society is unable to restrict the action of the government ("despotism")" (Woodruff 436) are equally undesirable, no less so to the anarchocapitalist than to anyone else.

For example, in the United States there is (as there wasn't two centuries ago) a settled conviction toward chattel slavery as a morally impermissible relationship. That is, Americans implicitly regard the control by human being A of human being B's body against B's will as intrinsically criminal. They so regard it no matter what any positive statute somewhere may say to the contrary. They hold that to seek to exercise such control is ipso facto to be criminally minded. The American polity or State, in the sense I am trying to clarify, is anti-chattel slavery. The libertarian argues for logically extending the range of that settled conviction to embrace all of justly held property. In so arguing, he shows his discourse to be commensurate with that of most non-libertarians. That is, it recognizes a common objective, namely, how to pursue our innumerable and diverse projects peacefully, how to cooperate even in the conduct of our rivalry, and how to deal with violent non-cooperators "so that men and nations differing in all other things could live in peace together."

I do not wish to overstate my case for Acton as a libertarian hero. While Acton doesn't believe that the government is the preferred means of satisfying the "claim on the wealth of the rich" that the poor allegedly have, neither does he rule it out as a necessarily objectionable means. He does believe the poor have a moral claim in "so far as they may be relieved from immoral, demoralizing effects of poverty." The claim is not that the poor man somehow owns part of another's wealth, but rather that when he "becomes destitute," presumably through no fault of his own, "it is a moral evil, teeming with consequences injurious to society and morality." (SWLA III 572) It is not so much the enforceable right of "the poor" as it is the moral duty of "the rich."

If there was one weakness in Acton's intellectual armory, it lay in his grasp of economics. To that ignorance I mainly attribute his conflating of the State in Rothbard's sense with the State as society's necessary political dimension.[210]

Yet this conflation, in which he was (and is) not alone, does not detract from the value of the radical libertarian potential latent in his thought. For no more than his Savior did Acton specify what, if anything, belongs to Caesar. Although Rothbard knew that Acton did not take the anarchist step, he

> saw clearly [Rothbard wrote] that any set of objective moral principles rooted in the nature of man must inevitably come into conflict with custom and with positive law. To Acton, such an irrepressible conflict was an essential attribute of classical liberalism: "Liberalism wishes for what ought to be [Acton wrote], irrespective of what is." ... And so, for Acton, the individual, armed with natural law moral principles, is then in a firm position from which to criticize existing regimes and institutions, to hold

---

[210] For example: "The materialistic socialist will improve h[istory] for the poor. Their best writer, Engels, made known the errors and horrors of our factory system." From a note, c. 1900–01, for his Regius inaugural lecture. Hill 399.

them up to the strong and harsh light of reason. (Rothbard cites Himmelfarb, *Lord Acton*, 204.)

Not enough, perhaps, to dub Acton an anarchist, but enough to spawn the conjecture that anarchism is where his thought leads.

"I never had any contemporaries," Acton once sighed. (Hill 276) But, as Professor Himmelfarb noted, he

> would be pleased to know how many he now has. For dissidents today, he stands as an exemplar of intellectual courage, recalling us to first principles that are even more unfashionable today than they were in his time and challenging us to reconsider how those principles may be incorporated into the practical realms of ethics and politics.[211]

Needlessly impoverished are those libertarians who fail to embrace him as one of their own.

---

[211] Himmelfarb, "Lord Acton: In Pursuit of First Principles."

Appendix
D

Is Anarchy a Cause of War? Some Questions for David Ray Griffin

This was first published by the Libertarian Alliance (London) in 2009

Unexamined Presuppositions

[T]he state of anarchy, in being the permissive cause of the war system, is thereby the permissive cause of empires. – David Ray Griffin

The site of this provocative assertion is a chapter by David Ray Griffin in *The American Empire and the Commonwealth of God: A Political, Economic, Religious Statement.*[212] All the world's peoples, its four authors assume, must have a "say" in

---

[212] David Ray Griffin, John B. Cobb, Jr., Richard A. Falk, and Catherine Keller. *The American Empire and the Commonwealth of God: A Political, Economic, Religious Statement.* Westminster John Knox Press, 2006 (hereinafter AECG). The prefatory quote is from page 107.

"running" the world. A democratic form of global governance, operating through the (no doubt well-intentioned) experts of non-governmental organizations (NGOs) and religious councils ("progressive," of course) is the sole morally acceptable alternative to the current American imperial version of such governance.[213] The reader is also left to wonder what NGOs are supposed to *do* beyond registering approval or disapproval of the net result of billions of choices made daily on free markets.

Since Neo-Malthusian gloom-and-doom also haunts AECG, fear quickly displaces wonder.[214] The "war system," however, is much more of an imminent threat to humanity than any looming ecological disaster, Griffin argues. That millennia-old system has culminated in a historically unprecedented borderless empire headquartered in Washington. Armed with nuclear weapons, it is a "much greater threat to divine purposes" than the Roman Empire ever was. Since one cannot target nuclear weapons to hit military assets exclusively, one is morally forbidden to launch them even "defensively," let alone preventively or preemptively (the evil that the American Empire's sycophants

---

[213] None of the authors defines "democracy" in this book, let alone acknowledges that its referent has critics. Griffin is working on a book that will at least do those two things. Before finishing that project, according to my email exchange with him in 2007, he intends to read Hans-Hermann Hoppe's *Democracy: The God That Failed* (Transaction Publishers, 2001), which I had brought to his attention.

[214] Developing a variation of the "public goods" argument against the free market, its authors (especially philosopher-theologian Cobb: see also his *For the Common Good* (Beacon Press, 1989, with economist Herman Daly; 2nd updated edition, 1994) maintain that the global economy is sawing off the branch of the ecological tree on which it is allegedly perched precariously. Why? It lacks the wise and benevolent superintendence of experts inspired by the vision of the common good promoted by Cobb *et al.* Left to themselves, free markets cannot allocate scarce resources optimally, if optimality includes an ecologically secure future for humanity. Now, sawing off the branch one is sitting on is certainly an unsustainable activity, and one is grateful to whoever sounds such an alarm. But even *if* the whistle-blowers were right about the danger, it would not follow that they have earned the privilege of regulating one's life. For all that our neo-Malthusians have shown to the contrary, "democratic governance" may only make things worse. A study of George Reisman's "Natural Resources and the Environment," comprising the third chapter of his *magnum opus, Capitalism* (Jameson Books, 1996), to mention no other work, drove me to the conclusion that their command of relevant fact is as weak as their grasp of theory.

brazenly rationalize). Given Christianity's birth in antagonism to empire, Griffin rightly finds irony and scandal in the spectacle of millions of Christians celebrating empire's most demonic instance, as one may witness in America today.[215]

The "War System": Civilization's Frankenstein Monster?

In making his case for global democracy, Griffin draws heavily upon Andrew Bard Schmookler's *The Parable of The Tribes: The Problem of Social Power in Social Evolution*.[216] The parable is supposed to shed light on the "war system" as a consequence of mankind's transition from hunting and gathering to civilization. According to Griffin's summary:

> The war system originated within the past ten to twelve thousand years. This origination was closely related to the rise of civilization, with its cities and agriculture. Prior to this, when people lived in small tribes that supported themselves by hunting and gathering, violence between tribes certainly occurred. Desires of revenge and other motives would have led tribes to carry out savage raids on each other from time to time. But the hunting-and-gather mode of existence would have provided no motive for a war system as such. . . .
>
> But the rise of civilization changed all this. Slaves could be assigned the drudge work involved in agriculture and the building of walls and water canals. Women captives, besides working in the homes and the fields, could bear children to build up the city's defensive and offensive capacity. The cities, with their cultivated

---

[215] By "demonic" Griffin means "diametrically opposed to divine values and powerful enough to threaten divine purposes" (154). That human action can threaten as well as carry out divine purposes is a tenet of Griffin's panentheistic philosophy. .

[216] S.U.N.Y. Press, 1995. One reviewer of Schmookler's *The Illusion of Choice: How the Market Economy Shapes Our Destiny*, S.U.N.Y. Press, 1993, pegged it "a perfect example of post-socialist scribbling." *The Quarterly Journal of Austrian Economics*, Vol. 2, No. 2, Summer 1999, 79. Freely available on mises.org.

lands and their domesticated herds, provided additional motives for attack. The rise of civilization brought the institution of war.

Once the war system began, every tribe was forced to participate. Even if one society wanted to be peaceful, any one society could force the rest to prepare for war or risk being subjugated or annihilated. (AECG 103-104)

A dilemma arises for each tribe or state as soon as it feels it must arm itself against possible aggression by others. "The point is not that you actually fight against everyone else," Griffin writes, "but that every other society is at least potentially your enemy" (105). Thus, intertribal or international anarchy is a condition of war that, unlike the human capacity for violence and propensity to live in societies, we can eliminate. How? By democratically appointing a supervenient governing body to fill the void that is anarchy. Griffin refers, however, not to "conditions" of the emergence of the "war system," but rather to the *causes* of its emergence, "permissive causes" to be precise. A permissive cause is "one that allows almost anything else to become an immediate cause of war" (105).

A Root Fallacy

As someone who once looked to Whitehead as well as Rothbard to organize his thoughts, I do not know how to ascribe causal power to a *state of absence*, which is then said to "allow" an event to occur or a system to emerge and evolve. To suggest that anarchy, a lack of centralized governance, could be a *cause* of any kind is, it seems to me, to commit the fallacy of misplaced concreteness.[217] I learned about that fallacy from Whitehead's writings. He defined it (I paraphrase) as the imputation to abstractions the causal efficacy that only actualities have. We may, for example, speak informally of an orchestra of crickets

---

[217] See the Wikipedia entry:
http://en.wikipedia.org/wiki/Fallacy_of_misplaced_concreteness

chirping but, strictly speaking, the chirping is in the individual crickets that comprise the orchestra. Libertarians often confront this fallacy in the form of methodological collectivism.[218]

More accurately, I learned about this fallacy from reading eminent expounders of Whitehead's philosophy, in the first place David Ray Griffin. "Anarchy" is an abstraction denoting an unrealized (even deliberately suppressed) potential that people have to be in a "relationship of State" to each other. A potential is a non-actuality. A non-actuality might be a negative *condition*, that is, the absence of obstacles to an actuality's action. A non-actuality cannot, however, be a causal agent. Therefore, anarchy could not be a cause, either of a particular war or of a "war system." If in noting Griffin's apparent lapse from his metaphysical principles I only demonstrated my ignorance, I beg his correction.[219]

---

[218] See Ludwig von Mises' authoritative discussion, "On the Rejection of Methodological Individualism," from the fifth chapter of his *The Ultimate Foundation of Economic Science*, Van Nostrand: 1962. Freely available on mises.org.

[219] In an email, a learned libertarian reviewer of an ancestor of this essay wrote: "Suppose someone's car stops suddenly and his head goes through the windshield. He wasn't wearing a seatbelt. Does it make sense to say that (part of) the cause of his going through the windshield is that he wasn't wearing it? You might say it doesn't, since the absence of something—his failure to do something—has no causal power. But I think that there is an ordinary language sense of 'cause' that this misses. Someone who makes the claim about the seatbelt means, 'If he had been wearing the seatbelt, he would not have gone through the windshield,' and this counterfactual claim doesn't imply that an absence has positive causal power. In like fashion, Griffin's claim can be read, 'If we had a world government, wars would be averted, and unless we do have one, we will continue to have wars.' This claim seems to me mistaken, but it doesn't fall into the logical fallacy that you attribute to it." In reply I wrote (I'm paraphrasing) that I would not be willing to give Griffin the "out" of ordinary language were he to ask for it, because he was not engaged in ordinary conversation. In proffering a *theoretical* remedy to the gravest of political woes (total war), he employed a term, "cause," with which, as a philosophical theologian, he has been professionally concerned for over fifty years. The unbuckled seatbelt of my critic's example is a *condition*, not a "permissive cause," of the driver's propulsion. In reading Griffin, I had at first hastily interpreted him as holding international anarchy to be a *condition* of war, but then realized that "condition" was not his term. Aggressors cause wars, and the notion that international anarchy is like an unfastened seatbelt, which locutions like "permissive cause" encourage, obscures that agency.

Griffin's Arbitrary Neo-Hobbesian Gambit

We are not here reviewing Schmookler's causal hypothesis about the rise of civilization and the "war system." We confine our attention to Griffin's raising anew of the classic problem of the defense of person and property, i.e., how to avoid "being subjugated or annihilated." As he acknowledges, the problem is prior to the formation of states. Hobbes proposed one solution (in the "state of Nature" people assign their rights to an absolute sovereign who defends them against aggressors), libertarians another (property owners contract with competing police and insurance agencies to deter, apprehend, try, and punish aggressors). I found it odd that Griffin, at least in this book, uncritically subscribes to Schmookler's Hobbesian description of the human situation as if critiques of Hobbes were not even worth a mention.

The increase in human productivity beyond the subsistence level issued in greater leisure and so made possible vastly more opportunities for good as well as evil, for trade as well as for aggression. Now, the moral imperative under all circumstances is to promote the good and oppose the evil. Griffin, however, seems to promote the evil of the State by globalizing it and dubbing it rather euphemistically "global democratic governance" (GDG). Should Griffin protest that by GDG he does *not* mean what Murray Rothbard meant by the State, namely, an enterprise that acquires its revenue by threatening violence, then in his next book he should explain just how (a) GDG would acquire its revenue and (b) its personnel would be restricted to *persuading* owners to use their property in allegedly more enlightened ways.

The use of force against, or to acquire control over, another's person or property defines the genus *crime*. Wars of aggression are but a species of crime. The "war system"—like the "the welfare system," like the "protectionist system," like the "inflation system"— is the *state* system. Therefore, to eliminate imperialist war from humanity's future, it will be necessary to eliminate states.

That is a bridge too far for Griffin. He wants to preserve states, but somehow also prevent them from starting wars. How GDG would avoid the poorer quality, higher costs, and moral hazards that attend every non-market monopoly is an issue he does not even hint at anywhere in his three chapters with their combined 190 substantial reference notes.

Anarchocapitalism: The Neglected Alternative

An anarchist society will differ from a statist one, not in the absence of crime, but rather in the presence of *legal sanction* for it. The anarchist further believes, however, that legal sanction for taxation, conscription, regulation, and aggressive war contributes to the *magnitude* of crime that afflicts a statist society: there would be less of it without the sanction. For the State teaches by example that we may violate any and every one of our hard-core moral imperatives—e.g., "Do not murder," "Do not enslave," "Do not steal"—if the interests of the State require it.

In his otherwise effective synopsis of the history of the American Empire, Griffin shows no interest in the question of the legitimacy of power and of its morally corrosive effects. Perhaps it is only natural that he who holds implicitly that the *demos*, the people, have the moral right to rule is not inclined to denigrate political power as such.

Cornering the Political Question

Whether anyone would really *own* anything under GDG, Griffin does not say. He no doubt believes human beings have the right to have their bodies used only in ways of which they approve. Does he, however, also believe, as do anarcho-capitalists, that moral self-ownership grounds the possibility of justly held property in all other classes of scarce resource? If self-ownership does that, then no scarce resource is morally available for "democratic global governance." By first-use appropriation and trade, persons will acquire rights to scarce resources, global democrats and other politically meddling types permitting. As Griffin is opposed the use of violent means to achieve ends (even the end of self-defense, it seems), perhaps he is equally opposed to GDG's possessing a monopoly of the use of legitimate force. The meaning of his rejection of violence will depend on how he understands, and affirms, the moral line of demarcation enshrined in property rights.

For no obvious reason Griffin decides to quote, as though from authority, the eminent historian William H. McNeill:

> To halt the arms race, political change appears to be necessary. Nothing less radical than [a global sovereign power] seems in the least likely to suffice . . . . The alternative appears to be sudden and total annihilation of the human species.[220]

Here are the words obscured by Griffin's ellipsis:

> Even in such a world [with a global sovereign power], the clash of arms would not cease as long as human beings hate, love, and fear one another and form into groups whose cohesion and survival is expressed in and supported by mutual rivalry. But an empire of the earth could be expected to limit violence by preventing other groups from arming themselves so elaborately as to endanger the sovereign's easy superiority. War in such a world would therefore sink back to proportions familiar in the preindustrial past. Outbreaks of terrorism, guerrilla action and banditry would continue to give expression to human frustration and anger. But organized war as the twentieth century has known it would disappear.

---

[220] William H. McNeill, *The Pursuit of Power: Technology, Armed Force, and Society since A.D. 1000*, The University of Chicago Press, 1984, pp. 383-84.

We may ask the perennial question of politics precisely in terms of the optimal arrangement for human beings who "hate, love, and fear one another." Just how shall the putatively peace-loving "empire of the earth" prevent other groups from endangering that "easy superiority" without monopolizing the means of the very violence it claims to forswear? How will it maintain "preindustrial" levels for weapons, but for nothing else? More questions unanswered because unasked.

The Global Logic of Statism . . . and of Liberty

Rothbard once challenged inconsistent libertarians to choose between (a) a single worldwide state and (b) a world without states. The argument applies to all peoples or to none: if North and South Dakotans ought not to exist in a state of anarchy, to use Rothbard's example, then neither ought North Dakotans and the residents of Satchkatchewan:

> Although it is true that the separate nation-States have warred interminably against each other, the private citizens of the various countries, despite widely differing legal systems, have managed to live together in harmony without having a single government over them. . . . It is all more curious . . . that while *laissez-faire* theorists should by the logic of their position, be ardent believers in a single, unified world government, so that no one will live in a state of "anarchy'" in relation to anyone else, they almost never are.[221]

If anarchy is rejected, there is no non-arbitrary stopping point short of One World Government. Rothbard's logic can cut the other way, however, and dissolve the mythical ties that bind individuals to less-than-global states.

---

[221] Murray N. Rothbard, *Power and Market*, Institute for Humane Studies, 1977, 4. Freely available on mises.org.

Griffin might shine a klieg light on Rothbard's *en passant* clause, "nation-States have warred interminably against each other." They have done so, Griffin claims, because no super-State prevents them. But if heretofore human rulers have not been good and faithful over a few things, why ought one expect their global democratic editions be good and faithful over many things, and thereby enter into the joy of the commonwealth of God?

A fatal defect in Griffin's plea for peace lies in his failure to distinguish defensive military action from military aggression. Just as we may analyze the former without remainder into an individual's right of self-defense, so we may also analyze the latter into individual aggression. Neither type of military action is rooted in any failure of people to relate "governmentally" to each other. Again, it is not war in general that is a species of crime, but rather military *aggression*, to which the just response may be military defense or liberation.

Conclusion: What Is to Be Done *Away With*?

The coherent goal of politics, then, is not the elimination of "the war system," but rather reduction of crime of *all* types. The "total war" of our unfortunate era is only crime's morally worst type. To eliminate states requires an understanding of crime, not as whatever happens to transgress some edict or statute, but as whatever deprives persons of their justly owned property.

What distinguishes the crime of military aggression from garden-variety gang warfare is that *states* commit them and bask in the legitimacy of states. To suffocate empires and their wars of aggression requires demystifying and delegitimizing the State as such.

About the Author

A native New Yorker, Anthony Flood graduated New York University and studied philosophy at the Graduate Center, City University of New York. Over the past forty years his writings have been published in *American Communist History, Journal of American History, C. L. R. James Journal, FrontPage Magazine, LewRockwell.com, Crisis: Politics, Culture & the Church, The Philosopher's Magazine, New Oxford Review, New International Review,* and *Science & Society.*

Sign up to be notified of future publications!

www.AnthonyGFlood.com